Modular Digital Multitracks

The Power User's Guide

Revised and Expanded Second Edition

by George Petersen

Foreword by Les Paul

6400 Hollis Street
Emeryville, CA 94608

06 05 04 03 02 01 00 99 98 97   6 5 4 3 2 1

Library of Congress Catalog Card Number: 97-073717

Book design, layout, and cover art: Linda Gough

Production staff
Mike Lawson: publisher, Lisa Duran: editor, Randy Antin: editorial assistant, Sally Engelfried:
copy editor, Don Washington: operations coordinator, Teresa Poss: administrative assistant,
Georgia George: production director, Tom Marzella: production assistant

6400 Hollis Street
Emeryville, CA 94608
(510) 653-3307

Also from MixBooks:
The AudioPro Home Recording Course, Volumes 1 and 2
I Hate the Man Who Runs This Bar!
How to Make Money Scoring Soundtracks and Jingles
The Art of Mixing: A Visual Guide to Recording, Engineering, and Production
500 Songwriting Ideas (For Brave and Passionate People)
Music Publishing: The Real Road to Music Business Success, Rev. and Exp. 4th Ed.
How to Run a Recording Session
The Songwriters Guide to Collaboration, Rev. and Exp. 2nd Ed.
Mix Reference Disc, Deluxe Ed.
Critical Listening and Auditory Perception
Keyfax Omnibus Edition
Modular Digital Multitracks: The Power User's Guide
Concert Sound
Sound for Picture
Music Producers
Live Sound Reinforcement

Also from EMBooks:
Making the Ultimate Demo
Tech Terms: A Practical Dictionary for Audio and Music Production
Making Music With Your Computer

Also from CBM Music and Entertainment Group:
Recording Industry Sourcebook
Mix Master Directory
Digital Piano Buyer's Guide

MixBooks is a division of Cardinal Business Media Inc.

Printed in Auburn Hills, Michigan

ISBN 0-918371-23-6

Contents

vi

Foreword
by Les Paul

ix

Preface

xi

Acknowledgments

1

Section One: Understanding MDMs and Digital Recording
Chapter 1   MDM: The Revolution Begins 2
Chapter 2   Basics: MDM Technology 6

9

Section Two: Akai A-DAM Format
Chapter 3   Akai A-DAM System 10
Chapter 4   A-DAM Maintenance and Troubleshooting 16

19

Section Three: ADAT Type I Format Recorders
Chapter 5   Alesis ADAT 20
Chapter 6   ADAT Accessories 28
Chapter 7   Secrets of the ADAT 36
Chapter 8   Fostex RD-8 38
Chapter 9   Alesis ADAT XT 46
Chapter 10 Panasonic MDA-1 52
Chapter 11 Fostex CX-8 54
Chapter 12 ADAT Maintenance and Troubleshooting 56

61

Section Four: ADAT Type II Format Recorders
Chapter 13 Alesis ADAT M20 62
Chapter 14 Studer V-Eight 66

69

Section Five: DTRS Format Recorders

Chapter 15 Tascam DA-88 70
Chapter 16 Secrets of the DA-88 80
Chapter 17 Sony PCM-800 82
Chapter 18 Tascam DA-38 84
Chapter 19 Tascam DA-98 90
Chapter 20 DTRS Accessories 93
Chapter 21 DTRS Maintenance and Troubleshooting 96

101

Section Six: Yamaha Format Recorders

Chapter 22 Yamaha DMR8/DRU8 102

111

Section Seven: The MDM Power User

Chapter 23 The Power Demo 112
Chapter 24 The Buddy System 114
Chapter 25 Analog Interfacing 115
Chapter 26 Digital Interfacing 120
Chapter 27 Cloning/Tape Backups 123
Chapter 28 Tape Tips 125
Chapter 29 MIDI Sync 129
Chapter 30 MIDI Machine Control 131
Chapter 31 Understanding SMPTE 132
Chapter 32 The Whys and Hows of Crossfades 134
Chapter 33 Digital Assembly Editing 136
Chapter 34 MDM: The DAT Editing Tool 139
Chapter 35 The Built-in -10/+4dB Converter 140
Chapter 36 Mix to MDM! 142
Chapter 37 MDM: The Multichannel Mix Format 143
Chapter 38 Track Bouncing, Revisited 145
Chapter 39 The Submix Sync Trick 147
Chapter 40 Megatracking Without Bouncing 148
Chapter 41 The Workstation-MDM Connection 150
Chapter 42 The No-Console Tracking Trick 152
Chapter 43 Track Delay: Who Needs It? 154
Chapter 44 Fun With Pitch Shifting 156
Chapter 45 The 20-/24-bit MDM 158
Chapter 46 The Suicide Auto-Mute Squeeze! 160
Chapter 47 MDM: The Next Generation 161

Foreword

by Les Paul

Les Paul in his home studio, circa 1949.

MULTITRACKING: IT WASN'T ALWAYS THIS EASY

My first attempt at multitrack recording was back in the late 1920s. My mother had a player piano, and much to her surprise, I would take her piano rolls and punch extra holes in the paper to create new intros and harmonies.

My next crack at multitrack was in 1933, when I built my first recording lathe. I was a tinkerer, fooling around with the idea of recording my trio. After one of our rehearsals, the other guys in the band had left, and I realized that I wanted to put down the rhythm for "Lime House Blues." I thought about it for a minute and decided to record the rhythm guitar part myself, so I could play along with it and practice. But there was no way to hear a playback of me playing to the acetate. I came up with the idea of spreading the grooves farther apart and putting down two tracks on one acetate. I cut one recording and then started the second recording between the grooves of the first. I tried to lock these two up so they'd be in sync—I'd have bass and rhythm guitar on one acetate with two playback heads on it to make a multiple recording.

It didn't work very well, although I once put demos of two songs on one side of a disc—one between the other—for a release I proposed to the president of Capitol Records. The record drove him crazy because when he went to listen to "How High the Moon," on came "The World's Waiting for a Sunrise." The next time he played it, he heard "How High the Moon." They were going nuts, but later Capitol even considered putting a record like that out. I wanted to do one for promotional purposes to screw up disc jockeys.

Eventually I built two machines and bounced

from one machine to the other. That way, I could record one part, play it back, then make a second disc and alternate back and forth. That's how I made my multitracks until the tape machine came along.

When the tape machine landed in my backyard in 1949, I sat down and wondered how I could do a multiple channel recording on this new machine instead of carrying my lathes around with me. The tape machine was far better than the discs, but I still needed two machines. So I looked at it and wondered if I could put a head prior to the erase head, the record head and the playback head. I followed the path on a piece of paper with my pencil and realized that I could do sound-on-sound with this simple setup.

> *When the tape machine landed in my backyard in 1949, I sat down and wondered how I could do a multiple channel recording on this new machine…*

My friend Wally Jones and I built this little four-input mixer that was powered from the guitar amplifier. I also had two pairs of Air Force earphones, one RCA 44DX microphone and a mic stand. That's what I used to make every record I did for Capitol.

Before Mary Ford and I drove to Chicago to play our first job together with a trio at the Blue Note, I called Ampex and asked them to send me another tape head. We finally arrived at the New Lawrence Hotel, and in comes this little package from Ampex. We called some guy out of the Yellow Pages to drill a hole in the recorder's top plate and put the head in there. When he introduced himself as Mr. Goodspeed, I knew we were going to be lucky. I said "Testing 1-2-3-4," and "Hello there, hello there," and they both came back! Mary and I were elated, and the multitrack was born.

When we went out on the road, we went as many as 37 dubs down, so we saved the parts that were most important until last. We had to know what we were doing. That's why we could go 24 dubs down on "How High the Moon." We were wise enough to put the most important parts on last, which were the lead voice in Mary's "glee club" and my guitar. The last dub was me balancing the thing out. I had many different types of tape spliced together and the level

might drop by 3dB at some point, so I had to run it by once more just to make the levels equal. I'd have to know that at the third bar of the second chorus I had to bring the level up 3dB at some particular note, then bring it back down.

The 8-track came along in 1953. We were filming, and I was taking a rest and looking up at the sky when my manager asked what I was dreaming about. I said that recording using sound-on-sound was crazy. There's a better way: Stack the heads one on top of the other, 1-2-3-4-5-6-7-8, and align them so we could do self-sync, with all the heads in line. My manager said the concept was beyond him but wondered if it was a good idea. When I told him, "I think it will change the world," he told me I should do something about it.

I went to California to see Westrex, but they didn't think it was a good idea and said it wasn't feasible. So I went up to Ampex. They leapt at the idea. And that's how the 8-track was born.

So what do I think of the multitrack today? I'm terribly excited to see what they are doing with the new multitracks. It's more than a step in the right direction—it gives the people out there a chance to see their dreams coming true, because they can do things that a few years ago we could only look out the window and wish for. Today, here it is.

Les Paul

1994

Preface

The arrival of any new technology, whether it's desktop publishing or Gutenberg's movable type, brings new and different ways of looking at the way we work. And while it hasn't exactly had a global impact, modular digital multitrack (MDM) technology is beginning to change the working structure of the entire industry of professional and semi-pro recordists.

Today, home and high-end studios have suddenly found themselves on equal footing in terms of access to state-of-the-art recording gear that ten years ago would have cost ten times as much. This new technology has spawned the project studio; a new generation of recording facility, where musicians using low-cost/high-performance equipment are capable of creating professional quality products in garages, basements and bedrooms.

I'm always saddened to hear musicians use lack of equipment as an excuse for not making and recording music. George Martin produced the Beatles' *Sgt. Pepper's Lonely Hearts Club Band* on a pair of analog 4-track decks. I'm certainly glad that they didn't cancel the project because the needed technology wasn't available! And when he wasn't busy inventing the solid-body electric guitar, music synthesizer and multitrack recorder, Les Paul cut all of his hit records at home with one mic and a four-input mixer!

Obviously, a little creativity can go a long way in the recording process. This book is intended for those who seek maximum results from a minimum amount of gear, whether they're budding novices or seasoned professionals.

In the hope that I can walk that difficult line between boring the advanced users and bewildering the beginners, I've made a few assumptions about you, the reader. I figure that if you've spent, or are about to spend, $3,000 or more on a tape recorder, then you must already know a little about the recording process and understand such basic concepts as overdubbing, punch-ins/-outs and how a mixing console works. If you need more help in these areas, don't despair: There are dozens of excellent texts and videotape courses on the subjects. In fact, the Mix Bookshelf catalog lists hundreds of such titles: call (800) 233-9604 or (510) 653-3307 for a free copy.

As the editor of *Mix*, the world's leading professional audio magazine, I've written over 600 articles covering every aspect of audio recording and music production. But there's never enough room in the confines of a magazine article to say everything you want, which led me to write *Modular Digital Multitracks: The Power User's Guide*. When it comes to using new technologies, such as MDMs, we're all beginners. This book is designed to guide and inspire you to develop your dreams into reality.

Acknowledgments

I would like to acknowledge some of the people who assisted me in assembling this second edition of *Modular Digital Multitracks: The Power User's Guide.* First of all, the manufacturers, without whom there would be no MDM revolution: I'd like to especially thank Allen, Dan, Jim, Jeff and Don at Alesis; Bud at Fostex; Roger and Yuan at Tascam; Marcus at Fast Forward Designs; and Peter at Yamaha. My support team at MixBooks has been great: a tip of the tape to Mike, Lisa, Linda and Georgia, as well as Brad at Hal Leonard Corp. I should also mention my wife, Merida, for putting up with me as I wrote this, and my studio partner, JJ Jenkins, who watched in horror as I bumped paying sessions aside so I could reconfigure our entire facility to try out yet another MDM system or technique. And I should not forget my mom, who brought music into our home via a Yamaha pump organ and took me to the foreboding alley known as Via San Sebastiano in Napoli when I was 12 to buy that all-important first snare drum. My life was never the same after that day.

Finally, I owe a debt of gratitude to Les Paul, who contributed the book's foreword but also, and more importantly, invented the solid-body electric guitar and devised the multitrack recording process that got me and countless others hooked on this curious blend of art and technology. Keep those great ideas coming, Les!

Understanding MDMs and Digital Recording

Chapter 1 MDM: The Revolution Begins

Chapter 2 Basics: MDM Technology

MDM: The Revolution Begins

Revolutions often occur where you'd least expect them. Who would have predicted that a surprise product unveiling at the annual expo of the National Association of Music Merchants (NAMM) would forever change the world of professional and semi-pro recording? The place: the Convention Center in Anaheim, California. The date: January 18, 1991. The product: the Alesis ADAT, a compact studio recorder that could store eight tracks of digital audio (at better-than-CD quality) on an S-VHS tape and could be interlocked with up to 15 other ADAT units to provide up to 128 tracks in all.

Certainly, the product represented remarkable technology, but what was most impressive was the original ADAT's $3,995 price tag. This was far lower than the $14,995 Akai A-DAM, an earlier modular digital multitrack (MDM) that recorded 12 tracks on 8mm videotapes; and the Yamaha DMR8, a $34,000 digital 8-track/digital mixer combination. After Alesis began putting ADATs into the stores and into the hands of anxious consumers, other low-cost MDMs came to market from Tascam, Fostex, Sony, Panasonic and Studer.

THE FORMATS

Today there are three current MDM formats:

- ADAT Type I is a 16-bit format (with 67 minutes maximum record time on a T-180 S-VHS tape) used by the (original) Alesis ADAT, Alesis XT, Fostex RD-8, Fostex CX-8 and Panasonic MDA-1.
- ADAT Type II (also referred to as PDAT) is a 20-bit format (with 67 minutes maximum record time on a T-180 S-VHS tape) used by the Alesis M20 and Studer V-Eight recorders.
- DTRS (Digital Tape Recording System) is a 16-bit format (with 108 minutes of record time on an NTSC-120 Hi-8mm videocassette) used by the Tascam DA-88, DA-38 and DA-98 and Sony PCM-800.

All of the above formats store digital audio on readily available consumer videocassette formats and provide the ability to interlock up to 16 8-track recorders in sample-accurate (±1/48,000 second) sync

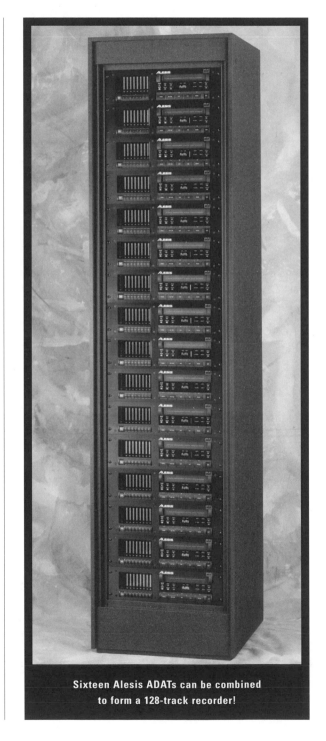

Sixteen Alesis ADATs can be combined to form a 128-track recorder!

for up to 128-track recording.

There are also two formats used by the now-discontinued Akai A-DAM and Yamaha DMR8/DRU8 systems. *Note: Detailed information on each of these recorders can be found in following chapters.*

THE MDM ADVANTAGE

Offering a tremendous cost-to-performance ratio, these modular digital multitracks spell a major recording revolution in the making. At current retail, a complete 24-track MDM system costs approximately $10,500, comparable to a 1-inch, analog 24-track or one-third the $30,000 (and up) cost of a professional 2-inch, 24-track analog machine. Meanwhile, prices for pro reel-to-reel digital multitracks begin at over $60,000 for a bare-bones, no-frills model and can run as high as five times that price for a decked-out, 48-channel system.

Videotape-based digital recording systems also provide a substantial savings in tape costs—up to 90 percent over professional analog systems. With an MDM, you can forget about spending $120 for a 2-inch, 24-track analog reel that runs a mere 17 minutes at 30 ips. At best, that's only four songs per tape, and tape costs can add up fast: Big budget, major-label recording projects sometimes use as many as 100 reels of 2-inch tape! Storage space for masters is another concern. But fortunately, all the tape for a complete album project recorded on an MDM, including the 2-track DAT mixdowns, could fit in a shoe box or two.

Having done sessions on just about every type of modular digital tape recorder (Akai, Alesis, Fostex, Tascam, Yamaha and a custom 4-track digital system

I've used since 1984), I can say that recording on such devices uses a lot more tape than you might initially think possible. For example, on a typical reel-to-reel 24-track music session, the band plays and erases over the basic tracks until a suitable take is recorded. Why? Tape costs money. A six-minute song on an analog 24-

The beauty of MDM designs is that multiple recorders (of the same format, of course) can be synchronized via a simple connection of one cable between each transport, and no audio tracks need be "wasted" on sync signals.

track consumes about $40 in 2-inch tape, so people tend to be picky about what becomes a "keeper." When your tape costs are cut to less than a twentieth of that amount (typical for an 8mm or S-VHS system), you tend to keep a lot more takes.

Pro commercial studio owners should be aware that when using MDMs, bands tend to record *lots* of versions of basic tracks, which turns into *lots* of band-in-the-control-room listening time, which translates

Tascam DA-88 8-track MDM

into higher revenues. Ditto for the pleasure of keeping all 64 guitar solos or lead vocal overdubs (filling eight 8-track tapes) and then spending hours listening to them *all* while the studio time meter is running. Add in another four or five hours patching together the "perfect" take via assembly editing on the multitrack or SMPTE, and you've discovered the secret solution to the studio recession.

On the more serious side, many pro studios, ranging from entry-level to world-class, have found a healthy market in catering to the home MDM user. It's a win-win situation for both sides: Working on an MDM at home, an artist can spend as much time as required to perfect the basic tracks, thus saving a fortune in hourly studio fees. (Also, performers tend to be less nervous when they don't have to worry about time or studio fees.) Later, by stepping up to the professional facility, the artist has access to exotic microphones for overdubs, plus high-end signal processing and consoles for the mix.

GETTING MODULAR
Another advantage stems from the modular aspects of MDMs, which by nature are both upwardly and downwardly compatible. Way back in the Neolithic analog days, if you recorded on a 16-track deck, you had to mix on a 16-track deck. With four recorders in an S-VHS or Hi-8mm MDM system, you can work on 8-, 16-, 24- or 32-track sessions. Similarly, a 24- or 32-track MDM system has no trouble playing back 8- or 16-track sessions. That trick is a lot harder to pull off using a conventional reel-to-reel multitrack.

In the same manner, if you need more tracks, you can always borrow or rent a couple of extra modules. Better still, link up with a friend who has a similar format machine: Each of you can work at home on an 8-track system and then occasionally pool your MDM resources to increase the number of available tracks when you begin overdubbing.

The ADAT and DTRS systems are based around 8-track modules that can be combined for up to 128 tracks. Two or three Akai A-DAM 12-tracks can be synched for 24- or 36-track recording, and the same is true for the 8-track Yamaha system, which is expandable for 16- or 24-track work.

SYNCHRONICITY
Analog recorders require the dedication of one audio track on each machine for storing synchronization signals, so two synched 16-tracks provide 30 tracks, rather than 32. Additionally, a hardware synchronizer (typically priced in the $2,000-and-up range) is needed to interlock two analog decks. The beauty of MDM designs is that multiple recorders (of the same format, of course) can be synchronized via a simple

connection of one cable between each transport, and no audio tracks need be "wasted" on sync signals.

Amazingly, the sync resolution of two or more MDM transports is sample-accurate (±1/48,000 second). Such performance was previously unheard of, even in the most accurate professional video-editing setups, and is over one thousand times tighter than a frame-accurate (±1/30 second) analog multitrack. How is this possible in a low-cost system?

The answer is electronic sync, rather than mechanical sync. As data is read by two machines in close mechanical sync, the digital information from the tape heads is temporarily stored in a RAM memory buffer. Word-clock timing information (carried

Fortunately, all the tape for a complete album project recorded on an MDM, including the 2-track DAT mixdowns, could fit in a shoe box or two.

on a multipin sync cable) from the master machine controls the release of data from the second deck's buffer, thus enabling sample-accurate interlock of two (or more) decks.

With this type of system, synchronizing an MDM to a video recorder for music scoring or other post-production chores is cost-effective and quite a simple matter. Available accessories for synching MDMs to video include plug-in sync cards for the Tascam DA-88 (SY-88), Sony PCM-800 (DABK-801) and the JLCooper dataMaster, Alesis BRC remote control/autolocator/synchronizer and the Alesis AI-2 synchronizer for the Alesis ADAT, Alesis XT, Fostex CX-8 and Panasonic MDA-1. The Alesis M20, Fostex RD-8, Studer V-Eight, Tascam DA-98 and Yamaha DMR8 provide built-in, chase-lock SMPTE synchronizers. All of the above sync features also include MIDI sync for locking your MDM to computers, synthesizers, drum machines, samplers and other MIDI gear, including MIDI-based console automation systems.

NEW POSSIBILITIES
Besides easy multimachine sync, MDMs also offer the ability to make flawless clones of tapes by using a single cable to connect the digital output of one machine to a second deck of the same format.

Beyond the obvious uses, such as archiving tapes with "safety" backup copies, the ease of cloning tapes offers many creative possibilities. For example, before attempting a difficult punch-in on a tricky passage (such as replacing a single note in the middle of a frenetic guitar solo), it's wise to make a backup copy, just in case you mess it up the first time through.

Long-distance recording sessions are another possibility. Want your cousin Guido in Napoli to do an accordion overdub on your next speed-metal hit? Make a clone of the session tape onto a digital multitrack cassette and, Federal Express willing, you'll have that hot performance you need in a couple of days. Very cool.

Unfortunately, all of the current formats use proprietary track schemes. Therefore, tapes recorded on an ADAT cannot be duplicated or backed up using standard S-VHS video decks, and the same is true for the 8mm A-DAM and Hi-8mm DTRS formats. But interformat adapters, which allow digital domain transfers from, say, a DTRS tape to the ADAT Type I format, are available from numerous vendors. A few of these include the Apogee Electronics (Santa Monica, CA) FC-8, the Otari (Foster City, CA) UFC-24 and the Spectral (Woodinville, WA) Translator.

The old school of recording required the purchase of a completely new recorder when you wanted to upgrade, which made retailers happy. Using MDM technology, you can start out with a modest 8-track system and then purchase more modules as your needs, or cash reserves, grow.

Perhaps more significant than price is that MDMs bring new ways of looking at the entire recording process. For example, a bass overdub in a typical digital recording session would previously have required a facility with an expensive digital multitrack, probably accompanied by a big-ticket console and a nice recording room. Time would be booked, and the producer, engineer, second engineer and bassist would all converge at the studio for a couple of hours. Add up the cost of studio time and salaries, and this quick overdub becomes an expensive proposition. As an adjunct, the acoustics of the recording room become an irrelevant fixture as soon as the bassist plugs into a direct box. With a modular system, the producer can give the bassist a "slave" (digital copy) tape with a scratch track and, working at a suitably equipped home studio, the player can lay down several tracks at a convenient time. Later, the player gets paid, the producer chooses from up to seven different bass takes, the slave tape is locked to the master and the selected track is digitally transferred. Megatracking becomes a reality. Clearly, MDMs offer a world of new possibilities in terms of recording creativity and flexibility.

Basics: MDM Technology

digital multitrack tape recorder has a lot in common with an analog multitrack recorder. Both machines allow the user to record on any number of tracks, either simultaneously or by overdubbing on additional tracks at a later time. As tape-based devices, both are linear recording mediums, meaning that information is stored chronologically on a long strip of magnetic recording material. Thus, when recording a song, the recorded information for Track one is stored on the tape somewhere near Track two, and so on. This differs from computer-based, nonlinear recording systems such as Digidesign's Audiomedia and ProTools or the Akai DR8, which may store information anywhere on a hard disk and still have the ability to play back audio data in perfect sync.

To get a handle on how modular digital multitracks work, it is important to understand a few digital audio basics. For detailed background reading on digital systems and technology, I highly recommend *Principles of Digital Audio* and *Advanced Digital Audio*, published by Howard Sams & Company. Written by respected digital authority Ken Pohlmann, these two texts cover theory, applications and practice of digital audio and present this difficult material in a straightforward and quite readable manner. In the meantime, here is a thumbnail description of some fundamental concepts involved in digital recording technology.

UNDERSTANDING DIGITAL RECORDING

You may already be familiar with the analog recording process, which transforms audio signals into a *continuous* voltage that can be stored on tape. Digital recording, on the other hand, uses a process known as sampling, whereby a signal is represented by a series of brief snapshots, or "samples," with each being a representation of the input or output signal at any one instant.

When this series of samples is played back, it recreates the original signal. In many ways, this process is similar to the technology used in motion pictures: The movie camera takes 24 still pictures per second on a strip of film, which are perceived by the viewer as continuous when played back. However, digital audio reproduction requires a lot more than 24 samples per second!

In fact, one of the basic tenets of digital audio, known as the Nyquist theorem, specifies that the highest reproducible frequency in a digital system is equal to or less than one-half of the sampling frequency. In real terms, if we want a digital system to reproduce the entire frequency range of human

To get a handle on how modular digital multitracks work, it is important to understand a few digital audio basics.

hearing—20 to 20,000 cycles per second (Hz)—then the system would have to sample the incoming signal at two times the highest input frequency, or 40,000 cycles per second (40kHz). This doubled figure is the sampling rate or sampling frequency. Generally, the higher the sampling rate, the greater the accuracy of the digital reproduction.

Theoretically, the highest frequency reproducible by a digital recorder operating at a sampling rate of 48kHz would be 24kHz. Similarly, a system such as a CD player operating at 44.1kHz would have an upper-end frequency limit of 22.05kHz. When frequencies going into a digital system exceed one-half the sampling rate, the result is an undesirable distortion component known as *aliasing noise*. One way to get around this limitation is by adding anti-aliasing filters—frequency-shaping filters that prevent signals higher than half the sampling rate from entering the system. The actual upper frequency response of a system is thus somewhat less than the Nyquist theorem would dictate, due to the real-world limitations of filter design technology.

All current MDM recorders employ pulse code modulation, a common method of encoding, transmitting and/or storing digital data. Abbreviated PCM, the name stems from the process of creating a string of electrical pulses to represent an input signal; the pulse chain is coded to increase the efficiency of data storage.

A key factor in defining the accuracy with which a PCM-based device records or reproduces a digital audio signal is the system's bit resolution. The num-

Example of 65-line screen reproduction

ber of available bits describes the number of steps available to represent a signal's level, in exponential increments: A 1-bit system has 2^1 (two) steps, an 8-bit system has 2^8 (256) steps, a 16-bit system has 2^{16} (65,536) steps, a 20-bit system has 2^{20} steps (1,048,576), etc.

These steps in resolution are directly related to audio quality. As an example, consider a 1-bit digital system controlling the level of a guitar amp. In this situation, we have a choice of either off or full-blast. A 2-bit system has four settings (off/low/medium/loud), and so on. Once we get to 16 bits, we have 65,536 variables. Digital audio works along the same lines.

To make another analogy, the bit resolution of a digital system is a lot like the printing process in which a series of black dots represent the myriad combinations of black, white and gray tones in a photograph. If you use a magnifying glass to compare the dot resolution of typical newspaper reproduction (65 lines per inch) to the 133 lines-per-inch resolution of the photos in this book, the difference in quality

should be obvious. Likewise, in digital audio, the greater the bit resolution, the more accurate the reproduction.

The ideal digital system would have a high sampling rate, such as 96kHz, combined with a high bit resolution of, say, 24 bits. This brings up the question, "Why would anyone design a 16-bit, 48kHz system when better technology is available?" The answer is a simple matter of dollars and sense: Digital converters with 20- or 24-bit resolution are far more expensive than their 16-bit cousins. Also, systems with more bits

Example of 133-line screen reproduction

and higher sampling rates have far greater memory requirements, and more memory equates to more money. For the time being, the 16-bit/48kHz systems offer a reasonable compromise with better-than-CD quality at an affordable price.

TAPE HEADS

Cost considerations have also led modular digital multitrack manufacturers to store digitized audio signals on videotape, using a rotary-head mechanism similar to that used in standard videocassette recorders. In such devices, the tape is pulled from the cassette and is partially wrapped around a cylindrical drum that houses the rotating video heads. The heads spin at a high rate, creating the equivalent of a high-speed tape, even though the actual tape speed is quite slow when compared to analog systems. Additionally, the tape heads are tilted at an angle, so the recorded material is laid down in long diagonal bands of data known as helical scans.

This helical-scan approach is a reliable storage method and is used in millions of consumer and professional VCRs worldwide, as well as computer data tape backup systems, DAT audio recorders and the specialized Sony PCM-1630 format used for mastering compact-disc releases. One obvious advantage of a rotary-head MDM design is that maximum record times are far longer than most analog recorders: 108 minutes for DTRS decks or 67 minutes for the ADAT Type I/Type II decks. Compared to the maximum record times of a professional analog multitrack running a 10.5-inch reel of tape at 15 ips (33 minutes) or 30 ips (16.6 minutes), MDM systems have the edge.

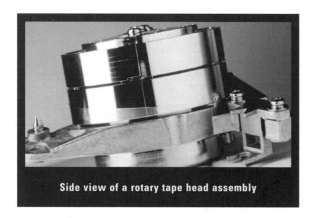

Side view of a rotary tape head assembly

The easily available tapes used in the videotape-based MDM systems can be quite convenient: When the creative urge strikes you at some odd hour and you've run out of tape, it's nice to know that a late-night drugstore may have what you need. If the same scenario occurs with reel-to-reel analog tape, you're probably out of luck, at least until weekday business hours. In any case, stocking up on your favorite brand isn't such a bad idea, especially when there's a sale at Walgreen's.

However, while rotary-head transports are a proven, cost-effective data storage technology, the combination of the long diagonal helical scans and the cassette medium precludes the use of tape splicing or other physical editing methods. Additionally, rotary-head assemblies are extremely fragile when compared to relatively impervious analog tape heads. Therefore, serious maintenance should be deferred to experienced professionals. The maintenance chapters in this book contain more information on basic maintenance and troubleshooting procedures.

It should be noted that the (now-discontinued) Yamaha DMR8/DRU8 digital system uses a proprietary tape type and a stationary head design. While more rugged than a rotary-head system, the stationary approach requires a much higher tape speed, thus limiting the record time of a single-machine sys-

tem to a maximum of 22 minutes. Although this is shorter than the rotary-head ADAT and Tascam machines, 22 minutes of recording time is still more than 25 percent longer than a 10.5-inch reel of 24-track tape running at 30 ips.

FORMATTING

One trait that all MDMs have in common is that, like floppy disks for a computer or MIDI sampler, MDM tapes must be formatted before use. The process takes place in real-time and is fairly simple. The user merely selects the required sampling frequency, usually 48kHz, although you may choose to work at 44.1kHz for special applications, such as digitally transferring material from 44.1kHz sources (CDs, pro DAT tapes, etc.). Another possible reason to format at 44.1kHz is that tapes formatted at this sampling frequency have a ten percent longer running time than tapes produced at 48kHz, although the recording quality will be reduced from "better-than-CD quality" to mere "CD quality."

Note: Formatting will completely erase any existing material on the tape, so it's always a good idea to double-check any tapes before formatting.

By the way, all current MDM recorders on the market allow a tape to be formatted while recording is taking place. Just to be sure, however, I make it a habit to have a couple of pre-formatted tapes on hand, and I usually format a tape or two while miking the drum set, emptying out the studio ashtrays or coiling microphone cables after a session. If you have a multimachine setup with similar-format MDM decks, you can always use an off-line machine (one that is not synchronized to the other decks) to format while you are recording on the other machine(s) in the system.

Akai A-DAM Format

Chapter 3 Akai A-DAM System

Chapter 4 A-DAM Maintenance and Troubleshooting

Akai A-DAM System

The first MDM: Akai's A-DAM system

istory was made in the sequestered back room of a hotel suite on the fifth floor of the New York City Hilton Hotel on October 16, 1987, during the 83rd Convention of the Audio Engineering Society. I was one of a handful of people to see the first prototype of the A-DAM (Akai-Digital Audio Multitrack), and I was instantly drawn to the possibilities of this expandable, 12-track system, which was publicly unveiled at the AES convention in Paris on March 17, 1988.

The machine's 80-pound, 7-rackspace chassis and $35,000 price (eventually reduced to a more affordable $14,995) may seem excessive by modern standards, but in a historical context, A-DAM was truly revolutionary. At the time, the least expensive digital multitrack available was the original Sony PCM-3324, which cost $140,000 and weighed approximately 500 pounds. With the introduction of A-DAM, more than three years before the debut of the Alesis ADAT, the dues for the elite club of digital multitrack owners had come down to a new level of affordability, and the concept of the modular digital multitrack was born.

Units began shipping to customers in May of 1989, and evidently I was not alone in my appreciation: In 1990, A-DAM was the recipient of a Technical Excellence & Creativity (TEC) Award in the category of Outstanding Technical Achievement, Recording Devices/Storage Technology. Although the A-DAM system was discontinued several years ago, more than 2,000 systems were sold worldwide, and many of these are still in operation today.

SYSTEM BASICS

A-DAM is a 12-track recording package offering up to 21.5 minutes of recording time on readily available, inexpensive 8mm videocassettes. While a 21.5-minute recording capacity may seem short, it's nearly 25 percent longer than a 2,500-foot roll of 24-track tape running at 30 ips, which only yields 16.6 minutes. This maximum running time is based on a 90-minute videotape at 44.1kHz; the maximum time at 48kHz is

Spotlight

Akai A-DAM

- Product Introduction: March 17, 1988
- Deliveries Began: May 1989
- Format: A-DAM proprietary, using standard 8mm videotapes
- Maximum Recording Time: 21.5 minutes (MP-90 tape)
- Track Capacity: 12, expandable to 24 or 36
- Digital System: Rotary head; 16-bit linear; selectable 44.1/48kHz sampling frequencies
- Analog Connections: Balanced +4dBu inputs/outputs on XLRs
- Digital Connections: Proprietary A-DAM 37-pin bidirectional digital input/output port; AES/EBU interface optional
- Dimensions: 12.25x19x24 inches (HxWxD of DR1200 recorder only); 79 pounds
- Retail (when last offered): $14,995, including autolocator and remote meter bridge

about ten percent shorter. Akai's research proved 120-minute tapes to be too thin for reliable operation, so the system automatically ejects such tapes.

As with other MDM systems, tapes must be formatted before recording, in the same manner that one would format a floppy disk on a computer. The process must be carried out in real time, and the user must select a sampling frequency (44.1 or 48kHz) for each tape prior to formatting.

System specifications state a frequency response of 20 to 20kHz (+1dB, -1.2dB), over 90dB dynamic range and 16-bit linear quantization. Features include selectable 44.1/48kHz sampling rates, balanced +4dBm XLR inputs and outputs, independent digital delay on each track (up to 66ms), ±6 percent pitch change (only operable at the 44.1kHz rate), a choice of four crossfade times for smooth punch-ins/-outs, frame-accurate auto-punch-ins/-outs, spot erase capability and storage of more than 100 cue points. An analog auxiliary track is provided for cueing or time code functions, such as synching to video and/or a MIDI system.

The recorder uses six rotary heads (three playback/three record), with a single head rotation equivalent to one frame of data. The heads rotate at 2,100 rpm, so the system's frame rate is 35 frames per second. This internal frame rate does not affect synchronization with other systems. Double Reed Solomon Code—the same error correction used in DAT machines—is employed, and digital data is recorded on the tape using a group interleave (channel scrambling) scheme, wherein data is spread out across three tracks, allowing continuous operation even if one of the playback heads is clogged or fails.

An A-DAM system is made up of the DR1200 recorder, the DL1200 programmable autolocator and the DM1200 meter bridge. As the DL1200 autolocator can control up to three DR1200 transports simultaneously (without an external synchronizer), users can

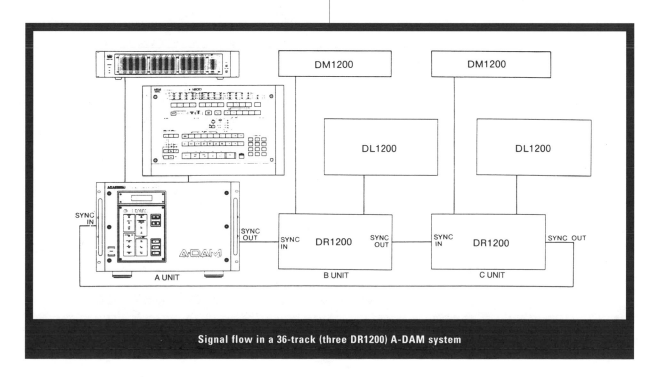

Signal flow in a 36-track (three DR1200) A-DAM system

The DR1200 contains the transport and recording electronics.

cleaning (at least once or twice daily). A removable top plate allows quick access to the head assembly, so a pull-out, drawer-style mount is a necessity if the machine is placed in a rack.

A-DAM OPERATIONS

In a quiet control room, A-DAM creates a discernible amount of fan noise, which, while not overwhelming, is as noticeable as a fairly loud computer hard drive. Supplied cables for the meter bridge and locator are about 25 feet long, allowing placement of the transport in the rear of the room or in an adjacent area. Akai offers optional cables that double the distance; both units use standard D-sub connectors (37-pin female for the meters, 50-pin female for the autolocator), so users can assemble custom cables for permanent installations.

The DM1200 meter unit features 15-segment LED meters for each of the 12 PCM tracks and a 12-segment level display for the aux channel. Front-panel switches allow the user to tailor meter characteristics, with a choice of two release times (a fast-acting 319ms or a more gradual 1,277ms), as well

upgrade the basic 12-track system to 24- or 36-track operation with the purchase of one or two additional DR1200/DM1200 units.

The transport's rear panel includes ports for an external error-rate counter, a proprietary 37-pin digital I/O connector (for making clone copies to/from another DR1200 or for connecting the optional DIF1200 AES/EBU digital interface adapter), internal sync ports for slaving multiple A-DAM units, ¼-inch analog auxiliary track in/out jacks (these are for the low-fidelity track, which is suitable for cue functions or SMPTE time code), connections to the meter bridge and autolocator and a 25-pin "D" port for an external video synchronizer. Regarding the latter, Akai recommends the TimeLine Lynx and Adams-Smith 2600 and Zeta models.

All of the components in the system are rackmountable, although at nearly 80 pounds, the DR1200 transport requires a fairly hefty rack. However, it's important to keep in mind that the DR1200's rotary heads and tape path need thorough, regular

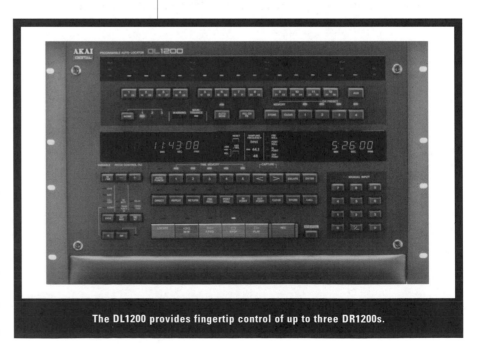

The DL1200 provides fingertip control of up to three DR1200s.

as auto peak reset (with peaks displayed for about 1.5 seconds) or continuous display of the highest peaks.

The DL1200 autolocator provides versatile control of record and transport parameters. Features include 105 memory points (five are single-button selectable, with 100 more available in "stack" memory), programmable pre-/post-roll times, frame-accurate auto-punch-in/-out, repeat and return modes, a "rehearsal" function for checking punch points before committing to tape, keypad entry or on-the-fly capture of locate and patch points, auto playback muting (selectable on any track), "trans-punch-in/-out" (digital track-to-track copying) and four programmable preset combinations of channel-mode (record/playback) settings. The LED readouts of minutes/seconds/frames have half-inch-tall characters, and the user can select time display in either absolute or relative modes (referenced from the start of the tape or from a chosen point).

Perhaps the most revolutionary aspect of the A-DAM is that all of this autolocation information can be stored in a "table of contents" (TOC) section on the head of the tape. This concept is taken a step further (with alphanumeric names available for locator points, song names, etc.) on the Yamaha DMR8, Alesis ADAT/BRC, Alesis XT and M20, Fostex RD-8/CX-3, Panasonic MDA-1 and Studer V-Eight systems, and allows location data to be loaded instantly, thus eliminating the need for tedious re-entry of locator points each time you work on a tape. When working on an Akai A-DAM system, take special note that the procedure to save autolocation points is nearly identical to the "format tape" command. Be sure you don't initiate the wrong procedure, particularly at the end of a late-night session.

Users can choose crossfade times of 12, 23, 46 or 93ms for seamless punches, and a "trans-punch" feature allows digital copying of entire or partial tracks. This is eminently useful in all kinds of situations; for example, a "safety" track of a guitar solo can be copied to an unused track before you begin a difficult punch, such as a single note in a complex riff.

Trans-punch also allows for digital editing capability. For example, one possible creative application is using three takes of a vocal performance (on three tracks) and copying various parts—say, the first and third verse from Track two, choruses from Track one and the second verse from Track three—into a "perfect" version on an unused track. Once the desired track is assembled, the three original tracks can be erased, providing more tracks for backing vocals or solos.

If you find yourself needing more than 12 tracks, you can stripe the analog auxiliary track with SMPTE time code or FSK sync signals for synching to MIDI. You can also premix the first 12 tracks to a DAT tape and then copy the 2-track mix onto a new A-DAM tape, providing ten additional tracks for vocals and solos, with minimal signal degradation caused by the bounce. Alternately, you can record ten tracks and mix them to the two unused A-DAM tracks; once you're satisfied with the mix, you can erase the original tracks to make room for more material. A final option is to expand into 24- or 36-track operation by adding additional DR-1200 units to the system.

Discontinued years ago, the A-DAM system has essentially vanished into oblivion; however, its role in proving the viability (and versatility) of the modular digital multitrack concept puts the system in a special place in recording history. Judging by the popularity of current MDM formats, it's a safe bet that A-DAM's influence will be felt for years to come.

Akai Professional
Box 2344
Ft. Worth, TX 76113
817-336-5114

Note: Turn page for diagrams of A-DAM front and rear panels.

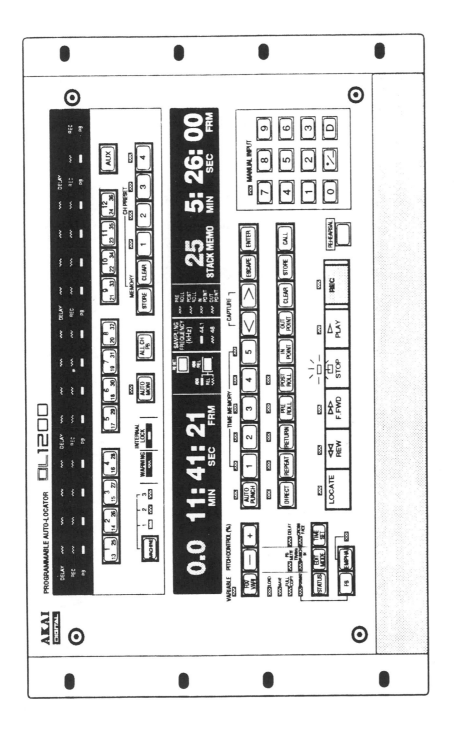

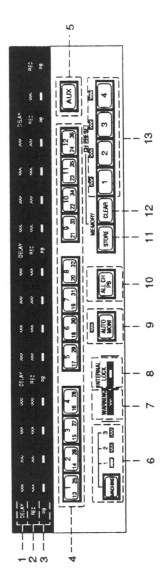

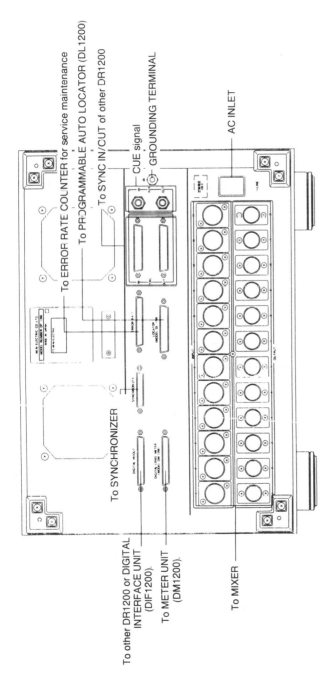

To SYNCHRONIZER

To DR1200 or DIGITAL INTERFACE UNIT (DIF1200).

To METER UNIT (DM1200).

To MIXER

To ERROR RATE COUNTER for service maintenance

To PROGRAMMABLE AUTO LOCATOR (DL1200)

To SYNC IN/CUT of other DR1200

CUE signal

GROUNDING TERMINAL

AC INLET

Akai A-DAM Operations

As the DR1200 recorder has no transport controls, A-DAM system operation is entirely dependent on the DL1200 programmable autolocator. Most of the functions, such as transport play, record and rewind, are self-explanatory; however, some of the DL1200 keys and indicators (numbered 1 through 13 in the front panel detail) deserve some elaboration.

1. Delay Indicators: Amber LEDs that glow when the track delay function is active on that particular channel.

2. Record Indicators: Red LEDs that glow when a particular track is in record mode; the LED flashes in record standby mode.

3. Playback Indicators: Green LEDs that glow when tracks are in "safe" (playback) mode.

4. Channel Select Keys: Used to switch channels between record and playback modes or select certain tracks for delay or editing functions.

5. Aux Key: Used to toggle the analog (cue or SMPTE) track between record and playback modes.

6. Machine Select Key: When synchronizing multiple DR1200s, this key changes the operation of the Machine Select keys to control Tracks 1-12, 13-24 or 25-36.

7. Warning LED: Indicates a system error, tape problem or improper transport condition.

8. Internal Lock: This LED lights to indicate when all transports in a multiple A-DAM system are in exact synchronization.

9. Auto-Monitor: This switches playback monitoring into auto mode, where monitoring is automatically switched from track playback to the new material during overdubs or punch-in/-outs.

10. All Channel Playback: Automatically switches all channels into "safe" playback mode.

11-13. Keys for storing new channel presets—such as delay time, crossfade time, pre-/post-rolls, etc.—deleting old ones or recalling other channel presets.

CHAPTER 4

A-DAM Maintenance and Troubleshooting

There are certain eventualities in life, and one of them is that every piece of audio gear is going to break down someday. This certainly applies to vintage digital recorders. Paying attention to some obvious things, such as using high-quality tapes, keeping your recorders in a clean, dust-free (and maybe smoke-free) environment and plugging the AC lines into a power conditioner—or at least a spike/surge suppresser strip—will go a long way towards keeping your recorders happy.

Keep a maintenance log on all the gear in your studio. I keep mine in a three-ring binder, with one sheet for each piece of gear. I list the name of the device, serial number, date of purchase, software version and any pertinent info, such as the dates when the software was upgraded or the heads were cleaned, the date and description of any repairs or modifications, etc. If anything ever goes wrong with your system, it's nice to have this information handy.

TAPE HEADS

One thing to keep in mind is that the rotating heads used in any videotape-based MDM—Alesis, Akai, Fostex, Panasonic, Sony, Studer and Tascam—usually need replacing after 1,500 to 2,000 hours of use (typically less than one year at a busy studio). DAT machines use a similar rotary-head technology, but as DAT decks aren't subjected to the constant looping, shuttling and endless punch-ins/-outs that multitrack recorders endure, the heads in DAT recorders often last longer than those of MDMs. Additionally, in most music sessions, a studio's DAT machine usually sits idle until the mixing phase, while the multitracks are active during the tracking, overdub-

bing *and* mixing stages.

Concerning rotary tape heads, Akai's original guarantee on the heads was for 1,500 hours, although Akai has reported that numerous sites have logged 3,000 to 4,000 hours before requiring replacement. Your mileage may vary: Tape head life can be extended beyond the 1,500-hour figure by avoiding dusty conditions and cleaning the tape heads and pathway on a regular basis.

An internal meter in the DR1200 transport (at the left rear of the mechanical block transport assem-

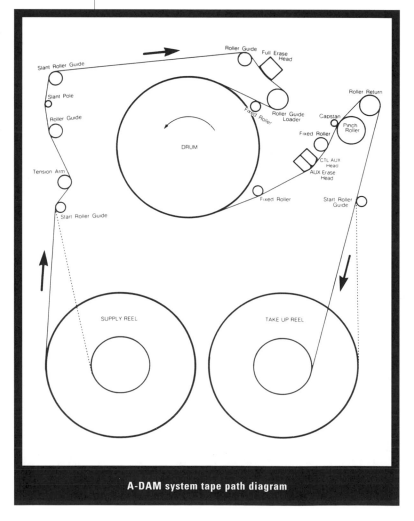

A-DAM system tape path diagram

bly) keeps track of usage, which may give you a rough idea of the remaining head life. Anyone buying a used A-DAM should take a peak under the hood and check the meter display before parting with any cash. The full scale of the head life meter corresponds to 3,000 hours; the halfway point represents 1,500 hours. Any other settings will require a bit of interpolation and guesswork.

The last time I inquired (several years ago), a new A-DAM head assembly was priced around $2,000. This is perilously close to the street price of a new Alesis ADAT XT or Tascam DA-38 and makes it higher than the $1,500 prices on used (original) ADATs.

Note: Since the head replacement process on an A-DAM involves changing the entire mechanical block and tape pathway, the swap can supposedly be handled by the average studio technician.

TRANSPORT/HEAD CLEANING PROCEDURES
In contrast to the fixed heads used on analog decks, the rotary tape heads used in the A-DAM and other MDMs (ADATs, DA-88s, etc.) are extremely fragile. However, unlike other MDMs (which typically go for lengthy periods between head cleanings), A-DAM heads require cleaning every eight to ten hours. Because they require such frequent cleaning, commercial head cleaning cassettes should *never* be used in an A-DAM system. Such products are mildly abrasive and, if used every day or so, would permanently damage the heads after a short while.

Other than explaining that no cleaning cassettes should be used, the instructions in the owner's manual are vague. Unless you have lots of money and time to drag the machine to a repair shop every day for a professional head cleaning, you'd better learn to do it yourself. With this in mind, the DR1200 transport has a door on the top for convenient access to the heads. If your A-DAM is mounted in a rack (at 80 pounds per transport, please make it a sturdy rack!), a pull-out, drawer-style mount is a necessity.

However, before embarking on the head cleaning endeavor, be aware that the insides of electronic devices carry potentially lethal voltages, and inexperienced hands mucking around in complicated electromechanical devices can seriously damage themselves and the equipment. It's all too easy to trash a $2,000 set of rotary A-DAM heads if you don't know what you're doing.

Cleaning the rotary head drum and the fixed control head is especially important before formatting tapes. Here is my recommended procedure for head and tape path cleaning.

You'll need some absolute (99+%) ethyl alcohol. This is commonly sold in drugstores as "denatured" alcohol, which is ethyl "grain" alcohol combined with

a trace amount of a chemical that makes it poisonous to keep people from drinking it. Do not use rubbing alcohol, which is typically a mixture of isopropyl alcohol combined with water. Note that ethyl alcohol is extremely flammable. Make sure it is sealed tightly after use. If it's left uncovered, it will draw water vapor out of the air and lose its purity.

The rotary heads should be cleaned using Kimwipes (which look similar to ordinary tissues, but

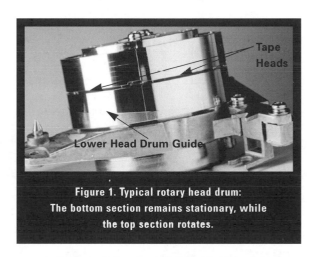

Figure 1. Typical rotary head drum: The bottom section remains stationary, while the top section rotates.

are sterile and lint-free) or deerskin (chamois) swabs. Do not use cotton swabs, as these shed lint and cotton particles, which will create havoc with rotary heads.

Begin by ejecting the tapes and disconnecting the power to the unit. Open the head access door on the top. Inside, the most prominent thing you'll see is the silver head drum, which looks similar to that shown in the photo in Chapter 2. Note that the side of the head drum has a slot cut into it that goes around the entire drum. The tiny rectangular bits that are in the slot are the video heads *(see Fig. 1)*.

Apply the absolute ethyl alcohol to the wipe or chamois and gently (but firmly) hold the wipe along the side of the head drum. Without moving the wipe, rotate the drum several times in one direction with your other hand and then reverse the direction. Do not move the wipe up and down. Allow five minutes for the head drum to dry before using the recorder. The key to the head-cleaning procedure is finding the right amount of finger pressure: There is a fine line between properly cleaning and permanently damaging the delicate rotary head. If in doubt, take the deck to an audio or video repair shop and ask them to show you the procedure for manual head cleaning before attempting it yourself.

I suggest using a dental mirror to inspect the heads and tape path before and after cleaning, and if you don't have success with ethyl alcohol, try a commercial aerosol video head cleaner.

Make sure you clean the lower head drum guide. This is an indentation in the head guide that the tape rests upon as it travels around the head. It runs at an angle to the head slot, providing the precise angle for laying the audio track information in helical scans. If you're careful not to touch the rotary heads, an alcohol-moistened cotton swab can be used. Although the lower part of the drum does not rotate, I turn the head drum several times as I clean the lower drum guide so that the heads are away from the section I'm cleaning. It is critical that this part of the tape path is absolutely clean, as any dirt or crud that accumulates can push the tape up slightly, causing the tape to mistrack, resulting in an unplayable tape.

You can also use denatured alcohol and cotton swabs to clean the rest of the tape pathway: the fixed auxiliary and full erase heads, tape guides (four fixed and eight roller), pinch roller and capstan. The lower head drum guide should be cleaned every 50 hours (or as needed). Unlike the rotary heads, these parts can be cleaned with an up and down motion; just be gentle with the fragile nylon roller guides.

The rubber pinch roller wheel should be cleaned with a cleaner designed specifically for rubber parts, as alcohols degrade the life of rubber. TEAC/Tascam makes an excellent rubber roller cleaner, which I highly recommend.

LOOKING FOR TROUBLE? AKAI ERROR MESSAGES

One possible source for mysterious A-DAM error messages is the type of tape you're using. I have had excellent results using Sony MP and Maxell HG-XM 8mm formulations but poor results with other brands of tape, including TDK. TDK makes very good VHS, DAT and analog cassettes, but their 8mm tapes just don't work well with the A-DAM system.

After using the A-DAM for a couple of days, you may encounter an "E 1 7" message on the autolocator's LED display. This translates as a read/write error (excessive block error rate) originating either on the tape or from the heads. Although there is the small possibility of mechanical/electronic problems, this usually indicates dirty heads or a bad or worn-out tape.

The Akai error messages include three characters, so an "E 1 7" code means there's an "Error on machine 1 of type 7." Here are the specifics of the error codes:

E __ 1 Mechanical or servo error occurred during transport.

E __ 2 Dew sensor indicates excessive condensation on head drum.

E __ 3 TOC data save/load malfunction.

E __ 4 Tape is not formatted or user is attempting to record audio in TOC area.

E __ 5 Record protect: The user is attempting to record on a tape that has its record-protect window closed. Slide the erase-protect door to "open" position to enable recording.

E __ 6 Sync problem: Check the sync cable and/or digital I/O cable (if error occurred during cloning).

E __ 7 Excessive block error rate caused by a poor-quality or defective tape, dirty rotary heads, etc.

ADAT Type I Format Recorders

Chapter 5 Alesis ADAT

Chapter 6 ADAT Accessories

Chapter 7 Secrets of the ADAT

Chapter 8 Fostex RD-8

Chapter 9 Alesis ADAT XT

Chapter 10 Panasonic MDA-1

Chapter 11 Fostex CX-8

Chapter 12 ADAT Maintenance and Troubleshooting

Alesis ADAT

I
t's hard to say whether ADAT is more important as a product or a phenomenon, since no device in the recent history of professional audio has created such controversy, speculation and conjecture. Announced in January of 1991, the system uses a modular approach to digital multitrack recording at a price comparable to the least expensive pro analog decks.

Immediately upon its debut, ADAT had the audio industry buzzing. ADAT's scheduled December 1991 release date came and went, and initial deliveries didn't begin until February or March of the next year, with large-scale production runs in the summer of 1992. During the 16-month period between the first ADAT announcement and widespread store deliveries, ½-inch analog 8-track sales came to a virtual standstill. Every conversation in the audio and music industry seemed to be centered around this

newcomer on the digital multitrack block. In October of 1992, Fostex announced an agreement with Alesis to develop ADAT-format recorders under the Fostex name, thus transforming ADAT from a simple model name into an accepted audio format.

The repercussions of ADAT were far-reaching indeed. Was it mere coincidence that as the first ADATs were delivered to retailers, the Society of Professional Recording Services recommended that record labels drop the ADD, DDD, etc., code designations indicating whether an album was recorded and/or mixed using analog or digital gear? After years of "educating" consumers to look for that all-important "DDD" tag, was the decision to abandon the code based on an affirmation of analog (particularly advanced analog techniques) as a viable medium, or was the availability of low-cost digital a perceived threat to the allure of a DDD sticker?

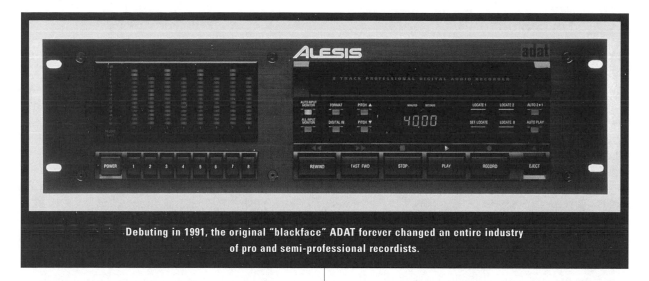

Debuting in 1991, the original "blackface" ADAT forever changed an entire industry of pro and semi-professional recordists.

SYSTEM BASICS

ADAT records on the ADAT Type I format, featuring 16-bit linear resolution, variable sampling rates of 40.4kHz to 50.8kHz, two location memories (plus return-to-zero), a looping/rehearse function and a choice of three digital crossfade times. From the start, Alesis made a conscious decision to keep ADAT at that magic under-$4,000 price tag; this required omitting certain features, such as MIDI sync, chase-lock to SMPTE time code, the ability to assign delays to indi-

Spotlight

Alesis ADAT

- Product Introduction: January 18, 1991
- Deliveries Began: March 1992
- Format: ADAT Type I, using S-VHS videotapes
- Maximum Recording Time: 40 minutes (T-120 tape), 54 minutes (T-160 tape)
- Track Capacity: Eight, expandable to 128 (in multiples of eight)
- Digital System: Rotary head; 16-bit linear; selectable 44.1/48kHz sampling frequencies
- Analog Connections: Unbalanced -10dBV ¼-inch; balanced +4dBu inputs/outputs on 56-pin EDAC multipin connector
- Digital Connections: Proprietary ADAT fiber-optic input/output ports using TosLink connectors; AES/EBU and S/PDIF interface optional
- Dimensions: 5.25x19x14 inches (HxWxD); 15 pounds
- Retail: Originally $3,995, including LRC remote control; when last offered, retail was $2,995, including LRC remote control

vidual tracks, digital assembly editing and advanced autolocation functions. If you need such features, they can be obtained by adding the Alesis BRC remote controller/synchronizer. Some of these functions are also available via add-on accessories from Alesis and a number of third-party suppliers.

Included with every ADAT is the LRC, a palm-sized remote control that duplicates all the transport controls. The LRC connects to the ADAT via a two-conductor, ¼-inch cord; the 8-foot cord attached to the LRC can be extended using a ¼-inch female-to-female "barrel" connector and a standard guitar cable.

The rear panel has sync in/out ports on 9-pin D-sub connectors and an output for an external meter bridge, which is an optional 19-inch rackmount unit that displays the levels on 32 channels (up to four ADATs) simultaneously. Fiber-optic in/out ports allow the cloning of safety copies (each ADAT includes the necessary glass fiber cable) and provide access to the digital audio datastream for connecting peripheral devices, such as the optional AI-1 AES/EBU-to-ADAT digital interface.

Any number of ADAT transports up to a maximum of 16 can be synchronized by simply daisy-chaining the units, with one 9-pin sync cable between each pair of machines. The first deck in the chain is automatically designated as the master deck, and all of the other decks in the chain will follow it with sample-accurate (±1/48,000 second) synchronization. Adding the BRC to the system adds some extra features and makes recording operations more convenient, but the BRC is *not* required for interlocking multiple ADAT transports.

ADAT's sample-accurate sync performance is achieved via electronic, rather than mechanical, sync. As data is read by two machines in close mechanical sync, the digital information is stored in a buffer. Word-clock timing information from the master machine (carried in the 9-pin ADAT sync cable) controls the release of data from the second deck's buffer, which enables sample-accurate sync. Other information carried via the 9-pin connections includes bidirectional MIDI data for MIDI Machine Control and Alesis-proprietary System Exclusive MIDI commands, sample address data and word-clock in/out.

Fig. 2 shows the results of testing ADAT's self-sync accuracy. To perform this test, I recorded two tapes with the same information—an instantaneous tone burst 40 seconds from the tail of the tape. I played the ADATs in sync, routing one output from each machine into a separate channel of a Digidesign Sound Tools system, recording the burst and examining the waveforms. The horizontal axis is divided into blocks of 64 samples, with each time period approximately 0.00145 seconds. As is clearly evident in the waveform display, the sync is rock-steady and far more accurate than any two analog tape transports.

Alesis sells the 9-pin sync cables for $11.95, but any D-sub 9-pin cable with pin-to-pin connections, male connectors on both ends and the shield connected to the connector shell on both ends will work. (Despite this ominously technical description, this is a fairly standard computer item. It's even carried by Radio Shack—part #26-116, $9.95.)

It's important to note that the transport synchronization scheme used in the Alesis ADAT, the Tascam DA-88 and other MDM designs does not require an audio track for SMPTE or other synchronization signals. When you lock up two ADATs, you get 16 usable audio tracks, and the same is true for synching two Tascam DA-88s, Fostex RD-8s or Yamaha DMR8/DRU8 units.

CONNECTIONS

Analog input/output connections include both ¼-inch jacks (-10dBV, unbalanced) and +4dBu balanced. However, to reduce manufacturing costs, ADAT's +4dBu I/O is provided on a single 56-pin EDAC (Elco-compatible) connector. These can be hard to find and fairly expensive but rugged, with large, gold-plated contact pins. These connectors are not unusual for professional audio gear, including certain Soundcraft, Neve and Soundtracs mixers, as well as the Alesis X-2 recording console.

Currently, there is no industry standard for the wiring of 56-pin EDACs, so using ADAT's +4dBu connections may require some lengthy soldering sessions. Luckily, Alesis had the forethought to print the connector's pinout on the back panel and in the manual. While this is not noted, the pinout diagram

refers to the *face* of the female connector or the *solder side* of the male plug. If your mixer has balanced +4dBu connections, the effort of wiring to the ADAT's EDAC is highly recommended: The hotter outputs require less console input gain, and the balanced lines reduce the possibility of noise/hum problems.

As an alternative, several companies are marketing EDAC-to-XLR and EDAC-to-¼-inch snakes. ADAT-compatible interface cables are manufactured by Clark Wire & Cable (708-272-9889), Hosa (714-522-5675), Pro Co (616-388-9675), Whirlwind (716-663-8820) and others. Also, Elco makes multipin connectors which are compatible with the ADAT-EDAC connectors. For more information about Elcos, EDACs and ADAT cabling, see Chapter 25.

Also on the rear panel is a ¼-inch jack for a punch-in/-out footswitch. Any momentary-contact, single-pole/single-throw (SPST) switch, such as a standard synthesizer sustain pedal, can be used for this function. Make sure the footswitch is connected to the ADAT when powering up; during the power-up procedure, the ADAT automatically senses whether the footswitch is closed or open and adjusts itself accordingly.

Speaking of powering up, you should know that ADATs output a noticeable audio "thump" every time they are turned on. Make sure that any ADATs in your audio system are turned on before you turn on the power amplifiers. This is good advice for any audio system: The power amps should always be LOFO (last-on/first-off) devices; conversely, ADATs are FOLO (first-on/last-off) units.

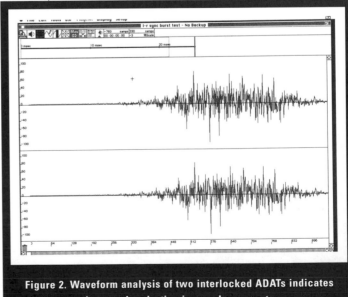

Figure 2. Waveform analysis of two interlocked ADATs indicates that synchronization is sample-accurate.

OPERATIONS

ADAT operations are extremely straightforward—anyone who has used a cassette multitrack should be able to figure out ADAT in a matter of minutes. One obvious exception is tape formatting, which involves writing time-address data onto the videotape, much like the procedure for formatting floppy disks. Formatting takes place in real time (40+ minutes per tape). In a multitransport ADAT system, you can format tapes on an unused transport (as long as it's not synchronized to the others) while recording tracks on another machine.

In an emergency, tracks can be recorded while formatting, but any gaps in the address data on the tape will result in unrecordable areas. For example, let's say you format a three-minute song while recording some basic tracks. Later, while overdubbing, the vocalist spontaneously decides to add an a cappella chorus to the end of the song. The performance is amazing, but unfortunately, since you stopped formatting at the 3:10 mark and the new vocal dub continued 30 seconds beyond that, the deck stopped recording at the 3:10 point. It's always possible to continue the formatting on a partially formatted tape by entering the format mode before the end of a previously formatted section, but the case described above is one of many reasons why pre-formatting is a good idea.

During the formatting process, a tape is divided into three sections: leader, data and the recordable area. These are shown on ADAT's LED time counter respectively as "LEAD," "DATA" and a minutes/seconds display. The LEAD section refers to a short length of leader at the beginning of the tape. If you are using an ADAT system without a BRC remote controller/synchronizer, you may wonder about the need for the 2-minute, 15-second DATA section at the beginning of each tape. While of little use in a non-BRC system, the DATA section allows the storage of hundreds of locator points, the names of the points and song titles, which can be recalled and displayed on the BRC's 2-line by 16-character, backlit LCD screen.

Other helpful ADAT counter displays include "noFo," indicating that the tape is not formatted, and "Prot" indicating that has had its erase-protect tab removed. The counter is also capable of displaying various error and status messages, which are explained in detail in Chapter 12.

PERFORMANCE

Intensive listening tests on high-end consumer and studio speaker systems indicate that the ADAT sounds very good. In fact, A/B comparison tests of the ADAT and a CD playback source revealed only extremely subtle differences between the two. In qualitative terms, I'd say it sounds equal to a good-quality DAT machine, so if you're pleased with the sound of DATs, you'll be quite happy with ADAT.

Of course, an ADAT doesn't sound much like an analog machine, but neither does a $250,000 Sony PCM-3348 digital multitrack. If you want a slightly different sound, try ADAT with an Apogee Electronics (Santa Monica, CA) or Manley (Chino, CA) outboard analog-to-digital converter. (This requires the optional ADAT optical-to-AES/EBU or S/PDIF interface.)

Without a doubt, the Alesis ADAT (mostly in terms of its then-revolutionary $3,995 pricing) forever changed an entire industry of semi-pro and professional recordists.

In terms of frequency response, Alesis specifies a figure of 20-20kHz, ±0.5dB. The ADATs I've tested have exceeded this spec by a considerable margin, with one deck measuring out flat to a tolerance of ±0.1dB and others in the range of ±0.2dB.

Alesis claims a THD+Noise spec of 0.009 (at 1kHz); this was confirmed to be extremely close, although one machine tested out insignificantly higher at 0.00952 percent. Even at 10kHz (ADAT's worst-case performance), THD+N measured below 0.02 percent, which is quite respectable.

One of digital's fundamental axioms is not to exceed 0dB on the meters, as digital clipping is an immediately apparent artifact. An 18dBV input lights the red clip LEDs, with the result being very audible, unpleasant harmonic distortion exceeding 5.6 percent. A word to the wise: Keep out of the red.

In the "don't try this at home" department, I've also disassembled a few ADATs. The layout of the transport and boards is clean and clear; access for servicing or routine maintenance should be fairly simple, especially in the transport section, which is designed for heavy use. I was surprised by the amount of room in the case. It didn't resemble the jumbled trappings of a consumer VCR, which is what I had expected.

The ADAT's digital-to-analog converter chips are Burr-Brown 1700s, and the analog-to-digital converters are Crystal CS5336s: good stuff. Some little touches, like Shottke protection diodes on the analog-digital converters, high-quality Wima capacitors and the placement of the switching power supply in a separate lower compartment (shielded from other components), indicate that a lot of care went into the audio design, and the measured specs confirm this.

A built-in lithium cell on the main board retains autolocator settings, even when the unit is unplugged or switched off. In my experience, such batteries last at least five years (usually eight or more), so around the turn of the century, if you encounter a senile ADAT, the problem may be nothing more than a dead battery.

I imagine that 16 synchronized ADATs would make a sizable racket, which is a good reason to hide the machines away in a separate machine room (or a very tall rack in a closet).

The ADAT transport is smooth, though sometimes a bit noisy from cassette shell noise, particularly when shuttling into play. When recording with two synched machines, the operating noise of the transports is noticeable in a quiet control room—about as loud as a hard disk whirring. It isn't unreasonably loud, but you can tell it's there. I imagine that 16 synchronized ADATs would make a sizable racket, which is a good reason to hide the machines away in a separate machine room (or a very tall rack in a closet) and use the BRC controller with a couple optional remote meter bridges for visual monitoring of the signals.

ADAT's front-panel layout is logical, with everything where you'd expect it. I would prefer a preset switch for changing the sampling rate from 48 to 44.1kHz; currently, the unit defaults to 48kHz, and changing the rate to 44.1kHz involves adjusting the +100/-300 cent pitch control by -147 cents.

Speaking of time, the deck requires about three to four seconds to switch into play or record from stop. If the heads are "engaged" (a pause-style mode where the tape is lightly held against the head drum), then going into play takes about one second. The tape can be shuttled forward or backward with the heads engaged, although long fast-forwards or rewinds should be avoided. Two presses on the Stop button disengage the heads, and the heads disengage automatically if no transport activity occurs for four minutes. A 40-minute tape rewinds in 112 seconds.

While the BRC provides a means of choosing from four crossfade times (10.67, 21.33, 32 and 42.67ms), the ADAT unit does not have a dedicated switch for this function. Nonetheless, non-BRC ADAT users can make a choice as well; press the Set Locate and Record buttons simultaneously and the display will read "FAd1," which means the 10.67ms setting is selected. Pressing the two buttons a second time brings up "FAd2," meaning 21.33ms, and so on for the 32ms and 42.67ms crossfade times. The unit defaults to the comparatively short 10.67ms setting, which is best for most applications; however, the longer crossfades are particularly useful on sustained notes and guitar, vocal and reverberant instrumental tracks.

TAPE TIPS

With ADAT's high operating speed, a 120-minute S-VHS cassette yields 40 minutes and 44 seconds of record time. However, the original ADAT's recording time can be extended to 54 minutes by using a 160-minute tape; the only drawback when using tapes longer than 120 minutes is that the tape counter display will be incorrect. This is easily corrected by putting the ADAT into the "160 Mode," by simply pressing the Set Locate and Format buttons simultaneously. When the two buttons are pressed, the counter display will toggle between the "Std" and "t160" settings to indicate your choice of mode. 160-minute tapes are manufactured on a thinner tape stock that is more fragile than the 120-minute tapes, so I would suggest using the shorter tapes unless you're working on a project that demands the extra running time.

But be wary of shorter cassettes as well: I once formatted a 20-minute, professional broadcast cassette, which, after recording the time address data, provided a net recording time of only six minutes!

Over the years, I've tested a variety of S-VHS tapes on the ADAT, including Ampex, 3M, BASF, JVC, Maxell, Sony, TDK, Alesis (identical to Ampex 489, but in a specially packaged version with the Alesis name) and other brands. So far, the most consistently high-quality, trouble-free tapes have been the Ampex 489, BASF, Maxell and TDK.

I once tried JVC's S-XZ, a top-of-the-line S-VHS formulation. (At a discounted street price of $12.99, this is the most expensive tape I've used.) Ironically, the $8.99 JVC S-XG tape worked better. In the middle of a live jazz session using the S-XZ, the ADAT started flashing "Er-7" and dropped out of record mode. Wondering what this referred to, I looked through the manual, but it was no help. Alesis prefers in such cases that you call their tech staff, but unfortunately this situation occurred during a late-night session. I put a pre-formatted Ampex 489 tape into the deck and continued recording for another two hours without incident.

An Alesis representative later explained that "Er-7" indicates a loss in control-track data and, since the machine worked afterward, perhaps it had been a faulty tape. He said that Alesis had tested dozens of tape formulations, ranging from "el cheapo" off-brands to exotic high-end stuff, with good results.

A few lessons can be learned from this incident:

1. If you're recording something really important, run two machines in tandem as a backup.
2. Always have a few extra formatted tapes available, just in case.
3. Find a good-quality tape you like and stick to it.

Although Alesis recommends using the best tape possible—especially since these tend to have the best mechanisms and shells—I decided to check out ADAT's performance with the worst tape I could find: a generic non-S-VHS tape from K-Mart. I pre-formatted the tape, but when I rewound and started recording, the blinking "Er-7" display came on immediately. I resorted to an old analog trick: exercising the tape (fast-forwarding and rewinding before the first use) and re-formatting. I hit the Record button and was surprised to see the system operate normally. And the playback was spot-on! So I set up a 20-second loop and let the machine cycle (play-rewind-locate-play…) for about 90 minutes, after which it still sounded great. Perhaps the old exercise trick applies equally well to digital multitrack cassettes—time will tell.

The ADAT manual provides good primer-level explanations of ADAT operations and recording principles, but it does not include schematics or a signal flow diagram. There are no head cleaning instructions either, but I've inspected ADATs after periods of 500-1,000 hours of use and found that in most cases, the tape heads and pathway remained remarkably clean. Any pro maintenance engineer versed in video head cleaning will have no problem cleaning the heads, drum and guides. Conversely, untrained hands getting into any precision mechanism can lead to possible equipment damage and/or electrocution.

If head cleaning is required, Alesis recommends the 3M ASD Series Model HC or Black Watch, two "dry" formulation cleaning cassettes that can be used every 800 hours or whenever the Advanced Information indicator glows steadily. This indicator is a green LED that looks like an additional decimal point, located at the lower right-hand corner of the "seconds" indicator on the time display. Alesis does not recommend any other cleaning methods; in particular, don't use "wet" cleaners, which typically involve putting a few drops of some cleaning liquid onto a VHS-sized cleaning mechanism. Such methods may permanently damage the ADAT heads and should *never* be used. If you are unsure of the number of hours, pressing the Set Locate and Stop buttons simultaneously will display the total elapsed hours of head drum operation on the time counter display.

MORE, MUCH MORE

The Alesis ADAT is undeniably an impressive piece of gear. However, there are many operations, such as multichannel editing, video and/or MIDI synchronization, multipoint autolocation, track delays, track bouncing, etc., that are lacking in the basic ADAT because the original price was kept as low as possible. The optional $1,495 BRC controller (more on this in Chapter 6) adds such essential functions like transforming one or more ADATs into a complete studio system, adding SMPTE time code read/write/generate, chase-lock sync, MIDI sync, MIDI Machine Control, fingertip transport control of up to 16 ADAT decks, up to 400 locate points, digital-domain track bouncing, automated assembly editing, independent delay of any or all tracks, record group assignments, auto-punch-in/-out, multimachine offset and more.

Without a doubt, the Alesis ADAT (mostly in terms of its then-revolutionary $3,995 pricing) forever changed an entire industry of semi-pro and professional recordists. Although it has been replaced with other machines, such as the Alesis XT, it's still compatible with newer ADAT systems, including the radical Alesis M20 and Studer V-Eight recorders. And with tens of thousands of these original ADATs in use throughout the world, I have a feeling we'll be seeing these in use for years to come.

Alesis Corporation
3630 Holdrege Avenue
Los Angeles, CA 90016
310-558-4530
http://www.alesis.com

Note: Turn page for diagrams of Alesis ADAT front and rear panels.

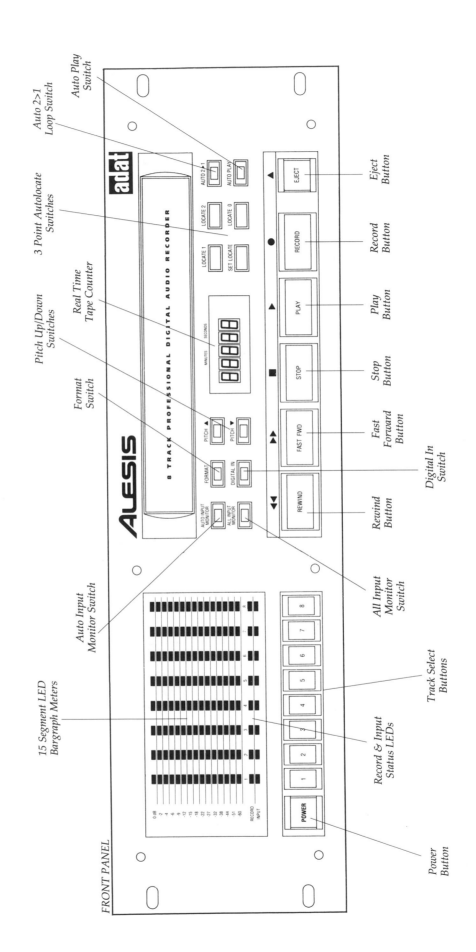

FRONT PANEL

Auto Play Switch

Auto 2>1 Loop Switch

3 Point Autolocate Switches

Real Time Tape Counter

Pitch Up/Down Switches

Format Switch

Auto Input Monitor Switch

15 Segment LED Bargraph Meters

Eject Button

Record Button

Play Button

Stop Button

Fast Forward Button

Digital In Switch

Rewind Button

All Input Monitor Switch

Track Select Buttons

Record & Input Status LEDs

Power Button

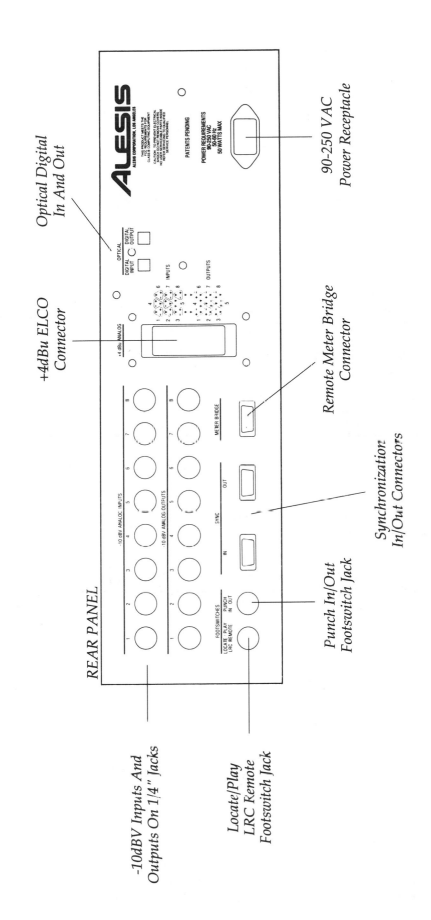

REAR PANEL

-10dBV Inputs And
Outputs On 1/4" Jacks

Locate/Play
LRC Remote
Footswitch Jack

Punch In/Out
Footswitch Jack

Synchronization
In/Out Connectors

Remote Meter Bridge
Connector

+4dBu ELCO
Connector

Optical Digital
In And Out

90-250 VAC
Power Receptacle

CHAPTER 6

ADAT Accessories

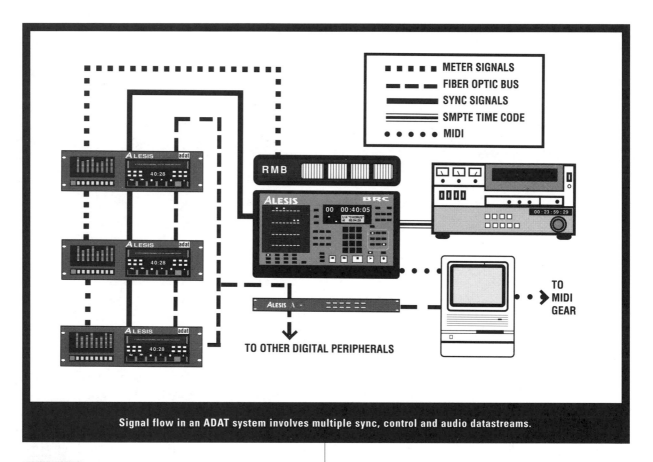

Signal flow in an ADAT system involves multiple sync, control and audio datastreams.

METER SIGNALS
FIBER OPTIC BUS
SYNC SIGNALS
SMPTE TIME CODE
MIDI

RMB

TO OTHER DIGITAL PERIPHERALS

TO MIDI GEAR

ALESIS BRC

Without a doubt, the Alesis ADAT is an impressive piece of gear. However, there are many operations, such as multichannel editing, video and/or MIDI synchronization, multipoint autolocation, track delays, track bouncing, etc., that are lacking in the basic ADAT system. The optional BRC controller ($1,495) adds such essential functions, transforming one or more ADATs into a complete studio system.

BRC is an acronym for Big Remote Control (the LRC, Little Remote Control, is included with each ADAT recorder). It performs all of the functions expected from any modern multitrack autolocator, plus far more. Standard features include SMPTE time code read/write/generate, chase-lock to any external SMPTE source, MIDI synchronization, MIDI Machine

Control, transport control of up to 16 ADAT decks (128 tracks), up to 400 locate points, digital-domain track bouncing, automated assembly editing, independent delay, record group assignments, auto-punch-in/-out, multimachine offset and more.

As if this weren't enough, the BRC also provides a few other clever tricks, such as the ability to name and display individual song titles, take numbers or regions, as well as storing such data (along with setup information, autolocator points and customized user defaults) on the head of each tape. By now, you should get the idea that the BRC's abilities go beyond those of a mere remote controller.

However, don't throw out your LRC just because you have a BRC, as the LRC can be connected to act as a remote control for the BRC itself. This can be useful if your BRC resides near the mixing console and you want to have a secondary remote elsewhere in the room, such as near a synth rack.

Before getting started with the BRC, you need to know a few things. In refining the BRC over the past couple years, Alesis added a lot of extra bells and whistles to the system beyond what they had originally envisioned. The bad news is that the BRC only works with ADATs whose internal control software is version 3.03 or higher. The good news is that Alesis will update your ADATs to the latest software at no charge; call Alesis for details. On most ADATs, this is a simple EPROM (software chip) swap; on some early units, this involves a chip swap and minor hardware modification. You can determine an ADAT's software version by pressing the Set Locate and Fast-forward buttons simultaneously; the number of the software version will be shown on the LED display.

Physically, the BRC is sizable, built into a hefty 12-pound, wedge-shaped box with a top panel measuring 10.5x17 inches. Beneath the removable end panels are rack ears for mounting in a standard 19-inch rack or an optional roll-around stand. The BRC also fits nicely on an industrial-duty music stand. The optional 32-channel Remote Meter Bridge (RMB) can also be mounted on top of the BRC. The BRC includes a 30-foot, 9-pin control cable for connection to the ADAT, but the 6-foot AC power cord seems too short. I substituted a 12-foot cable in my system, which is more convenient.

Speaking of cables, BRC cables have been tested reliably up to lengths of 300 feet using a twisted pair, pin-to-pin, grounded and shielded cable at both ends. It is critical for the cable be a twisted pair to avoid any interference which could interrupt the clock signal and possibly corrupt the command chain. Sync cables are available in three different lengths from Alesis' parts department. Pinouts are available through Alesis Technical Support for any users who would like their own custom cable built.

The BRC's rear panel has ¼-inch jacks for locate/play (the LRC) and an optional punch-in/-out footswitch; SMPTE in and out (both +4 and -10 signals are accommodated); 48kHz clock in/out and video sync input on BNC connectors; and MIDI in/out ports. That's more connections than the usual autolocator setup, so I suggest using cable ties to create a custom "snake" for BRC connections that avoids the "rat's nest" effect of tangled cables. This is highly recommended for any BRC user.

The front panel is similar to any other professional transport autolocator, and anyone familiar with such devices can work with the BRC immediately. The

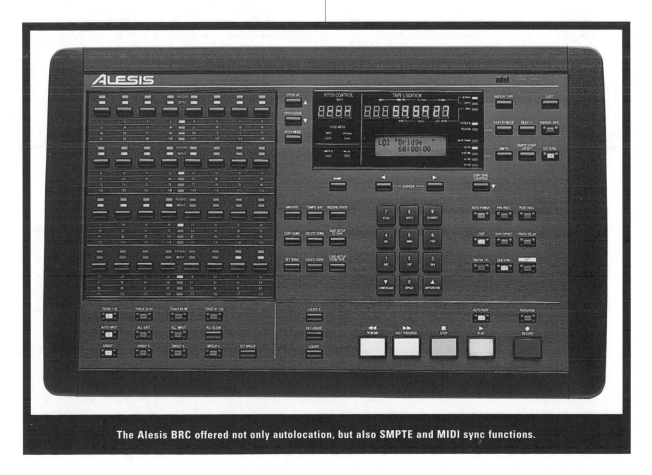

The Alesis BRC offered not only autolocation, but also SMPTE and MIDI sync functions.

Track Arming/Record-Play select buttons on the left allow the user to monitor status and control any number of ADATs simply and efficiently. The transport buttons are illuminated, as are many of the function and editing buttons. For some reason, the button that takes the BRC in and out of edit mode is marked in blue, a color that's hard to read. (The color was changed in later BRCs.) Fortunately, its location makes it easy to find, as this button plays a vital role in BRC operations.

Tape location is provided on an hours/minutes/seconds/frames display with ½-inch LEDs; this read-out can be switched to display normal (absolute or relative) time, SMPTE locations, or musical bars/beats/sub-beats. A switch selects any of six SMPTE formats, and a 2-line by 16-character alphanumeric LCD readout indicates location points/addresses, edit mode information and song names. As with many LCD readouts, the BRC's display has a contrast control to optimize viewing from any angle.

Information is entered into the BRC via a 10-key alphanumeric pad that allows names to be created quickly, while two Up/Down Arrow keys enable instant changes from upper- to lower-case text. This approach is light-years ahead of the scroll-through-the-entire-alphabet-twice routine that most programmable gear requires. When you are in a mode that requires purely numerical entry, such as defining offsets or SMPTE times, the keypad responds as a standard 10-key device.

The BRC provides for the creation of 20 "songs," each defined as a particular set of parameters, with up to 20 location points (and their names), pre-/post-roll times, auto-punch points, loop points, track delays, tape offsets, track groupings, tempo maps, and user defaults for MIDI and/or SMPTE synchronization settings. Location points can be set on the fly or entered manually.

Various editing windows set the parameters for BRC functions. For example, punch-ins/-outs and machine-sync offsets are frame-accurate events, but by entering the "fine-tune" window, they can be defined to occur with subframe (1/100 frame) or sample accuracy.

Continuous play allows multiple ADATs to operate in a relay fashion for a virtually unlimited amount of record/play time: As one deck stops recording, another seamlessly begins from that point. The process requires twice the number of machines (two ADATs for an 8-track recording; four for 16 tracks, etc.) and requires careful pre-planning and an involved setup procedure, but it does the trick when you have to record a really *looooooooooong* event, such as a live concert.

The BRC offers extensive control of the Alesis Digital Bus, a proprietary fiber-optic chain that allows the creation of perfect clones of important sessions, assembly editing and track bouncing. And while the BRC acts as a central *controller* for data traveling between multiple ADATs, all digital data stays within the digital bus. To take full advantage of the digital bus, the fiber-optic ports of all ADATs in the system must be interconnected in a daisy-chain. In a 24-track system, the digital out of ADAT #1 would feed the digital in of ADAT #2; deck two's output would feed deck three's input and, to complete the chain, deck three's output would be connected to deck one's input.

Tracks can be bounced (copied) from any single ADAT to any other machine in the chain. The procedure is straightforward, and any source tracks can be copied to any record-enabled tracks. For example, Tracks 2, 7 and 8 on ADAT #1 (as indicated via track-select buttons) could be copied to Tracks 12, 15 and 23, with the lowest-numbered source track automatically routed to the lowest-numbered destination track, etc.

One of the BRC's most powerful features is assembly editing, providing nondestructive editing capability in the digital domain. While the off-line, video-style assemble editing process on the BRC is not as fast as a typical disk-based workstation—and lacks some of the features, such as playlist editing—it nonetheless offers great creativity and flexibility.

I often use multitrack assembly editing to manipulate or change the structure of a song after I've cut the basic tracks, cutting and pasting at will to create several versions or tighten up an arrangement. However, the BRC's assembly editing capability is also useful for editing 2-track material, such as DAT mixes. In fact, two ADATs teamed with a BRC and the Alesis AI-1 digital interface can form a simple, effective system for editing and/or sequencing tunes from DAT tapes.

As an example, a song I produced recently, called "International World", is a 9-minute rock anthem for global unity with verses in six languages. I needed an under-5-minute, which required deleting a verse and two choruses, trimming the solo and moving a couple of the other parts around, for a total of about seven edits. For the first edit, I began by transferring the entire 2-track mix to ADAT #1. Next, I copied the intro and first verse from ADAT #1 to ADAT #2, using the fiber-optic digital bus cable. By adjusting the sync offset between the two machines, I deleted the second verse on the new copy by delaying the third verse on #1 to follow the first verse on #2. For such an operation, the essential offset and punch-in/-out times can be tweaked in the edit page before auditioning an auto-punch with the rehearse function.

BRC assembly editing is much easier to fathom if you think of the auto-punch-in point as the end of the section you're adding to and manipulate the offset of the source ADAT to define the other side of the edit point. The fine-tune pages in edit modes allow sample-accurate nudging of edit points, like a workstation, and the rehearse function lets you preview edits as many times as you need. (This is another place where the ADAT's selectable crossfade times come in handy.) Once you determine the exact edit you need, just turn off the rehearse key and hit the Record button to make it permanent.

The assembly-editing process can also be applied to individual tracks (to create a seamless vocal or instrumental performance from several different takes) or to entire multitrack sections, such as rhythm tracks. You can also combine assembly editing with subsequent track bouncing (or vice versa) for even more complex manipulations.

Other parameters available in the ADAT's edit pages include pre- and post-roll times (up to 20 seconds) and track delay. The latter offers the ability to individually delay the playback of any track by up to 170ms. The BRC manual recommends this function for shifting certain instruments into and out of "the pocket," but track delay is also an invaluable method of making phase adjustments to compensate for variances in mic technique and distances.

Here's an example of the creative use of track delays: On a guitar solo overdub, I combined three sources—a Tech 21 SansAmp preamp/processor, a close-miked guitar cabinet and a tube mic placed across the room—recorded on individual tracks. Each sounded fine alone, but when mixed together, the results were disappointing. Adding delays to the SansAmp (19ms) and close mic (23ms) tracks "aligned" their signals with the far-field tube mic, yielding a punchy and tight sound. Similar results were obtained when combining a direct-box input and an amp mic on a bass guitar. Drums also benefit when close-miked signals are delay-aligned with the overhead and room mics. It's an amazing difference. As a rough guideline, remember that sound travels about one foot per millisecond, and you'll be on your way to all kinds of track-delay fun.

Sync is also no problem under BRC control. The system slaves to incoming SMPTE time code at 24, 25, 29.97 or 30 fps, with the latter two selectable to standard or drop-frame varieties. However, you should verify what the source code type is; the BRC cannot tell the difference between 29.97 and 30 fps, even though the system can automatically detect and sync to incoming code. Video sync (composite or black burst) and word-clock in/out ports are also provided, and BRC's SMPTE in/out ports can be switched to operate at +4 or -10dB levels.

The BRC also offers sync to MIDI sequencers using either MIDI time code or MIDI Clock/Song Position Pointers. Tempo maps can be created (and stored with individual song information) with relative ease, and the BRC tape location readout can be switched to display events in bars/beats/sub-beats, which is a nice touch.

Besides providing a convenient place for storing location points and song defaults (including tempo maps), the data section on the head of each ADAT tape is also capable of sending and receiving MIDI data in the form of SysEx dumps. This means that backups of the BRC data can be loaded to or from outboard MIDI devices, such as sequencers or the Alesis DataDisk. The data section has a capacity of approximately 20KB, opening up interesting possibilities for future use.

The BRC also supports MIDI Machine Control and many sequencing programs (and some forward-thinking console manufacturers) include MMC transport controllers as onscreen or hardware features.

THE REMOTE METER BRIDGE
Sooner or later, your ADAT system will expand to the point where you have too many transports to keep track of and not enough space in your control room for all the meters to be within sight. Another complication might be that the operating noise of 4, 8, 12 or 16 ADAT transports can add up to a major ruckus. Since the units can be controlled remotely via the

The Alesis Remote Meter Bridge (RMB)

BRC, you might want to tuck them away in a closet or machine room somewhere. And while your mixer might accommodate 32, 64 or even 128 inputs, your console probably won't have enough meters to handle a growing population of ADATs.

Enter the Alesis Remote Meter Bridge (RMB), a $995 accessory that puts 32 tracks of metering anywhere you need it. The RMB can be placed atop a mixing console, mounted in a signal-processing rack or attached to the BRC controller. The unit is in a 2-rackspace enclosure and provides four banks of eight meters (each bank connects to the recorder via a 9-pin D-sub cable) that use the same 16-segment LED level displays as the ADAT.

One major difference between the RMB and the standard ADAT meters is that the RMB includes front-panel switches that give the user complete control over all metering operations. Two peak modes are available: The "momentary" setting (the same as standard ADAT metering) holds peaks for approximately 1.5 seconds, and the "peak hold" mode continuously displays the highest peak on each track until the "peak clear" switch is pressed.

Meter decay time is also adjustable, and users have a choice of the fast decay of the standard ADAT meters or a slow of one-half of the normal ADAT meter

is another serial protocol developed jointly by Sony and Philips (hence the "S/P" designation) for carrying two channels of digital audio over a single line, with either RCA (phono jack) or fiber-optic terminations. Note that the S/PDIF optical interface is incompatible with the ADAT fiber-optic digital bus.

Priced at $895 and housed in a single-rackspace box, the Alesis AI-1 combines a sample rate converter with an Alesis fiber-optic-to-AES/EBU and S/PDIF digital interface. Thus, the AI-1 provides the pathway for bringing signals from other digital audio devices —such as recorders, digital-to-analog and analog-to-digital converters, CD players, CD recorders, workstations and an increasing number of digital signal processors—directly into the ADAT format without leaving the digital domain, eliminating signal loss (as long as the peripheral is equipped with a digital output port). The AI-1 works with 32kHz (a seldom-used radio broadcast standard), 44.1kHz and 48kHz sampling rates, so it will be able to handle conversions such as transferring a sound effect from a CD player's digital output (44.1kHz) to an ADAT tape recorded at the default rate of 48kHz.

In addition to loading information from DAT and CD sources, the AI-1 is essential for transferring material to and from digital workstations and editing

Now discontinued, the Alesis AI-1 converted various digital signals to/from Alesis Lightpipe format.

speed. In the slow decay mode, the meter operation resembles slower-reacting mechanical VU meters.

Note: The Alesis RMB only works with the original Alesis ADAT and Fostex RD-8 machines. Due to a later proliferation of 8-bus consoles on the market (with extensive meter bridges), the RMB connection was deleted from the second generation ADATs, such as the ADAT XT, Panasonic MDA-1 and Fostex CX-8.

THE ALESIS AI-1

In addition to the Alesis fiber-optic digital bus, several other digital audio transfer standards are in use. The AES/EBU digital standard is a serial protocol adopted jointly by the Audio Engineering Society and the European Broadcasting Union for transferring two channels of digital audio along a single line, using a 3-conductor cable with XLR connectors. Originally intended for use in home stereo equipment, S/PDIF

systems not equipped with the ADAT-format fiber-optic connectors.

As mentioned earlier, AES/EBU and S/PDIF ports transmit digital audio information serially in stereo pairs. When connected to an ADAT (via the AI-1), audio information from the source device will be routed to any enabled tracks, as long as the recipient ADAT's digital input switch is enabled and the daisy-chained digital bus is connected between all ADATs in the system. Conversely, audio information from any two adjacent ADAT tracks can be sent to an outside digital peripheral via the AI-1.

One useful application for the AI-1 involves using an ADAT as a combination tracking and mixdown system. You could record six tracks on a single ADAT (or 14 tracks on a 2-deck system), mix through your console and route the finished mix to the two unused ADAT tracks. Later, using the AI-1, the mixes

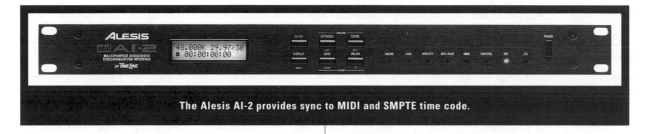

The Alesis AI-2 provides sync to MIDI and SMPTE time code.

could be transferred to DAT or a workstation system for final assembly and editing.

The AI-1 can also be used without an ADAT as a stand-alone digital sample rate converter, for applications such as digitally transferring the output of a 44.1kHz CD to a consumer DAT deck operating at 48kHz.

THE ALESIS AI-2

Another useful ADAT accessory is the AI-2 synchronizer ($995), developed jointly with TimeLine (Vista, CA). Used with an ADAT system (with or without the BRC), the single-rackspace AI-2 can act as a stand-alone synchronizer for chase-locking to incoming SMPTE time code from any source. Other features include a time code reader with support of -10dBV and +4dBu input levels, reshaped time code output, MIDI Time Code output, MIDI Machine Control support, MIDI merging, word-clock in/out, video sync or black burst reference input and a 9-pin interface (Sony P2), providing VTR emulation for control via a TimeLine Lynx, Lynx-2 or Microlynx video editing system.

In 1995, the AI-2's software was upgraded to version 2.00, adding major new features, the most significant of which was "Local Play." This provides the ability to use a master ADAT (ID 1) and an AI-2 as a controller with SMPTE time code and MIDI Time Code (MTC) generation. For example, press play on your master ADAT, and the AI-2 will output MTC and/or SMPTE Longitudinal Time Code (LTC) relative to the location of the ADAT's tape. Any ID'd ADAT slaves will chase and lock to the AI-2 as well.

Other new features include acting as a master source for LTC (linear SMPTE) and MIDI Time Code, the ability to generate any time code based on the AI-2 time code offset and returning the AI-2 to chase/slave mode via the ADAT front panel.

Local Play Mode is supported by original ADAT versions 4.00 and higher, and all ADAT-XT versions. All versions of the Panasonic MDA-1 and Fostex CX-8 ADAT-compatible multitrack recorders will also accommodate the AI-2's Local Play feature.

THIRD-PARTY ACCESSORIES

A large user base has encouraged third parties to develop hardware accessories, custom modifications and peripherals to work with the ADAT system. Covering all of these would require more pages than this entire book, so here's a partial list with thumbnail descriptions of some of the available products, along with telephone numbers and Website addresses (if available).

Aardvark
313-665-8899; http://www.aardvark-pro.com
• Studio12—12-channel I/O card for loading ADAT tracks into a PC

Akai Professional
817-336-5114; http://www.akai.com/akaipro
• DR8—8-channel disk recorder with optional ADAT interface
• DR16—16-channel disk recorder with optional ADAT interface

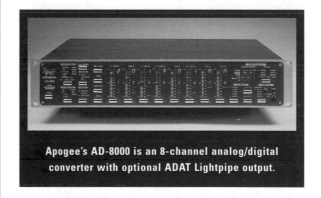

Apogee's AD-8000 is an 8-channel analog/digital converter with optional ADAT Lightpipe output.

Apogee Electronics
310-915-1000; http://www.apogeedigital.com
• AD-8000—8-channel analog-to-digital converter ADAT output
• AD-1000—analog-to-digital converter with mic pre-amp and ADAT output
• FC8—format converter for transferring tracks to/from ADAT to Tascam TDIF format

BASF/JRPro Sales

805-295-5551

- BASF ADAT Master Tape is available in 40- or 60-minute lengths.

CreamWare

604-527-9924; http://www.creamware.com

- TDAT-16—PCI card with two ADAT interfaces for 16 channels of I/O between an Intel Pentium PC and ADAT optical interface

Digidesign

415-842-7900; http://www.digidesign.com

- ADAT Interface—interface for connecting ADAT to its ProTools and Session-8 workstation products

Digital Audio Labs

612-559-9098; http://www.digitalaudio.com

- V8—8-channel I/O card for PCs, with optional ADAT I/O

Digital Labs/Horizon Music

314-651-6500

- ADAT Upgrade Boards—plug-in replacement circuit cards for the analog electronics in original ADATs

E-mu Systems

408-438-1921; http://www.emu.com

- Darwin—8-channel disk-based recorder editor with optional ADAT I/O

Ensoniq

610-647-3930; http://www.ensoniq.com

- Paris—disk-based digital recorder/editor with optional ADAT interface

Fostex

310-921-1112; http://www.fostex.com

- CX-8—ADAT-compatible recorder (now discontinued)
- RD-8—ADAT-compatible recorder (now discontinued)
- Foundation—line of disk-based workstations with ADAT I/O

FutureVideo

714-770-4416; http://www.futurevideo.com

- Editlink AV 2110—ADAT-compatible edit controller for Windows
- Media Commander 100—ADAT-compatible edit controller for Windows

Hohner Midia

707-578-2023; http://www.hohnermidia.com

- ARC 88—PCI-based PC recording card with analog, ADAT lightpipe and S/PDIF digital I/O; cascade more cards for more I/O

JLCooper DataMaster synchronizer

JLCooper

310-306-4131

- Cuepoint—remote controller for ADAT & compatibles
- DataSync2—sync box for slaving MIDI tracks to ADATs
- DataMaster—SMPTE and MIDI chase sync box for ADATs

Korg

516-333-9100; http://www.korg.com

- 168RC—A 16x8x2 digital console with ADAT I/O
- 1212I/O—multichannel ADAT I/O card for PCs
- Trinity—synthesizer with on-board sequencer and optional digital disk recorder with ADAT interface

Kurzweil DMTi digital interface

Kurzweil

310-926-3200; http://www.youngchang.com/kurzweil

- DMTi (Digital MultiTrack interface)—ADAT to/from AES/EBU, S/PDIF or Kurzweil K2500 sampler interface and sample rate converter

Mackie Designs

206-488-6843; http://www.mackie.com

- Digital 8-Bus—digital console with optional ADAT I/O interfaces

Mark of the Unicorn

617-576-2760; http://www.motu.com

- Digital Timepiece—ADAT to MIDI Time Code and SMPTE sync interface
- MIDI TimePiece AV—ADAT to MIDI Time Code and SMPTE sync interface

Merging Technologies

619-675-9703; http://www.merging.com

- Pyramix—disk-based recording/editing system with optional ADAT I/O

Millennia Media

916-647-0750

- HV-3—two channel mic preamp with analog, ADAT and AES/EBU outputs

Opcode Systems

415-856-3333; http://www.opcode.com

- XTC—MIDI/SMPTE sync box with ADAT and computer interfacing

Otari

415-341-5900; http://www.otari.com

- UFC-24—24-channel universal format converter ADAT to AES/EBU, S/PDIF, TDIF and vice-versa
- Radar—24-track digital disk recorder/editor with optional ADAT I/O

Panasonic/Ramsa

714-373-7277

- MDA-1—ADAT-compatible digital multitrack
- WR-DA7—digital mixer with optional ADAT I/O

Rane

206-355-6000; http://www.rane.com

- RC24a—PAQRAT 20/24-bit recording adapter for ADATs

Roland

213-685-5141; http://www.rolandus.com

- DIF-800—digital interface (ADAT format) for Roland's DM-800 workstation

RSP Technologies

810-853-3055; http://www.rocktron.com/rsp

- Project X—large format digital console with optional ADAT I/O

Silicon Graphics

800-800-7441; http://www.sgi.com

- PCI-AUD-8C—Optional ADAT I/O on PCI cards for importing audio into SGI's OCTANE and 02 systems

Sonorus

212-253-7700; http://www.sonorus.com

- STUDI/O™—PCI card interface with 16 channels of ADAT optical interfaces for PC workstations

Soundscape

805-658-7375; http://soundscape-digital.com

- SSHDR-1—digital workstation with optional ADAT interface
- SS8IO—An 8 in/8 out box with ADAT lightpipe, Tascam TDIF and Superclock/Wordclock I/Os on rear panel

Soundtracs

Distributed by Korg, 516-333-9100

- Virtua—digital mixing console with optional ADAT I/O

Spectral

206-487-2931; http://www.spectralinc.com

- Translator Plus—ADAT to/from AES/EBU, S/PDIF, TDIF and Spectral interfaces

Steinberg

818-993-4091; http://www.steinberg_na.com

- ACI—MIDI sync and MMC adapter for Alesis ADAT

Studer

615-399-2199; http://www.studer.ch/studer

- D19 MicAD—mic preamp with analog and ADAT outputs
- D19 MultiDAC—multichannel digital-to-analog converter with ADAT input, analog outputs
- V-Eight—Alesis Type II (M20 compatible) 16/20-bit recorder

Timeline

619-727-3300

- AI-2—ADAT-compatible SMPTE sync interface

Vestax

707-427-1920

- HDRV8—8-channel digital hard disk recorder with optional ADAT interfaces

Yamaha

714-522-9011; http://www.Yamaha.com

- O2R—Digital console with optional ADAT I/O
- 03D—Digital console with optional ADAT I/O

CHAPTER 7

Secrets of the ADAT

lthough the original Alesis ADAT has only 12 specialized function buttons on its front panel, the machine is capable of numerous "hidden functions," accessible by pressing various combinations of existing keys. These were designed especially for the original ADAT, but many of them also work with other ADAT-compatibles (Fostex, Panasonic and Studer machines), as well as the ADAT XT and M20 models. Simultaneously press any of the following and here's what you get.

SET LOCATE + FAST FORWARD
Display Software Version
This briefly displays the ADAT's software version. Real insiders know this is a tribute to Marcus Ryle from the company Fast Forward Designs, who developed much of ADAT's operational software, so it's appropriate that one of the keys to press to determine the software version is Fast Forward.

SET LOCATE + PITCH
Access +200 Cent Pitch Shifting!
Although the ADAT normally has a pitch shift limitation of +100 cents, you can instantly set the pitch shift up to +200 cents by pressing these keys. This is the only way to set the pitch up to +200 cents. And if you want to access +199 cents, you're out of luck, as whenever the pitch button is pressed while in +200 cents mode, the ADAT automatically reverts back to its +100 maximum. Unfortunately, this feature cannot be selected in the middle of a recording, but this is one of the best hidden ADAT functions of all.

SET LOCATE + PITCH
Instantly Set Pitch Down to -300 Cents
Pressing these instantaneously sets the ADAT's pitch to -300 cents with no ramping. Not allowed while recording.

PITCH UP + PITCH DOWN
Instantly Reset Pitch to Normal
Pressing these instantaneously changes pitch of ADAT to a setting of 000 (no pitch shifting), with no ramping. Not allowed while recording.

SET LOCATE + RECORD
Access Longer Crossfade Times
While the BRC remote controller provides a means of choosing from four crossfade times (10.67, 21.33, 32 and 42.67ms), the original ADAT does not have a switch dedicated for this function. Nonetheless, non-BRC ADAT users can make a choice as well; press the Set Locate and Record buttons simultaneously and

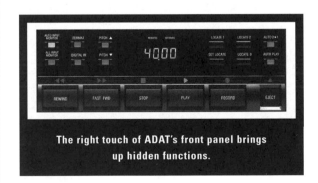

The right touch of ADAT's front panel brings up hidden functions.

the display will read "FAd1," which means the 10.67ms setting is selected. Pressing the two buttons a second time brings up "FAd2," meaning 21.33ms, and so on. The unit defaults to the comparatively short 10.67ms setting, which is best for most applications; the longer crossfades are particularly useful on sustained notes and guitar, vocal and reverberant instrumental tracks.

SET LOCATE + DIGITAL IN
Digital 48kHz Master Clock Select
For master ADATs with the Digital In button selected, pressing these keys toggles the internal digital 48kHz clock on or off. When enabled ("diG"), the *external* digital 48kHz clock will be used if it exists. Otherwise, the *internal* 48kHz clock is used. When disabled ("int"), the internal 48kHz clock is always used, regardless of whether a digital (external) 48kHz

clock exists or not. The master ADAT must disable the 48kHz clock ("int" mode) when it receives digital input from any of its slave units. Power-On reverts the clock to normal ("diG") mode.

SET LOCATE + RECORD 1
Display Record Tab Status

Pressing these will display the record tab status of the currently loaded cassette. A "rEcd" display means the tape is record enabled, and a "Prot" display indicates the tape is record write protected.

SET LOCATE + AUTO INPUT MONITOR
Enable Monitor Selection

Pressing these during recording toggles the ADAT between "source input" and "tape" monitoring.

SET LOCATE + ALL INPUT MONITOR
Audio Pathway Selection

Pressing these toggles the monitor pathway from input/output source to listening through ADAT's digital converters.

SET LOCATE + AUTOPLAY
Display Number of Loops Played

While the ADAT is in infinite loop mode, pressing Set Locate and Autoplay displays the number of completed loops, up to a maximum of 9999 loops (requires version 3.0 or higher software).

SET LOCATE + FORMAT
Enter T-160 (Longer Tape) Mode

As a way of getting around the 40-minute, 44-second record time limitation of T-120 (120-minute) tapes, original ADATs could extend their running time to 53 minutes by using 160-minute video tapes; unfortunately, the counter information would be incorrect. By pressing these two keys, two things could happen, depending on your software version. On earlier ADATs, pressing these toggles the machine between "Std" and T-160 mode. On later ADATs, pressing these toggles the ADAT between "t60" (T-60 format for T-60 cassettes), "t120" (the default setting for T-120 cassettes), "t160" (for T-160 tapes) and "t180" (T-180 tapes). Newer version ADATs automatically determine which tape is used when the tape is loaded. However, if you are using T-160 tapes, you should specify the "t160" mode after loading the tape. The ADAT reverts back to the T-120 mode whenever a tape is ejected.

SET LOCATE + EJECT
Master Eject Mode

This automatically ejects the tapes from all slaves. Highly useful if you've got a big system with lots of transports.

SET LOCATE + PLAY
Unit ID Display

Press these on any ADAT in the chain to see its Unit ID number.

SET LOCATE + REWIND
ADAT Brake Activate

Used only when there's no tape in the transport, pressing these will activate the deck's brakes as part of the ADAT brake service procedure. This function is no use to anyone except service centers, but I included it in case you accidentally pushed these buttons and wondered what the display meant.

SET LOCATE + RECORD 2
Record Tab Override

Hate using sticky masking tape to cover a missing record tab on a tape you want to record on? Press these keys to toggle between the "PrOn" (Protect Tab "On") mode and the "PrOF" (Protect Tab "Off"). Requires Version 4.03 Software and above.

SET LOCATE + STOP
Display Hours on Head Drum

Here's your key to accessing the ADAT's built-in "odometer." If you are unsure of the number of hours on your ADAT—or if you're buying a used one— pressing the Set Locate and Stop buttons simultaneously will display the total number of elapsed hours of head drum operation on the time counter display.

RECORD 1 + RECORD 8 (DURING POWER-UP)
Enter Auto Self Test Mode

Press these during power-up, and your ADAT will enter its Automatic Self Test mode.

RECORD 1 + RECORD 7 (DURING POWER-UP)
Enter Selective Self Test Mode

Press these during power-up, and your ADAT will enter its Selective Self Test mode.

RECORD + PLAY (DURING POWER-UP)
User Soft Reset

This is the famed ADAT re-initializing procedure. Hold down the Record and Play keys while powering up to, as Alesis puts it, "initialize memory to a known state without resetting drum head time." As for me, I try this procedure first, whenever my ADATs have glitches or odd software displays. About 90 percent of the time, this is all you need to do, and your ADAT will be just fine afterward.

CHAPTER 8

Fostex RD-8

The Fostex RD-8 was the first non-Alesis ADAT.

 t the Fall 1992 Audio Engineering Society Convention in San Francisco, Fostex announced that it was entering the modular multitrack milieu with a digital recorder compatible with the Alesis ADAT format. From the Fostex perspective, supporting the Alesis format made sense—certainly, the scenario of Fostex siding with arch-rival Tascam seemed an unrealistic partnership and it was also evident that any new (and incompatible) MDM format would likely go the way of the 8-track cartridge, Betamax tapes and the vinyl record.

Unveiled to the public on April 19, 1993, at the Convention of the National Association of Broadcasters in Las Vegas, the Fostex RD-8 uses the same S-

VHS transport and record electronics as the Alesis deck but adds sophisticated synchronization and control features. Initial deliveries of the recorder began in December of 1993. Due to the flexibility of its onboard MIDI and SMPTE synchronizer, the product stayed in production for approximately three years, even after Fostex was shipping its (ADAT XT-based) CX8.

FEATURES AND FUNCTIONS

Completely compatible with the Alesis ADAT, the RD-8 can be used as a master or slave deck (using the same D9-sub sync connector as the Alesis) and tapes recorded on the two machines are completely interchangeable. With any ADAT system, a 120-minute S-

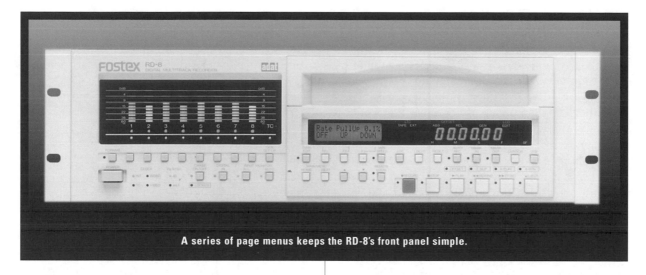

A series of page menus keeps the RD-8's front panel simple.

VHS cassette yields 40 minutes, 44 seconds of record time. The RD-8 also offers a T-160 mode, where it is possible to use 160-minute videotapes.

The RD-8 offers 16-bit linear digital resolution, variable sampling rates (44.1 or 48kHz) and a choice of four digital crossfade times. Other features in this three-rackspace deck include an onboard SMPTE chase-lock synchronizer/reader/generator (24/25/29.97/30 frames, in drop-frame or non-drop-frame versions), RS-422 (Sony P2 9-pin) control for interfacing with video editors, video sync input, word sync in/out, pull up/pull down (44.056 and 47.952kHz sampling for 29.97 fps resync), MIDI Machine Control, onboard 170ms track delay, multimachine offset and ±6 percent pitch shift capability.

Among the RD-8's autolocation-specific functions are a 100-locator-point memory, return to zero, a choice of time code, relative or absolute time displays, programmable pre-/post-roll times and the ability to create "zones" that temporarily restrict transport activity to a user-defined section of the tape.

Any number of Fostex RD-8s—up to 16 transports in any combination—can be synchronized by simply daisy-chaining the units with one 9-pin sync cable between each recorder, just like the Alesis ADATs. (See Chapter 5 for details on daisy-chaining.) The RD-8's sync performance is achieved via electronic rather than mechanical sync: As data is read by two machines in close mechanical sync, the digital audio information is stored in a buffer. Word-clock timing information (carried in the 9-pin sync cable) from the master machine controls the release of data from the second deck's buffer, thus enabling sample-accurate synchronization.

This transport-synchronization scheme (used in the Alesis ADAT, Fostex RD-8 and other MDM designs) does not require an audio track to recording SMPTE or other synchronization signals. When you lock up two RD-8s you get 16 usable tracks.

The RD-8's front panel has the transport, track arming, tape monitor and locator buttons found on the Alesis ADAT, but adds additional controls for track manipulation (delay and machine offset) features, as well as extensive MIDI and SMPTE time code synchronization functions. As an adjunct to the large ten-digit LED readout of hours/minutes/seconds/frames/subframes, 35 colored LEDs indicate operational status at a glance.

Spotlight

Fostex RD-8
- Product Introduction: April 19, 1993
- Deliveries Began: December 1993
- Format: ADAT Type I, using S-VHS videotapes
- Maximum Recording Time: 40 minutes (T-120 tape), 54 minutes (T-160 tape)
- Track Capacity: Eight, expandable to 128 (in multiples of eight)
- Digital System: Rotary head; 16-bit linear; selectable 44.1/48kHz sampling frequencies
- Analog Connections: Unbalanced -10dBV RCA/phono-type; balanced +4dBu inputs/outputs on 25-pin D-Sub multipin connector
- Digital Connections: Proprietary ADAT fiber optic input/output ports using TosLink connectors; word-clock, MIDI and SMPTE time code I/O standard
- Dimensions: 5.25x19x14 inches (HxWxD); 20 pounds
- Retail: Originally $4,795, including Model 4312 remote control

One important function that the RD-8 offers (lacking in the Alesis ADAT) is the ability to punch-in/-out of recording on one or more tracks while recording continues on other tracks. For example, while music is being laid down on Tracks one through five, you can punch in a short synth pad, guitar riff or horn stab, and then punch out on those tracks while the other tracks continue. This feature could be a real time-saver in the post-production environment: You might be laying back an edited music bed—say, from a workstation—and while everything is synched to picture, you could also punch in a couple of sound effects or narration cues.

Like the Alesis BRC controller, the Fostex RD-8 has a 2-line by 18-character LCD window that displays multiple pages of software access for operational data (incoming/outgoing SMPTE rates, sync status, sampling and/or clock rates, etc.), as well as autodiagnostics and locator info. Data in the LCD window also includes take numbers and other production information. Any information displayed, along with the machine's 100 locator memories and user-default settings for sync and operational parameters, can be stored in a table of contents section on the head of an ADAT tape. This information can be loaded back into the RD-8 at any time. As with many LCD readouts, the RD-8's display has contrast control that optimizes viewing from any angle.

Unique to the RD-8 are "user bits," specific pieces of information (memos of up to eight characters in length, date/time stamps, etc.), which are embedded within the time code track and displayed on the LCD screen in a page of the time code generator menu. User bits are generated and read with the data on every frame of time code and are ideal for indicating take numbers and other production data.

BACK VIEW

The RD-8's rear panel contains the -10dBV analog audio inputs (on RCA phono jacks); +4dBu inputs and outputs on D25-sub multipin connectors; fiber-optic digital I/O (in the ADAT format); MIDI In and Out; BNC video input (for locking to VITC time code, black burst or composite video sync sources) with 75-ohm termination switch; time code input and output on balanced XLR jacks; 9-pin output to the Alesis RMB meter bridge; ¼-inch jack for the Model 8312 remote control; ¼-inch jack for optional punch-in/-out footswitch; 9-pin sync jacks for interlocking with other RD-8s or ADATs and a 9-pin RS-422 interface. The latter is designed to emulate a Sony BVU-950 professional VTR and uses the Sony P2 serial communications protocol for controlling the RD-8's transport functions from a video editor.

The rear-panel fiber-optic in/out ports allow the cloning of safety copies with two RD-8s, two ADATs or one RD-8 and one ADAT. Each RD-8 includes the necessary glass fiber cable. The optical-transfer ports provide access to the digital audio datastream for connecting peripheral devices, such as the Alesis AI-1 AES/EBU-to-ADAT digital interface. (See Chapter 6 for more details on ADAT accessories.)

Also on the rear panel is a ¼-inch jack for a punch-in/-out footswitch. Any momentary-contact, single-pole/single-throw (SPST) switch, such as a standard synthesizer sustain pedal, can be used. The footswitch must be connected to the RD-8 when the recorder is powered up; during the power-up procedure, the RD-8 automatically senses whether the footswitch is normally closed or open and adjusts itself accordingly.

Included with the RD-8 is the Model 8312, a compact remote that duplicates the transport controls and adds buttons for input monitor select, locate mark in/out, locate zero, auto record and auto return/auto play. Except for the layout of the transport keys and the functions of several buttons, the 8312 is similar to the Alesis LRC remote. It connects to the RD-8 via a two-conductor, ¼-inch cable; the 8-foot cord attached to the 8312 can be easily extended using a ¼-inch female-to-female "barrel" connector and a standard guitar-type cable. *Note: When using the 8312, locator points 00-99 are inaccessible—you can only locate to zero, the mark-in point or the mark-out point.*

One look at the RD-8's crowded back panel and it's obvious why Fostex used the D25-sub multipin connectors instead of a bank of 16 XLR jacks for the +4dBu analog inputs and outputs—there's not enough space! There are already over 30 connectors on the rear of the RD-8, and adding 16 more would have been impossible. If you want to access the balanced +4dBu connections, you'll need two snakes with XLRs on one end and the D25-subs on the other. A number of third-party companies make the snakes; more information on these (as well as instructions on making your own cables) is provided in Chapter 25.

TRANSPORT AND ELECTRONICS

As with other MDM recorders, tapes must be formatted before recording in the Fostex RD-8. Tape formatting in the RD-8 writes time address information on the videotape, along with a header ("DATA") section on the head of the tape. However, formatting takes place in real time (40+ minutes per tape), so this should be done while setting up for a session or while running cassette dubs at the end of a session. If you have several MDMs available, you can format tapes on an unused transport while recording tracks on other machines.

Tracks can be recorded while formatting, although

it's always best to pre-format tapes. A unique feature on the RD-8 is a format search function, which searches for the location on a partially formatted tape where the formatting ends and then begins extending the formatting from that point.

When the formatting process is complete, a tape is divided into three sections: leader, data and the recordable area. These are shown on ADAT's LED time counter as LEAD, DATA and a minutes/seconds/frames display. The LEAD section is a short length of leader at the beginning of the tape and the recordable section is self-explanatory; the two-minute, 15-second DATA section at the beginning of each tape allows the storage of locator points, the names of locator points and song titles, which can be recalled and displayed on the RD-8's LCD screen.

Both the Fostex RD-8 and the Alesis ADAT send out a noticeable audio "thump" when they're turned on. Make sure that any MDMs in an audio system are turned on before you turn on the power amplifiers. Actually, this is always good advice: In any audio system, the power amps should always be LOFO (last-on/first-off) devices; conversely, RD-8s are FOLO (first-on/last-off) units.

The record electronics on the RD-8 and Alesis ADAT are identical and provide a frequency response of 20-20kHz, ±0.5dB, although machines I've tested have exceeded this spec by a considerable margin (typically in the ±0.1 or ±0.2dB range). The recorders' THD+Noise spec at 1kHz meets the published claims of 0.009 percent. Even in the worst case (at 10kHz), THD+N measured below 0.02 percent, which is excellent. The digital-to-analog converter chips are Burr-Brown 1700s, and the analog-to-digital converters are Crystal CS5336s—high-quality, reliable components.

As is the case with the Alesis ADAT, the Fostex RD-8 requires approximately three seconds to go into Play or Record from Stop. If the heads are "engaged" (referring to a pause-style mode where the tape is lightly held against the head drum), then going into Play occurs in a second. The tape can be shuttled forward or backward with the heads engaged, although long fast-forwards or rewinds should be avoided. Two presses on the Stop button disengages the heads, or they disengage automatically when no transport activity occurs after four minutes. In the engaged mode, the rewind time for a 40-minute tape is about four and a half minutes, as compared to the disengaged rewind time of under two minutes.

GOLDILOCKS AND THE THREE REMOTE CONTROLLERS

Do you remember the story of Goldilocks and the three bears? Here's the Fostex RD-8 version: The Model 8312 remote is functional, although somewhat limited, lacking useful features such as track arming and a remote time display. "It's too small!" says Goldilocks.

The RD-8 is also compatible with the Alesis BRC remote, a $1,495 unit that has all the required transport and track arming controls, but also adds features such as MIDI and SMPTE synchronization, track delays and offsets. These are unnecessary since the RD-8 already includes these functions. "It's too big!" says Goldilocks.

JLCooper CuePoint controller

Luckily, JLCooper Electronics of Los Angeles offers the CuePoint, a $799.95 autolocator/transport control unit that uses MIDI Machine Control and is able to control up to eight MMC-compatible tape recorders (such as the RD-8), MIDI sequencing programs and serial- or parallel-control protocol tape transports. Also compatible with Alesis ADAT, Tascam DA-88 and many hard-disk recorders, CuePoint provides conventional transport controls, a shuttle wheel and track enable/grouping functions for up to four 8-track MDM transports. Other features are auto-punch-in/-out, 99 locate points, SMPTE-MTC conversion and a SMPTE reader/generator with an LED hours/minutes/seconds/frames readout, which is switchable to a bars/beats display. Options include a dataCard for synching to an ADAT without losing a track (not required with an RD-8) and RS-422, RS-232 and Apple Desktop Bus communications modules. "It's just right!" says Goldilocks.

RD-8 OPERATIONS

Operationally, the Fostex RD-8 can be set up as simple or as complex as required by the user. Rather than filling the front panel with dozens of buttons, the RD-8 provides a Main Menu for selecting specialized features. The parameters within the Main Menu page are selected by pressing the Home and Next buttons, which reveals nine pages. These are the two functions on each of the pages:

1. Sampling Rate   Pull Up/Pull Down
2. MIDI Data Dump   TOC Load/Save
3. Time Code Level   Time Code Frame Rate
4. TC Rewind   User Bits
5. Zone Start   Zone Length
6. Crossfade Time   MIDI Machine Control
7. Date Set   Time Set
8. T-120/-160 Select   LCD Contrast Adjust
9. Error Rate   Software Version

Once the desired page is displayed, the user can manipulate the parameters by using the three "soft" function keys (F1, F2, F3) beneath the display to select a desired parameter and the data up/down arrow keys to change the value.

The process is a lot easier to do than to describe. For example, if you want time code to be output during rewind and fast-forward operations, just call up menu #4. Choose either of the two selections—TC Rewind or User Bits—by pressing the function key that's under the feature you want to enable; toggle the function on or off using the up/down keys; and you're done.

A similar procedure provides access to various menu pages that accompany most of the functions that have dedicated front panel buttons. Pressing the Data Edit button and any of the following controls will bring up a specific menu for that function:

- Format   Format Search Page
- Track 1-8   Track Delay Page
- Gen Setup   TC Generator Setups
- Chase On/Off   Chase Menu Pages
- Vari Speed   Vari Speed Edit Page
- Remote/Local   Remote Menu
- Digital In   Channel Assign
- Auto Rec   Auto Record Menu
- Mark In   Mark In Edit Page
- Mark Out   Mark Out Edit Page
- Loc   Locator Functions Menu

So, despite the apparent complexity of the RD-8, any function or parameter can be accessed or manipulated with a minimum of keystrokes. For example, Vari Speed (pitch control) is adjustable ±6 percent (in 0.1 percent increments) from either the 44.1 or 48kHz sampling rates. By entering the Vari Speed edit page, not only can the amount of pitch shift be varied, but also the parameter value can be changed from ±6 percent to +101/-107 cents. (In musical terms, each cent is defined as 1/100 of a semitone or 1/1200 of an octave.)

Clicking onto the Track Delay page allows the user to delay the playback of any track by up to 170ms, in 1ms increments. Explained in Chapter 43, track delay offers creative and practical uses, such as time-shifting certain instruments in and out of "the pocket," making phase adjustments to compensate for variances in microphone techniques and fine-tuning (time-slipping) elements, such as dialog and sound effects, in the video/film post-production environment.

Speaking of video/film post, the RD-8 offers a variety of features catering specifically to that market. The unit slaves to incoming SMPTE time code at 24, 25, 29.97 or 30 fps, with the latter two selectable to standard or drop-frame varieties. Among the external time code sources that the RD-8 can sync to are longitudinal time code, Sony 9-pin (serial protocol) or vertical-interval time code. The latter is a specialized, high-tech method of recording SMPTE time code information into the vertical blanking interval area between the video frames. Unless you spend a lot of time working at state-of-the-art teleproduction facilities, you are unlikely to encounter VITC. The longitudinal time code is more commonly used and can be recorded on the audio channel of any VTR or multitrack recorder. Word-clock in/out ports are also provided, and the RD-8's SMPTE in/out ports can be adjusted to operate at levels ranging from -10 to +4dB.

Additionally, the RD-8's sample rate can be adjusted by ±0.1 percent to compensate for the timing differences between film shot intentionally for video release at 30 fps (or 24 fps film transferred to video at 30 fps via a telecine) and the USA color TV standard (NTSC) frame rate of 29.97 fps. The RD-8's "pull up/pull down" feature makes the 0.1 percent change in the speed of the tape while leaving the time code format and frame rate unchanged. In Europe, which has adopted the 25 fps PAL television standard, video cameras and film cameras (when shooting for TV) run at 25 fps so nobody has any weird time code or pull up/down problems.

MIDI In and Out ports on the RD-8's rear panel can output MIDI Time Code for synching the recorder to a MIDI sequencer. MIDI Machine Control is also supported, allowing the RD-8's transport and record functions to be controlled from a sequencer that supports the MMC standard.

DIGITAL TRANSFER OPTIONS

The RD-8 offers extensive control of the Alesis Digital Bus, a proprietary fiber-optic chain that allows perfect clones of important sessions, track bouncing and assembly editing.

One of the RD-8's most powerful capabilities,

assembly editing, combines digital copying and offset features, thus providing nondestructive editing capability in the digital domain (two RD-8s are required for the process). A complete explanation of digital assembly editing can be found in Chapter 33, but suffice to say that the ability to create new versions of songs by copying (or deleting) verses or choruses offers great creativity to the producer. Best of all, the edits are done on a copy tape, so the original tracks are unaffected and, as copying occurs in the digital domain, there is no audio degradation when using these methods: The user is free to create as many variations as possible.

While intended for use with multitrack material, there is no reason why these assembly-editing methods couldn't also be used with 2-track material, such as DAT mixes. And a two-RD-8 system, with an Alesis AI-1 digital interface, could be the basis for a flexible system for editing and/or sequencing songs from DAT tapes.

Transferring two channels of digital data from external AES/EBU- or S/PDIF-equipped devices, such as DAT machines or workstations, can be accomplished by connecting the RD-8 to the Alesis AI-1. Housed in a single-rackspace chassis and priced at $895, the AI-1 provides not only an Alesis fiber-optic-to-AES/EBU and S/PDIF digital interface, but also sample rate conversion functions. The latter are especially useful when you are working at 48kHz and need to transfer material from a 44.1kHz source (such as a sound effects CD) to an RD-8 tape in the digital domain. Digidesign offers a bidirectional 8-channel ADAT fiber-optic-to-Session 8 or ProTools interface that transfers both digital audio and sync data.

Meanwhile, Fostex has included an ADAT-format fiber-optic digital input and output on its Foundation workstation, an expandable 8- to 48-track disk-based system that combines recording, editing, mixing and signal processing functions.

THE BOTTOM LINE

Retailing at $4,795, the Fostex RD-8 offers an impressive combination of features ideally suited for incorporating this recorder into the post-production suite, project room or MIDI studio. By adopting the ADAT standard, Fostex entered the MDM world with a deck that's compatible with a large base of users and adds useful functions such as time code chase and enhanced autolocation. Single-ADAT owners may find that expanding their system with an RD-8 as the master deck will add extra flexibility at an affordable price.

Fostex Corporation
15431 Blackburn Avenue
Norwalk, CA 90650
310-921-1112
http://www.fostex.com

Note: Turn page for Fostex RD-8 front and rear panels.

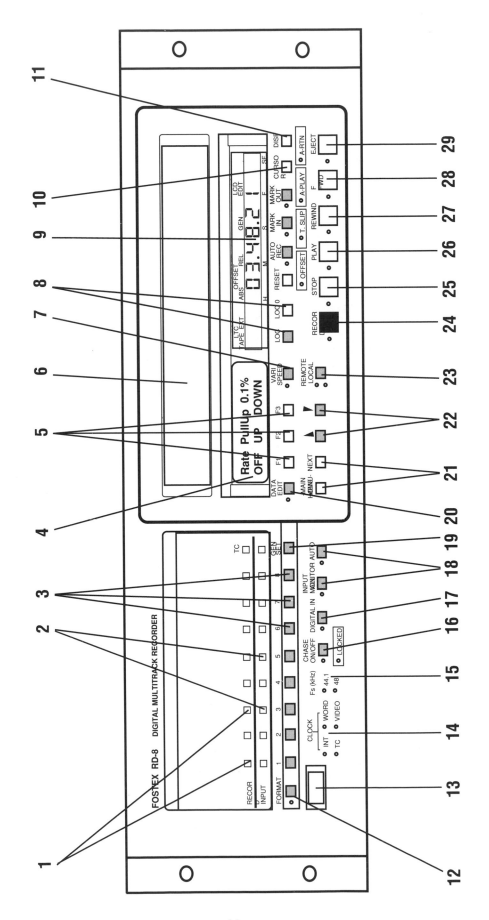

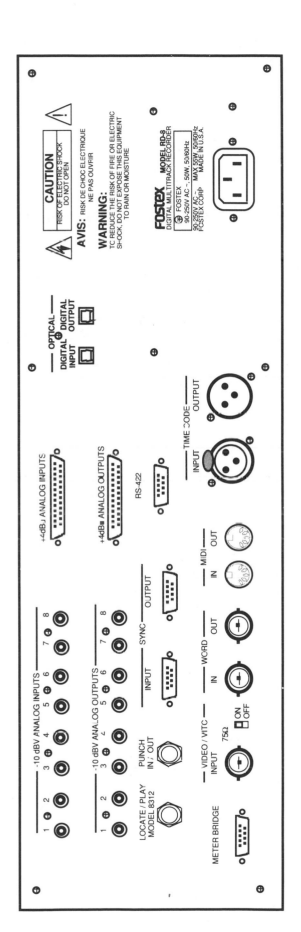

Fostex RD-8 Operations

FRONT PANEL

1. Record Status Indicators
2. Input Status Indicators
3. Track Arming Switches
4. LCD Status Screen
5. Function Keys
6. Tape Well
7. Vari Speed Key
8. Locator Keys
9. Time Display

10. Cursor Key
11. Time Display Selector
12. Format Key
13. AC Power Switch
14. Clock Source LED Indicators
15. Sample Rate LEDs
16. Chase On/Off Switch
17. Digital Input Selector
18. Tape Monitor Mode Switches
19. Time Code Generator Set Key

20. Data Entry Key
21. Main Menu Home/Next Select
22. Increment Up/Down Keys
23. Remote/Local Control Switch
24. Record Button
25. Stop Button
26. Play Button
27. Rewind Button
28. Fast-Forward Button
29. Eject Button

CHAPTER 9

Alesis ADAT XT

 our years and 70,000 MDMs after the first ADAT recorders were delivered to the audio industry, "ADAT: The Next Generation" arrived. And it was worth the wait. The Alesis XT adds 20 new features and functions and is priced at $3,495, which is $500 less than the original price of the ADAT. But Alesis didn't stop there: The new machine is built into a sleek, robust chassis that's more solid and more compact than the original, while it also improves transport control with faster locate/lockup times and provides better audio performance.

XT looks different, but it's an ADAT at heart. The tape format—(eight tracks on an S-VHS tape) is unchanged, and XT is fully compatible with tapes recorded on any ADAT system, including the original ADAT, Fostex RD-8, Fostex CX-8 and Panasonic MDA-1. And, like other ADAT-format modular digital multitracks, XT offers sample-accurate sync of up to 16 transports for up to 128 tracks.

XT definitely has that new generation look: The flat black front panel has been replaced with a brushed silver, extruded aluminum faceplate. Alesis has always been on the forefront of using custom display technologies such as those used in the Q2, SR-16 and QuadraSynth, but the XT goes much further. On the left side of the unit, a large, multicolored, custom vacuum fluorescent display shows the tape locator data, meters, status indicators and other session data.

On the rear panel, the ¼-inch unbalanced -10dBV

connectors have been replaced with RCA jacks, while the 56-pin EDAC connector, with eight channels of balanced +4dBu I/O, is the same as the original. There is one subtle variation with XT's balanced interfacing: The outputs are now servo balanced, so no level loss occurs when the balanced outs are connected to an unbalanced mixer. Also used on certain Soundcraft, Neve and Soundtracs mixers, as well as the Alesis X-2 recording console, the 56-pin EDACs connectors are rugged, with large, gold-plated contact pins. By the way, all Alesis ADATs—XT and original recipe—have been using 56-pin EDAC connectors for several years now, and the XT manual erroneously refers to the multipins as "Elcos," which are compatible with the EDACs, but made by a different company.

The remote meter bridge connector has been eliminated on the XT. With the availability of consoles with expanded metering capabilities, Alesis felt the remote meter bridge option was unnecessary. Other than these changes (and a cast "Alesis" logo), everything else on the back panel (sync, BRC, LRC, punch-in/-out jack and optical digital I/O connectors) is similar to the original ADAT.

Physically, the 20-pound unit is three units high but feels beefier than the first ADAT, with a shallower front-to-back depth and two scooped out sections along each side that fit exactly into the hands when lifting the unit. Four removable, rubber, nonskid feet protect tabletops or counter surfaces from scratching. The front panel sub assembly attaches to a heavy, one-piece, die-cast aluminum chassis. The design objective of this central chassis block was to remove variations in tooling of separate metal pieces by creating a rigid, single-section frame for mounting the power supply, electronics and transport components.

Included with every XT is the LRC, a palm-sized remote controller that duplicates all the transport controls. The LRC connects to the ADAT via a two-conductor, ¼-inch cord; the 8-foot cord attached to the LRC can be extended using a ¼-inch female-to-female "barrel" connector and a standard guitar cable.

The XT's LRC controller

DON'T TRY THIS AT HOME!

With such a slick outside package, I had to see how the insides stacked up. As with the ADAT, access to the transport and electronics comes by removing the top cover, which in the case of the XT requires only 5, rather than 12, screws. The transport is cleanly laid out, with plenty of finger room for cleaning and maintenance. On the underside of the chassis are two doors that provide easy access to the power supply and the capstan drive belt.

By the way, the XT and all other ADATs employ a switching power supply that runs cool and does not require a fan. One obvious plus of the switching supply is that it will operate at any AC line voltage from 90 to 250 volts, either 50 or 60Hz. ADAT recording should

be "no problemo," whether your recording exploits take you to Beijing, Benelux or Beruit.

The left side of the recorder houses the electronics. The main board has a socketed EPROM containing the XT control software, the transport control and logic circuitry. Also on the board is a lithium cell that retains autolocator settings, even when the unit is unplugged or switched off. In my experience, such batteries typically last at least five years (a cell in my Korg PolySix programmable analog synthesizer recently gave out after 15 years!), so around the turn of the century, if you encounter a senile ADAT, the problem may be no more than a dead battery. Lastly, the audio I/O boards (balanced and unbalanced) are mounted along the rear wall.

SYNC/LOCKUP SPEED TESTS

XT also increases the intelligent control of transport operations with servo control of the deck and microprocessor monitoring of the braking and motor action. The "intelligent" part refers to XT's ability to "learn" how to compensate for changes in transport dynamics. Let's say the system slightly overshoots a locate point: The first time this occurs, there is a slight delay while it makes the adjustment; but the next time, XT automatically compensates for the overshoot and parks the tape right on the money.

The XT's transport mechanism is the same as the original ADAT; however, improved software control makes it significantly faster in terms of the wind speeds. In "wrapped" mode, the original ADAT shuttled at approximately ten times play speed. XT is about four times faster, shuttling at about 40 times play speed. The only drawback here is that when shuttling tape, the XT's transport is considerably louder than the ADAT's. Given the choice of the two, I'd prefer a faster machine and put up with a little extra noise.

One of the main complaints about the original ADAT was the unbearably long times that were often

Spotlight

Alesis ADAT XT

- Product Introduction: October 5, 1995
- Deliveries Began: February 1, 1996
- Format: ADAT Type I, using S-VHS videotapes
- Maximum Recording Time: 40 minutes (T-120 tape), 54 minutes (T-160 tape)
- Track Capacity: Eight, expandable to 128 (in multiples of eight)
- Digital System: Rotary head; 16-bit linear; selectable 44.1/48kHz sampling frequencies
- Analog Connections: Unbalanced -10dBV RCA/phono-type jack; balanced +4dBu inputs/outputs on 56-pin EDAC multipin connector
- Digital Connections: Proprietary ADAT fiber-optic input/output ports using TosLink connectors; AES/EBU and S/PDIF interface optional
- Dimensions: 5.25x19x11 inches (HxWxD); 20 pounds
- Retail: $3,495, including LRC remote control

required to get all the decks in a multimachine setup to achieve exact sync. Typically, on a 24-track session, I would press Play and then wait about 10-12 seconds before all the tracks were in sync. From a dead stop, a 24-track XT system locks up in approximately two seconds; rewinding that same system two minutes back to a locate point with auto play requires four seconds.

Here are some machine lockup times we found in a typical studio setting. (Note that the XT times were consistent, so only one lock time is shown.) The original ADAT lock times varied considerably when rewind/fast-forward/locate operations were involved, so the lock time in the chart presents a range from the shortest to the longest times we measured. Also, the fast-forward times to locate points were slightly longer than the rewind times we measured.

16-TRACK LOCKUP RESULTS		
Configuration	Operation	Lock Time
XT-XT	Play from dead stop	2 seconds
ADAT-ADAT	Play from dead stop	4-9 seconds
XT-XT	Rwd 2 min. to locate point, play	4 seconds
ADAT-ADAT	Rwd 2 min. to locate point, play	5-12 seconds

24-TRACK LOCKUP RESULTS		
Configuration	Operation	Lock Time
XT-XT-XT	Play from dead stop	2 seconds
ADAT-ADAT-ADAT	Play from dead stop	9-12 seconds
XT-XT-XT	Rwd 2 min. to locate point, play	4 seconds
ADAT-ADAT-ADAT	Rwd 2 min. to locate point, play	13-20 seconds

Many ADAT owners will want to add XTs to an existing setup and, depending on what you're doing, you may want to do some interchanging of the setup during the session for best results. When doing a 16-track XT and original ADAT session, I start out by recording the first eight tracks on the XT. When I need to add more tracks, I designate the original ADAT machine as the master and have the XT slave to it. There are a couple of reasons for this:

1. The XT has better analog to digital converters than the original ADAT, and you should always use the best converters available whenever recording.

2. By designating the XT as the slave, it can lock up to the original XT almost instantaneously. If the original ADAT were the slave, the time-to-exact-sync would be much longer.

Of course, the fastest 16-track production in a combination XT-ADAT setup is by using the submix sync trick found in Chapter 39.

If you can swing it, the best possible solution is to use an all-XT system. The bottom line is that once you've used an XT, you probably won't want to go back to a standard ADAT, for a lot of reasons, such as...

SONIC QUALITY

The XT boasts new-generation Philips converters, 18-bit ADCs (120-times oversampling) and 20-bit ADCs (8-times oversampling). A single converter chip is used per channel to eliminate the chance of crosstalk and improve channel separation. My critical listening tests with the XT consisted of feeding identical program material (rock, classical, jazz) simultaneously into an XT and an ADAT, which were interlocked in sample-accurate record/playback. This allowed the luxury of making instantaneous A/B comparisons between the two machines. The results from a panel of engineers/producers (including myself) were identical: In every case, the XT demonstrated a noticeable improvement in sonic detail over the original ADAT. This was most evident in upper-end clarity, particularly with high percussion (cymbals, bells, triangle, hi-hat) and the top end reproduction of harmonic-rich instruments such as violins, cello, piano and acoustic guitars. Reverb tails also seemed much more detailed on the XT, with natural decays.

FEATURES AND COMFORTS

In January 1991, when ADAT was first unveiled to the world, Alesis' intent was to produce an affordable digital multitrack. With this goal in mind, some of ADAT's more esoteric features, such as individual track delay, digital track routing and multimachine offset, were shifted to the BRC controller. Now XT includes these and 20 other new features at a price that's less than the original recorder.

Despite the added features, most of the XT's recording functions are simple, straightforward operations. Below the meter display are the 8-track arming buttons, but, unlike the first ADAT, the XT allows punching in/out of any tracks while recording continues on others. Essential in many post-production applications, this is a welcome improvement on the XT.

The new machine now offers ten locate points, all easily set on the fly and editable to 1/100-second accuracy. The ten locate keys also double as a numeric keypad for quickly entering locate or edit points from the front panel. XT's rehearse mode allows safe, nondestructive previewing of auto-punch recording operations. The pitch up/down buttons also double as data increment/decrement keys during editing operations, and a front panel Clock Select key chooses a 44.1 or 48kHz sampling rate.

Many of the XT's improvements come by merely simplifying basic routines. The XT includes an extended recording time offset mode, which allows long recording times (such as two hours) by record-

BRC and the Alesis XT

The BRC, as well as the original ADAT, are completely compatible with the ADAT XT. As the BRC offers numerous features such as assembly editing, tape offsets, track delay, rehearse punch-ins/-outs, etc., you may wonder why you'd use a BRC with an XT. However, the BRC is a master controller over all the ADATs in a chain, while the XT's front panel functions only affect its settings.

To use a BRC with the XT, however, the BRC's software version must be 2.03 or higher. BRCs that are version 2.00 or higher may be updated by software alone by swapping an internal EPROM chip. BRC versions below version 2.00 require hardware modifications which must be performed at a local service center or at the Alesis factory.

The XT has the capability to bounce tracks digitally—both internally and to other units. The fiber-optic cable carries information for up to eight channels of digital audio simultaneously. The XT can be instructed to designate source tracks on the fiber-optic bus. These tracks are then received in order on the armed tracks. For example, by selecting Tracks 3 and 6 as the source tracks and arming Tracks 11 and 12 with "Digital Input" selected, Track 3 will be recorded on Track 11 and Track 6 will be recorded on Track 12.

---

ing on one deck and having a second take over when the first tape ends. Previously, this was only available by using two ADATs, a BRC and a tedious list of keystrokes. Thankfully, the operation is much simpler now and can be performed using only two XTs.

Many other small additions are a nice touch, such as a "write protect override" (when you need to record onto a tape whose record tab is removed) and the fact that pitch shift values are displayed in both percents and musical cents. These don't exactly change the world, but they definitely make life easier in the studio.

The XT's custom vacuum fluorescent display is a major upgrade that improves the ADAT interface, with more flexibility in customizing the deck's display to user preferences. For example, the user now has control over the selection of hours/mins/secs/hundredths of a second, indicated in absolute or relative time. The meters are multicolored displays in 13 3dB steps, from -48 to 0dB. The peak hold feature can be set to momentary (2-second hold), infinite (with peak-clear switching) or bypassed entirely—again, the choice is up to the user. I also like the fact that the track number is illuminated under each meter. On more occasions than I wish to recall, I'd have to look twice at the old ADAT display and count the meters to verify the track number that accompanied the meter, especially in dimly lit control rooms.

Here's a slick XT trick that's sure to impress your friends: By pressing the Peak Clear and Pitch Down buttons simultaneously, you can reduce the brightness of the vacuum fluorescent display; just press Peak Clear and Pitch Up to restore the display to full brightness. For more XT hidden features, see Chapter 7.

And speaking of the display, ADAT's blinking decimal point "error correction" indicator has been replaced with a small flashing star on XT's vacuum fluorescent display. For more detailed information, a hidden mode allows monitoring the actual error count of any tape. This feature also provides the user with a means of running objective comparisons of various tape formulations and brands.

One of the nice things about XT is how it can integrate into an existing ADAT system. If a user has one ADAT and adds an XT, this not only provides additional tracks but, by assigning the XT as the master deck and accessing its machine offset feature, the system becomes capable of digital assembly editing. Suddenly, multiple takes of basic tracks (or instrumental/vocal takes) can be combined into one seamless performance that incorporates the best sections of many takes. Additionally, data from one or more XT track(s) can be digitally routed and copied to different tracks on the XT itself or a second ADAT transport. Before performing a difficult punch on a vocal track, you can make a digital "safety" copy within the machine itself to any number of additional tracks. Previously, such functions were only accessible via the BRC controller.

With the debut of the XT, Alesis has added significant new performance improvements to its line of ADAT-format recorders. But, perhaps more importantly, XT makes a strong statement regarding the future of the ADAT format, as well as the company's commitment to maintaining compatibility with tens of thousands of existing ADAT users worldwide.

Alesis Corp.
3630 Holdrege Ave
Los Angeles, CA 90016
310-558-4530
fax: 310-836-9192
http://www.alesis.com

Note: Turn page for diagrams of Alesis ADAT XT front and rear panels.

FRONT PANEL

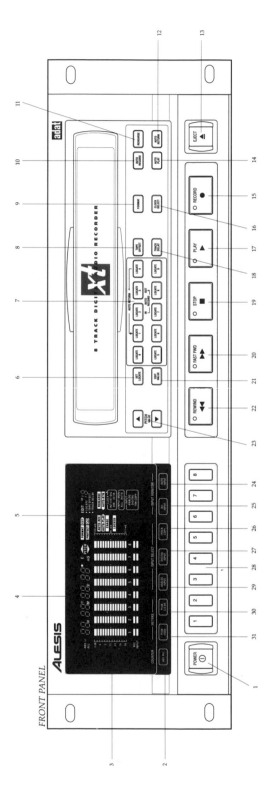

1. Power switch turns the unit on and off.
2. ABS/REL button switches the TIME counter between Absolute Time and Relative Time modes.
3. Peak Meters indicate the input and playback levels for all eight tracks. When editing Track Delay, the meters will indicate each track's delay amount.
4. Time counter displays tape position. When the PITCH ▲/▼ buttons are used, the pitch setting is momentarily displayed here. In Edit mode, it displays parameter values.
5. The display contains many icons that indicate the status of various features. In Edit mode, some of these icons indicate which feature is selected for editing.
6. SET LOCATE button is used to store tape positions into any of the 10 LOCATE buttons.
7. LOCATE buttons store tape positions for instant access. In Edit mode, these buttons select and display their stored tape positions for editing in the display. When the EDIT VALUE button is held, these buttons act as a 10-digit keypad (0-9) for editing parameter values in the display.
8. TAPE OFFSET button turns the Tape Offset feature on and off (for use in a multiple ADAT system only). In Edit mode, this button selects the Tape Offset amount for editing.
9. FORMAT button turns Format mode on and off.
10. AUTO RECORD button turns the Auto Record feature on and off. This lets you automatically record (punch-in/-out) without actually recording.
11. REHEARSE button turns Rehearse mode on and off. This allows you to audition an automatic recording (punch-in/-out) between the stored LOCATE 2 and LOCATE 3 tape positions.
12. AUTO RETURN button turns the Auto Return feature on and off. This makes the transport automatically return to the stored LOCATE 1 position upon reaching the stored LOCATE 4 tape position.

13. EJECT button ejects the tape.
14. AUTO PLAY button turns the Auto Play function on and off. This makes the transport automatically enter play mode after completing a locate command.
15. RECORD button initiates recording, when pressed while PLAY is held.
16. CLOCK SELECT button lets you choose between two different internal clock sample rates (48kHz and 44.1kHz) and a digital clock (for recording from the DIGITAL IN).
17. PLAY BUTTON initiates play mode. During record mode, pressing PLAY will punch-out of record.
18. TRACK DELAY button turns the Track Delay feature on and off. In Edit mode, this selects the Track Delay amounts for editing in the display.
19. STOP button stops the transport.
20. FAST FWD button initiates fast-forwarding of the tape. If pressed while PLAY is held, cue mode is initiated.
21. EDIT VALUE button turns Edit mode on and off. When this button is held, the LOCATE buttons may be used as a 10-digit keypad (0-9) for editing parameter values in the display, and the ▲/▼ buttons may be used to select a specific digit in the display for editing with the 10 LOCATE buttons.
22. REWIND button initiates rewinding of the tape. If pressed while PLAY is held, review mode is initiated.
23. PITCH ▲/▼ buttons are used to adjust the Pitch amount, which also controls playback speed. When either of these buttons is pressed, the display briefly indicates the current Pitch amount. When held, the Pitch amount is changed either up or down.
24. AUTO INPUT button turns Auto Input mode on and off. When off, any record-enable tracks will always monitor their input. When on, record-ready tracks will only monitor their input while in record or stop modes. This is a useful feature when punching in and out over a previous recording.

25. ALL INPUT button turns All Input mode on and off. When on, all tracks will monitor their inputs, regardless of their record-ready status.
26. TRACK COPY button selects Track Copy mode. This allows you to bounce the audio between tracks on the XT without the need for external patching.
27. DIGITAL INPUT button selects Digital Input mode. This allows you to record from the DIGITAL IN.
28. RECORD ENABLE buttons [1] through [8] toggle each of the eight tracks between record-ready mode and safe mode. This may be done before or while recording. When editing Track Delays, these buttons select one of the eight tracks for editing its Track Delay amount in the display.
29. ANALOG INPUT button selects Analog Input mode. This allows you to record from both the unbalanced and balanced analog inputs.
30. PEAK CLEAR button clears the meters' peak LED when either Continuous or Momentary Peak modes are selected.
31. PEAK MODE button lets you select between three Peak Modes for the meters: Continuous, Momentary or Off.

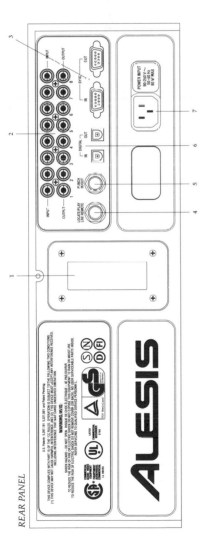

1. +4dBu Balanced inputs/outputs (Elco multipin connector).

2. -10dBu Unbalanced inputs/outputs (phono connectors).

3. SYNC IN/OUT connectors for linking multiple ADATs.

4. LOCATE/PLAY/LRC REMOTE jack is for footswitch-controlled locating or playing, or for use with the LRC handheld remote control.

5. PUNCH-IN/-OUT jack is for footswitch-controlled punching or for use with the LRC handheld remote control.

6. DIGITAL IN/OUT connectors for recording and playing back digital audio from/to other ADATs or ADAT-compatible devices.

7. Power Input AC power connector.

LCD DISPLAY

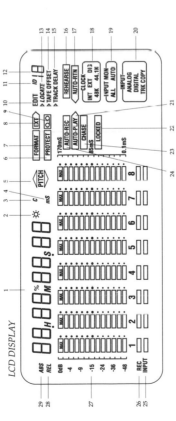

1. TIME counter displays tape position. When the PITCH ▲/▼ buttons are used, the pitch setting is momentarily displayed here. In Edit mode, it displays parameter values.

2. Interpolation Indicator flashes when errors have been detected and corrected using a proprietary interpolation method. It is a good idea to clean the tape heads and/or make a backup copy of your tape if you ever see this icon light.

3. Cents icon lights when adjusting Pitch controls use the PITCH ▲/▼ buttons.

4. Milliseconds icon lights when adjusting Track Delay amounts.

5. PITCH icon lights when editing Pitch controls and the Pitch amount displayed in the TIME counter. ▲ icon lights whenever the Pitch amount is greater than 0. ▼ icon lights whenever the Pitch amount is less than 0.

6. PROTECT icon lights when a tape is inserted that has its write-protect tab removed.

7. FORMAT icon flashes when a blank, unformatted tape is inserted, and lights solid when Format mode is turned on (by pressing the FORMAT button).

8. EXT icon will light along with the FORMAT icon whenever performing a format extend.

9. ⬚⬚ icon will light whenever a tape is in the transport.

10. EDIT icon will light whenever Edit mode is selected (by pressing the EDIT VALUE button). Below it are three icons, only one of which will be lit at any one time. These include: LOCATE. TAPE OFFSET and TRACK DELAY.

11. ID icon lights when the XT is first turned on, or if it is connected to a multi-ADAT system. The number appearing to the right of the ID icon will indicate the ID number of the unit (1-16).

12. Edit Number. In Edit mode, this indicates either the selected track (1-8) when editing Track Delay amounts or the selected Locate (0-9) being edited. If connected to a multi-ADAT system, this will indicate the ID number of the unit (1-16) on power-up.

13. LOCATE icon indicates that you are editing a Locate Point's address, which will appear in the TIME counter. A number (from 0-9) will appear next to the EDIT icon to indicate which Locate Point is being edited.

14. TAPE OFFSET icon lights when the Tape Offset function is turned on with a value that is not equal to 0:00:00. This function is only available when the XT is a slave within a multi-ADAT system. When in Edit Mode, this icon indicates that you are editing the Tape Offset amount, which will appear in the TIME counter.

15. TRACK DELAY icon lights when the Track Delay function is turned on. When in Edit Mode, this icon indicates that you are editing a track's delay amount, which will appear in the TIME counter. A number (from 1-8) will appear next to the EDIT icon to indicate which track is being edited. The peak meters will also show a bar-graph representation of the current delay values for all eight tracks.

16. REHEARSE icon lights when the Rehearse function has been turned on.

17. AUTO RETURN icon lights when the Auto Return function has been turned on.

18. CLOCK group of icons indicates which clock source is being used. The [CLOCK SELECT] button lets you toggle through the various options, including INT 48K (internal clock at 48kHz), INT 44.1K (internal clock at 44.1kHz), DIG 48K and DIG 44.1K (external clock source connected to the [DIGITAL IN] connector on the rear panel). If the XT is a slave in a multiple ADAT system, the EXT icon will light, indicating that the XT is deriving its clock from the master ADAT in the system.

19. INPUT MON group includes two icons: ALL and AUTO. The ALL icon will light whenever the All Input function is enabled (by pressing the [ALL INPUT] button). The AUTO icon will light whenever the Auto Input function is enabled (by pressing the [AUTO INPUT] button).

20. INPUT group of icons indicates which input source is being used. The ANALOG icon will light whenever the Analog Inputs are selected (by pressing the [ANALOG INPUT] button). The DIGITAL icon will light whenever the Digital Inputs are selected (by pressing the [DIGITAL INPUT] button). The TRK COPY icon will light whenever the Track Copy function is selected (by pressing the [TRACK COPY] button).

21. AUTO PLAY icon lights when the Auto Play function has been turned on.

22. LOCKED icon lights when a tape is in play or record and sample lock is achieved.

23. CHASE icon lights when a slaved XT is searching in fast wind mode to lock to the position of the master ADAT in a multiple ADAT system.

24. AUTO RECORD icon lights when the Auto Record function has been turned on.

25. REC LEDs (1-8) indicate which tracks are monitoring their inputs (on) and which are monitoring tape (off).

26. REC LEDs (1-8) indicate which tracks are in record-ready (flashing) or in record (on) and which tracks are safe (off).

27. 13-segment Peak Meters (1-8) indicate the levels of each of the eight tracks. MAX LED will light to indicate clipping.

28. ABS icon lights whenever Absolute Time mode is selected (by pressing the [ABS/REL] button).

29. REL icon lights whenever Relative Time mode is selected (by pressing the [ABS/REL] button).

CHAPTER 10

Panasonic MDA-1

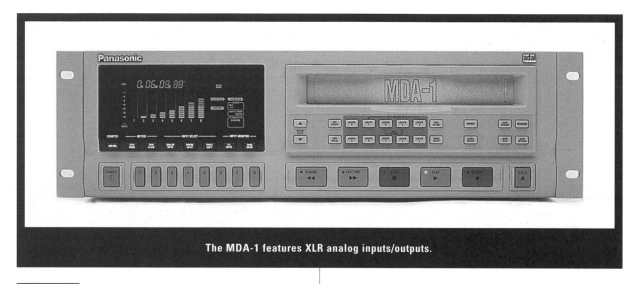

The MDA-1 features XLR analog inputs/outputs.

I t should come as no surprise that Panasonic became involved in the Alesis ADAT format. In November 1994, a year before the unveilings of the Alesis ADAT XT and the Panasonic MDA-1, the Panasonic Broadcast and Television Systems Company (PBTSC) announced that it would support the ADAT format and work with Alesis in the co-development of future ADAT products. Matsushita, Panasonic's parent company, is the world's largest manufacturer of S-VHS editing and duplicating equipment. It offered Alesis its high-end multimotor transports, which are now used in the Alesis ADAT M20 and Studer V-Eight 20-bit ADAT Type II recorders.

But there was more going on behind the scenes. Sony, Panasonic's rival in the industrial and broadcast video market, had joined with Tascam to make the Sony PCM-800 machine in the DTRS (DA-88) format. Panasonic needed an affordable, high-performance digital multitrack to include in package sales of large video installations, preferably a digital multitrack with the Panasonic name. Specifying a Sony (their chief audio competitor) or Tascam (a rival in the studio DAT market) recorder into an all-Panasonic installation did not fit into its view of success. Besides, Panasonic had a long history of audio excellence,

particularly with live performance consoles, wireless microphone systems and its SV-3700 studio DAT recorders—it certainly would not be considered a stranger in the field of professional audio recorders.

Immediately following the Alesis XT unveiling, new ADATs, all based on the XT, were announced by Fostex and Panasonic. Priced at $3,499, the Panasonic MDA-1 is similar to the XT with a few added twists. Although both machines have nearly identical front panels, the real differences between them are apparent by investigating the rear panel and by looking inside the unit.

Keeping the needs of broadcast and video users in mind, the MDA-1's analog interfacing offers an essential ingredient: individual balanced inputs and outputs. In the studio, individual outputs are less of a necessity, as most connections are generally left in one place and in one configuration. Also, balanced connections are de rigueur in applications where long audio lines run through electronically hostile environments, especially when video lighting (a troublesome source of hum and noise) is in use. For these reasons, nearly all audio connections in a broadcast facility use balanced lines.

Rather than provide a multipin connector (such as the XT's 56-pin EDAC) for access to the servo-balanced analog inputs and outputs, the MDA-1's rear panel has a set of eight XLR inputs and outputs. In many situations, eight separate I/O connectors may be easier to deal with than a large multipin. For convenience, a set of eight unbalanced RCA/phono-type

Keeping the needs of
broadcast and video users in
mind, the MDA-1's analog
interfacing offers an
essential ingredient:
individual balanced inputs
and outputs.

analog inputs and outputs are provided, along with the standard Alesis Lightpipe fiber-optic digital input and output. The outputs are servo balanced, so no level loss occurs when the balanced outs are connected to an unbalanced mixer.

Other than these changes, everything else on the back panel (sync, BRC, LRC, punch-in/-out jack and optical digital I/O) is identical to the ADAT XT.

One difference between the ADAT XT and the MDA-1 (you'd have to look inside to see) is that the MDA-1 also incorporates muting relays on the outputs, which avoids power on/off transients and improves the deck's signal-to-noise performance while the machine is in Stop mode. Also, like the XT, the MDA-1 is built into a stylish yet sturdy chassis that's more solid and compact than the ADAT classic and improves transport control, faster locate/lockup times and better audio performance.

The tape format (eight tracks on a S-VHS tape) is unchanged, and the Panasonic MDA-1 is compatible with tapes recorded on any ADAT Type I system, including the ADAT classic, ADAT XT, Fostex RD-8, Fostex CX-8 and Panasonic MDA-1. Like other ADAT-format modular digital multitracks, the MDA-1 offers sample-accurate sync of up to 16 transports for up to 128 tracks.

The MDA-1 includes an MDA-1R, a compact remote controller that duplicates the transport controls and connects to the MDA-1's rear panel via a two-conductor, ¼-inch cord.

Other than the hookup and analog interfacing changes noted here, the Panasonic MDA-1 is virtually identical to the Alesis XT. More information regarding MDA-1 features and operations can be found in Chapter 9.

Panasonic Pro Audio
6550 Katella Avenue
Cypress, CA 90630
714-979-7277

Spotlight

Panasonic MDA-1
- Product Introduction: October 5, 1995
- Deliveries Began: May 1996
- Format: ADAT Type I, using S-VHS videotapes
- Maximum Recording Time: 40 minutes (T-120 tape), 54 minutes (T-160 tape)
- Track Capacity: Eight, expandable to 128 (in multiples of eight)
- Digital System: Rotary head; 16-bit linear; selectable 44.1/48kHz sampling frequencies
- Analog Connections: Unbalanced -10dBV RCA/phono-type; balanced +4dBu XLR inputs/outputs
- Digital Connections: Proprietary ADAT fiber-optic input/output ports using TosLink connectors; AES/EBU and S/PDIF interface optional
- Dimensions: 5.25x19x11 inches (HxWxD); 22 pounds
- Retail: $3,499, including MDA-1R remote control

CHAPTER 11

Fostex CX-8

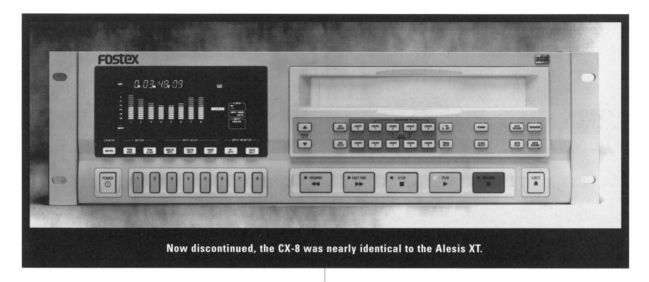

Now discontinued, the CX-8 was nearly identical to the Alesis XT.

he Fostex CX-8 was announced immediately following the unveiling of the Alesis XT. Priced at $3,500, the CX-8 is identical to the Alesis unit, save for front panel cosmetics and the replacement of the XT's 56-pin EDAC connector (for balanced line analog I/O) with the D-25 sub connector used on the Fostex RD-8 ADAT.

Unlike the earlier RD-8, which bore little resemblance to the original ADATs, with its onboard SMPTE and MIDI synchronization capability, the Fostex CX-8 wasn't a different enough product to compete against the Alesis XT, Panasonic MDA-1 and Tascam DA-88. The RD-8 was discontinued in 1996; the CX-8 disappeared early in 1997, about a year after it first shipped.

In any case, if you have a Fostex CX-8 and are looking for operational hints, check out the Alesis XT section in Chapter 9. For specifics on connecting the CX-8 to your studio system using the D-25 sub connectors, see Chapter 25.

Today, Fostex continues as a major supplier of professional quality, 2-channel DAT recorders for studio and location use, with an emphasis on high-performance stereo recorders with SMPTE time code capability for video production. Fostex has shifted its multitrack efforts into modular hard disk recorders,

Spotlight

Fostex CX-8

- Product Introduction: October 5, 1995
- Deliveries Began: Spring 1996
- Format: ADAT Type I, using S-VHS videotapes
- Maximum Recording Time: 40 minutes (T-120 tape), 54 minutes (T-160 tape)
- Track Capacity: Eight, expandable to 128 (in multiples of eight)
- Digital System: Rotary head; 16-bit linear; selectable 44.1/48kHz sampling frequencies
- Analog Connections: Unbalanced -10dBV RCA/phono-type; balanced +4dBu inputs/outputs on 25-pin D-sub multipin connector
- Digital Connections: Proprietary ADAT fiber-optic input/output ports using TosLink connectors; AES/EBU and S/PDIF interface optional
- Dimensions: 5.25x19x11 inches (HxWxD); 20 pounds
- Retail: $3,500, including remote control

such as the D-90 8-track, which can slave multiple units for 16- or 24-track recording or integrate into an existing MDM setup via its ADAT Lightpipe digital I/O ports. Fostex also offers the D-160, a 16-channel hard-disk-recorder-in-a-box and the high-end Foundation 2000 RE digital audio workstation, both products equipped with ADAT Lightpipe interfacing.

Fostex Corporation
15431 Blackburn Avenue
Norwalk, CA 90650
310-921-1112
http://www.fostex.com

CHAPTER 12

ADAT Maintenance and Troubleshooting

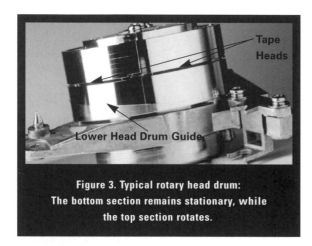

Tape Heads

Lower Head Drum Guide

**Figure 3. Typical rotary head drum:
The bottom section remains stationary, while
the top section rotates.**

In any studio, downtime is a fact of life, and modular digital multitrack systems are not immune to this rule. However, in contrast to earlier digital systems, MDM reliability looks pretty good. The first 3M digital 32-tracks were usually accompanied by a full-time maintenance tech just to keep them running! Early Sony and Mitsubishi digital multitracks also had a tendency to breakdown, despite being priced in the $140,000-180,000 range.

However, if you're prepared that your ADAT system will someday "go south," you're way ahead of the game. Fortunately, with a multi-MDM rig, if one recorder goes out, you can remove the bad deck and continue the session.

GENERAL CONSIDERATIONS

An ounce of prevention is worth a pound of cure as the old saying goes. Doing some obvious things, such as using high-quality tapes; keeping your ADATs in a clean, dust-free environment; and plugging the AC lines into a power conditioner (or at least a spike/surge suppresser strip) will go a long way toward keeping your recorders happy.

You should keep a maintenance log on all the gear in your studio. I keep mine in a three-ring binder, with one sheet for each piece of gear. I list the name of the unit, serial number, date of purchase, software version and any other pertinent info, such as dates when software was upgraded or the heads were cleaned or the date and description of any repairs or modifications. If anything ever goes wrong, it's nice to have this information handy.

THIS DOESN'T WORK

Check the easy things first. Cables have a peculiar tendency to come loose at inopportune times. This is a frequent cause of MDM problems, particularly when those tiny screws on the D-sub intermachine sync cables aren't tightened all the way. Even the removable AC power cables can find a way to wiggle out of their sockets, and an intermittent connection here can cause all kinds of unexplained maladies. Make sure the lockdown screws on the analog I/O multipin blocks are secure if you're using the EDAC/Elcos on ADATs or the D-25s on the Fostex machines. Audio problems can sometimes be solved by simply tightening the connections, perhaps using a touch of cleaner/deoxidizer/conductivity enhancement treatment such as DeoxIT from Caig Laboratories (619-457-1799) on the contact pins.

Having made hundreds of recordings on all types of MDM systems, I can conclusively state that tape is an important factor. Experiment a little, find a brand that works and stick to it. But no matter what you use, be aware that tapes will occasionally fail, jam or simply disintegrate. Backup tapes are a part of life in the digital lane, and if you care about your work, take the time to make safety copies. If you're having strange symptoms, such as a continuous or flashing error light, try playing another tape before calling the service department or dismantling your recorder.

HEAD GAMES

Once again, prevention, rather than cure, is preferable when caring for your modular digital multitracks. The rotating heads used in ADATs usually need replacing after 2,000 to 3,000 hours of use (typically, less than one year at a busy studio), but tape head life may be extended beyond that figure by avoiding dusty conditions and cleaning on a regular basis.

Also, when it comes to tape guides, cleanliness *is*

godliness. I've troubleshot dozens of MDM problems, and dirt particles trapped in the corners of the guide rollers cause tape misalignment and sticking, leading to all kinds of mysterious maladies, even when the heads are clean.

Unlike the heads on analog decks, MDM tape heads are extremely fragile. Unless you are thoroughly trained in the methods of cleaning rotary-head assemblies, you'd better forget about popping the top on an MDM to do head cleanings. Besides, there are a couple of other issues to consider:

- Dismantling an MDM will void your warranty.
- The insides of such devices carry potentially lethal voltages.
- Worst of all, inexperienced hands mucking around in complicated electromechanical devices can seriously damage the equipment; it's all too easy to trash a very expensive set of rotary heads if you don't know what you're doing.

Alesis recommends using "dry" tape head cleaning cassettes. Do not use the "wet" cleaners, which typically involve putting a few drops of cleaning liquid into a videotape-sized cleaning mechanism. These can permanently damage ADAT heads and should not be used. Alesis recommends the 3M VHS-HC Black Watch video cleaning cassette.

When to clean heads is subject to a variety of criteria, such as the conditions of operation (dust/humidity/temperature levels) and the type of work you do, such as constant shuttling over short sections of tape. Also, certain formulations of tape shed less particles than others, so once you find a tape you like, stay with it. My rule of thumb is to clean heads on an as-needed basis, such as when the ADAT's error light flashes frequently or stays on for long periods.

Keep a maintenance log and note how often your heads require cleaning. Check the number of hours on an ADAT by pressing the Set Locate and Stop buttons simultaneously. On a DA-88/DA-38, hold the Play and Stop buttons while powering up. This will display the total number of elapsed hours of head-drum operation on the time counter display. This hour display is useful not only for scheduling routine service but also for checking the "odometer" when you're looking at a used machine.

Another important point about head cleaning is that it should only be performed as required. Don't overdo it. Heads that are cleaned too frequently can wear out prematurely. If your MDM's heads or pathway need very frequent cleaning, perhaps it's time to look for a new brand of tape.

If you really want to clean your ADAT heads thoroughly, you should learn to do a complete manual tape assembly cleaning. What follows is my recommended procedure for head and tape path cleaning.

There are numerous commercial preparations available for head cleaning, but I like using absolute (99+%) ethyl alcohol. This is commonly sold in drugstores as "denatured" alcohol, which is ethyl "grain" alcohol combined with a trace amount of a chemical that makes it poisonous to keep people from drinking it. Do not use rubbing alcohol, which is typically a mixture of isopropyl alcohol combined with water.

Note that ethyl alcohol is extremely flammable. Make sure it is sealed tightly after use. If it's left uncovered, it will draw water vapor out of the air and lose its purity.

The rotary heads should only be cleaned using Kimwipes (which look similar to ordinary tissues, but are sterile and lint-free); deerskin (chamois) swabs; or synthetic chamois swabs, such as Chamois Tips™ made by Chemtronics (800-645-5244). The latter are carried by broadcast and pro audio dealers and are available in convenient 15-swab packs. Do not use cotton swabs, as these shed lint and cotton particles, which will create havoc with rotary heads.

If an error code tells you that the carburetor in your MDM has an improper air/fuel mixture or that one of the Venturi is blocked, should you head in with a soldering gun and an air hammer?

Begin by ejecting the tapes and disconnecting the power to the unit. Open the ADAT's top cover Inside, the most prominent thing you'll see is the silver head drum, which looks similar to that shown in the photo in Chapter 2. Note that the side of the head drum has a slot cut into it that goes around the entire drum. The tiny rectangular bits in the slot are the video heads (*see Fig. 3*).

Apply the absolute ethyl alcohol to the wipe or chamois and gently (but firmly) hold the wipe along the side of the head drum. Without moving the wipe, rotate the drum several times in one direction with your other hand, and then reverse the direction. Do not move the wipe up and down. Allow five minutes for the head drum to dry before using the recorder. The key to the head-cleaning procedure is finding the right amount of finger pressure: There is a fine line between properly cleaning and permanently damaging the delicate rotary head. If in doubt, take the deck to an audio or video repair shop and ask them to show you the procedure for manual head cleaning before attempting it yourself.

I suggest using a dental mirror to inspect the heads and tape path before and after cleaning, and if you don't have success with ethyl alcohol, try a commercial aerosol video head cleaner (if you use one of these, spray the aerosol cleaner onto the wipe, never directly onto the heads).

Make sure you clean the lower head drum guide. This is an indentation in the head drum that the tape rests upon as it travels around the head. It runs at an angle to the head slot, providing the precise angle for laying the audio track information in helical scans. If you're careful not to touch the rotary heads, an alcohol-moistened cotton swab can be used. Although the lower part of the drum does not rotate, I turn the top of the head drum several times as I clean the lower drum guide, so that the heads are away from the section I'm cleaning. It is critical that this part of the tape path is absolutely clean, as any dirt or crud that accumulates can push the tape up slightly, causing the tape to mistrack and resulting in an unplayable tape.

You can also use denatured alcohol and cotton swabs to clean the rest of the tape pathway: the fixed auxiliary and full erase heads, tape guides and capstan. Unlike the rotary heads, these parts can be cleaned with an up and down motion; just be gentle with the fragile nylon roller guides.

The rubber pinch roller wheel should be cleaned with a cleaner designed specifically for rubber parts, as alcohols degrade the life of rubber; TEAC/Tascam makes an excellent rubber roller cleaner, which I highly recommend.

THE ADAT IDLER WHEEL

If your ADAT shows symptoms such as sluggish rewind, dropping out of sync, dropping out of record, or mysteriously displaying the Nofo, Full, Er7, Er8 or Er9 error messages, you may need to clean or replace the idler wheel.

The idler wheel is a white plastic disk with a black rubber ring circling it, located within the ADAT transport assembly between the supply hub and take-up hub. During fast forward, rewind, play and record operation, the idler transfers the reel motor rotation to the hubs. However, after a period of time, the idler's outer rubber ring can become coated with tape oxide and other crud, causing it to lose traction.

Here's how to clean the idler wheel in a Type I ADAT:

1. Eject the tape.
2. Turn the ADAT off and disconnect the power cable.
3. Remove the ADAT's top panel.
4. Using a swab dipped in rubber cleaner, scrub the idler's outer ring until its finish becomes dull. (The idler wheel is between the supply hub and the take-up hub.)
5. Note where the two black reel hubs contact the idler, and scrub them with rubber cleaner until they're clean.
6. Replace the ADAT's cover and reconnect the AC power.

If cleaning doesn't cure the symptoms listed above, the idler should be replaced. Genuine OEM idler wheels are inexpensive and available through the Alesis parts department. They have a typical life that ranges from 300 to 750 "Drum On" hours as indicated on the ADAT front panel (press the Set Locate and Stop simultaneously to note the number of "Drum On" hours). Since the idler is inexpensive and easy to replace, it should be replaced as part of scheduled maintenance or whenever performance suffers.

Unlike the heads on analog decks, MDM tape heads are extremely fragile.

The idler wheel in ADAT-XTs (part kit #8-50-0053) are a different size and material from the part kit #8-50-0028 idler used in the original ADATs. The parts are not interchangeable, and both kits include installation instructions.

THE GERIATRIC ADAT

All modular digital multitrack recorders store operational data, such as autolocation information, crossfade times and pitch-shift settings, in battery-backed memory, even when the units are switched off or unplugged. This useful feature operates thanks to a built-in lithium cell, which constantly supplies power to the onboard RAM. In my experience, such batteries last at least five years (a battery in my vintage Korg Polysix synthesizer recently died after 15 years!) so around the turn of the century, if you encounter a senile ADAT, the problem may be nothing more than a dead battery.

AUTODIAGNOSTIC ROUTINES AND QUICK FIXES

ADATs include autodiagnostic circuits that display various error code messages to inform the user of potential problems. Should these appear on your machine, it's best to call the manufacturer's service department and get their advice. Unfortunately, many problems occur on weekends, late at night, holidays and other times when such phone help is unavailable.

Later in this chapter, I've included some of these messages, along with what problems they might indicate. So if an error code tells you that the carburetor in your MDM has an improper air/fuel mixture or that one of the Venturi is blocked, should you head in with a soldering gun and an air hammer? Probably not, but sometimes an error code message may indicate something that you *can* fix, such as replacing a defective tape or checking sync cables and I/O connections. At 3:00 a.m., it's reassuring to know whether an error signals a major breakdown that can stop the session or merely an inconvenience that can be worked around until morning.

ADAT TROUBLESHOOTING

ADAT machines (Alesis/Fostex/Panasonic/Studer) share a common tape format and display similar error messages. Many simple problems can be remedied by reinitializing, which is similar to rebooting a computer. To reinitialize, turn the power off, and then hold the Play and Record buttons simultaneously while powering up. Release after five seconds. In a multimachine and/or BRC system, reinitialize all components in this order: BRC first, then ADAT 1, 2, 3, etc.

The Alesis ADATs have a tiny light, known as the Advanced Information Indicator, located at the lower right-hand corner of the "seconds" indicator on the time display. It's a green LED that looks like an additional decimal point.

This LED lights whenever the error correction circuitry is active, and it may blink occasionally when a tape is playing. However, if it stays on for long periods of time or appears repeatedly, the tape heads may need cleaning. This condition can also be caused by poor-quality or defective tape, so before you blame the problem on dirty heads, play a different tape and watch the Advanced Information Indicator. If it stays on, dirty tape heads are probably at fault (unless both of your tapes were defective). If it returns to normal, then the first tape most likely was bad.

COMMON ADAT ERROR MESSAGES

As already stated, should error code messages appear on your machine, it's best to call the manufacturer's service department. However, your session may occur at a time when such phone help is unavailable. With that in mind, here is a listing of some of these messages and what problems they might indicate, so that you'll know whether you should stop the session or work around the problem until the service department is available to help you.

-du-: This indicates excessive humidity or condensation in the recorder. Leave the deck powered up, and let the machine heat up gradually.

Prot: Tape is protected against erasure: Its erase protect tab is removed. Recording cannot occur unless the open erase tab hole is covered.

FULL: The serial buffer is full and has no space for additional data. As a remedy, reinitialize the ADAT and/or clean the idler wheel.

noFo: No formatting present. This message sometimes appears when a cassette stops on the clear plastic leader at the end of a tape: There's no tape coating, so there's no formatting. In this case, rewind the tape. This may also indicate that a tape needs formatting: In this case, reformat the tape.

Er 0: The Tape Load switch has indicated improper loading/unloading of a cassette. Try reinserting the cassette gently and let the recorder pull it inside the deck. This may also indicate a tape whose adhesive label is applied outside of its designated area. Try another tape or a tape with no label.

Er 1–Er 3: These indicate threading errors or internal switch problems, such as dust blocking the microswitch that tells the ADAT the tape is threaded properly. This may also indicate a tape that's binding. Eject the tape and try a different one. If everything's okay, retry the first tape, perhaps after fast-forwarding it to the end and then rewinding it. If this doesn't cure the problem, try reinitializing the machine.

Er 4: The head drum isn't spinning when tape is threaded. If reinitialization doesn't improve the situation, it could be a motor problem requiring expert service.

Er 5: A head drum/capstan servo problem, such as too fast or too slow head-drum speed relative to tape speed. May occur when slaving to external clock source. Check sync cable connection; check optical I/O cables when deck is in "Digital In" mode. This can also indicate some physical problem that creates resistance in the tape path, which may be an unevenly wound cassette or warped/misaligned cassette shell. (Didn't your mother ever warn you about storing master tapes on your dashboard on summer days?) One solution that may work is "exercising" the tape: Fast-forward and rewind the tape a couple of times, then try playing it again.

Er 6: Problem reading information from data section of tape. This is sometimes caused by powering up the BRC before the ADAT transports.

Er 7: Excessive error correction during playback. Usually preceded by a lighting of the Advanced Information Indicator. May indicate poor-quality or defective tape (too many dropouts) or dirty tape heads. (See "Head Games" earlier in this chapter.)

Er 8: Loss of sync during recording. Several possible causes: loose or damaged sync cable, incoming time code has excessive jitter or dropouts, or dirty linear head. Error 8 may also be displayed at the end of tapes, since the plastic leader at the end of the tape carries no sync data; in such cases, there is no need for concern.

Er 9: Nonfunctioning take-up reel. This can be caused by a bad or dirty idler wheel that turns the take-up, a jammed take-up reel inside the cassette shell or a broken tape. Eject tape and try again with unimportant tape.

If these errors occur only with a certain tape or are rarely displayed, there is little cause for alarm. Errors 1, 2, 3 and 9 indicate conditions that may damage a tape; the other errors won't damage the tape or the recorder.

The following errors only apply to XT-family recorders, all of which can be cured by reinitializing the recorder.

Er 10: Record enable lights when track isn't in record mode. Reinitialize recorder to cure problem. *Note: Errors 11, 12, 13 and 16 are currently not used and are saved for future use.*

Er 14: Crossfade buffer problem. Reinitialize recorder to cure problem.

Er 15: Channel error or crossfading state error. Reinitialize recorder to cure problem.

Insider's Tip

Number your machines! Put a small number (using one of the adhesive numbers included with a videotape's label page) your deck's front panel. With a studio full of ADATs (meaning two or more), you can easily become confused as to which recorder is which. By referring to the stick-on number, you can keep track of the age, software version or minor eccentricities that recorders develop over time. Also, once the machines are numbered, you should develop a regular schedule of rotating the transports. If you have three decks in a rack, the top deck (Tracks 1-8) will get more use than the second, and that deck gets more than the third. Occasionally rotate the decks so all the machines get the same use. At the end of the year, you may end up with three decks with 1,000 hours each, rather than one with 2,500 hours, one with 400 hours and one with 100 hours.

Er 17: Tape-end sensor error. Reinitialize recorder to cure problem.

WHEN DISASTER STRIKES

Occasionally (fortunately, *very* occasionally) a tape will become lodged inside the ADAT (typical causes are a damaged or poor-quality tape) and will not eject, which means the tape may be jammed or wound around the transport mechanism.

Before you do anything rash, power down the deck and pull it out of the rack for easier access. Remove the deck's top cover. Now power up, while depressing the record enable buttons for Tracks 1 and 7, which causes the machine to display "CAP," and enter the capstan test mode. We're not really interested in running the capstan test. We just want to get the tape out of the machine. When you press Auto Play, the first part of the capstan test will eject the tape. Unthread the tape from the transport and head assembly, being careful not to touch the tape surface with your fingerprints. Now, carefully slide the tape loop out through the front panel cassette door.

At this point, hold the tape so that its door faces away from you. By pushing the small rectangular button on the right side of the tape, the door can swing upwards and you can manually reel the tape into the cassette. If the tape is not too damaged, a few fast-forward/rewind cycles will help straighten out minor wrinkles, and you can (hopefully) make a safety copy. Before you use the ADAT again, inspect its tape pathway and look for dirty rollers or guides that may have caused the tape to jam. Clean the deck thoroughly before reuse: You don't really want to go through this twice, do you?

BRC PROBLEMS AND CURES

The BRC functions only with ADATs that are software Version 3.03 or higher. Alesis can update pre-3.03 ADATs to the latest software; call the company for details. You can determine an ADAT's software version by pressing the Set Locate and Fast-forward buttons simultaneously; the number of the software version will be shown on the LED display.

Also, in a multi-ADAT system controlled by a BRC, the ADAT with the *oldest* software version should be the master deck, so if you have three decks (V3.03, V3.04 and V3.05) then the master should be the 3.03 ADAT.

If your BRC is acting quirky, you should first try the BRC initializing procedure: Hold the Play and Record buttons while powering on. However, this procedure will clear any song or location point memory in the BRC's memory, so try storing any important locator information to tape (for later download) before reinitializing the BRC.

ADAT Type II Format Recorders

Chapter 13 Alesis ADAT M20

Chapter 14 Studer V-Eight

Alesis ADAT M20

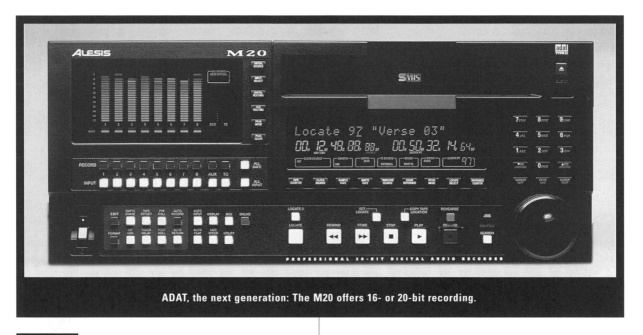

ADAT, the next generation: The M20 offers 16- or 20-bit recording.

arch 21, 1997: On the eve of the 102nd Convention of the Audio Engineering Society in Munich, Germany, Alesis and Swiss high-end pro audio manufacturer Studer announced an alliance for the development of ADAT Type II, a new 20-bit recording system based on the S-VHS ADAT format. Released in the fall of 1997, the first two Type II recorders are the Alesis M20 and the Studer V-Eight.

The Type II format provides 20-bit linear recording (up to 67 minutes on a T-180 tape at 44.1kHz), as well as a mode that switches the new machines to 16-bit operation. The latter mode provides Type II decks with full compatibility for the recording and/or playback of tapes made on the 100,000 machines using the original 16-bit ADAT format. The 20-bit tapes will not be playable on the Alesis, Fostex and Panasonic Type I ADAT decks. However, up to 16 ADAT decks (of any vintage) can be interlocked for as many as 128 tracks, in sample-accurate sync, merely by connecting the standard Alesis 9-pin sync cables between transports.

The M20 includes a Fostex RD-8-compatible dedicated time code track (time code can also be derived from the machine's absolute-time counter) and an analog auxiliary track for cueing or other purposes. The deck also offers onboard SMPTE/EBU time code chase-lock sync (all frame rates are supported), video reference and word-clock in/out.

Video/film post-production pros will appreciate the M20's "pull-up/-down" feature, which adjusts the sample rate by ±0.1 percent to compensate for film shot intentionally for video release at 30 fps (or 24 fps film transferred to video at 30 fps) and the standard NTSC frame rate of 29.97 fps. This makes a 0.1 percent change in the speed of the tape, while leaving the time code format/frame rate unchanged.

Among the M20's standard amenities are up to 170ms of delay on each track, auto-punch with rehearse mode, digital routing to/from any track on a machine or within a system and internal input/output trim pots for precisely matching operating levels to your console. Other features include a choice of 32 crossfade times (5.4ms to 1.486 seconds, depending on record sampling rate); switchable digital output (20-bit, 16-bit, dithered 16-bit); saving/offloading autolocator data to/from tape (in BRC format); MIDI sync; programmable pre-/post-roll; auto-punch-in/-out with rehearse mode; tape offset assembly editing; one-button record on/off; and external control via Sony P2 (9-pin) or MIDI Machine Control.

One of the M20's slick tricks is its ability to simultaneously record through its analog and digital inputs in adjacent channel pairs, so, for example, it's no problem to record two tracks via an outboard analog converter on Tracks one and two (perhaps for a piano or other delicate instrument), while using the onboard converters for other tracks.

The M20's rear panel can have as many as 45 connectors.

THE NEW ADAT ON THE BLOCK

From one glance at the ADAT M20, you can be sure something's different. Housed in a die-cast, four-rackspace chassis (1.75 inches taller than the original ADAT or XT), the M20 has the look and feel of a pro video editing deck, with a large jog/shuttle knob, illuminated transport buttons and a keypad for entering SMPTE addresses or the 100 locator points.

System status, locator information and metering are on two large fluorescent displays, with double the space provided on the Alesis XT. The M20's operational and autodiagnostic messages are far more descriptive and less cryptic than those on the ADAT classic or XT.

The front panel controls are extensive. The 80-plus controls include 9 function buttons, 5 illuminated transport keys, 4 locate-related keys, 15 editing switches, 20 track arming and input select buttons (2 each for the 8 digital audio channels, SMPTE time code and analog aux tracks) and 25 additional function buttons. Although this barrage may seem formidable, most are single-function keys, so you won't spend all your time getting lost in endless submenus, wondering how to reset a certain key back to some specific function.

No less than 37 connectors (45 with the optional AES/EBU interface installed) grace the M20's back panel. All analog interfacing is via balanced +4dBu XLRs (including time code and aux tracks) or the 56-pin EDAC (Elco-compatible) connector used on all previous Alesis ADATs. ADAT Lightpipe digital in/out ports are standard; an expansion slot accommodates an optional 8-channel AES/EBU digital I/O interface card.

The rear panel's selection of remote/sync connections borders on vast and includes two 9-pin D-sub ports (one in, one out) for sample-accurate ADAT sync (interlocking multiple transports); MIDI In/Out; RJ-45 jack for the CADI autolocator/controller and RMD 32-channel remote meter display; two ¼-inch jacks for the LRC small remote and (optional) punch-in/-out footswitch; 9-pin connector for Sony P2 protocol input; two pairs of BNCs for word-clock in/out and video sync in/thru (with 75-ohm termination switch); and two +4dBu balanced XLRs for time code in/out, supporting the following frame rates: Absolute time (ADAT 32-bit), SMPTE (30 and 29.97 DF and NDF), 25 fps EBU and 24 fps film.

Spotlight

Alesis ADAT M20
- Product Introduction: March 21, 1997
- Deliveries Began: Fall 1997
- Format: ADAT Type II, using standard S-VHS videotapes
- Maximum Recording Time: 67 minutes (T-180 tape at 44.1kHz)
- Track Capacity: Eight, expandable to 128
- Digital System: Rotary head; switchable ADAT Type I (16-bit linear encoding) or ADAT Type II (20-bit linear encoding); 44.1/48kHz sampling frequencies
- Analog Connections: Audio: balanced +4dBu inputs/outputs on 16 XLRs and 56-pin EDAC (Elco-compatible) multipin; two XLRs (+4dBu) for aux (cue) track I/O
- Digital Connections: ADAT Lightpipe (eight channels in and out on TosLink fiber-optic connectors); 8-channel AES/EBU interface optional on plug-in card
- Dimensions: 7x19x14.5 inches (HxWxD); 35 pounds
- Retail: $6,999, including LRC remote, standard rack ears and one fiber-optic digital dubbing cable

LET'S LOOK UNDER THE HOOD

Under the hood, both machines feature the Matsushita "IQ" transport used in Panasonic's high-end video editing systems and operate twice as fast as the Alesis XT. A 40-minute (T-120) tape rewinds in just over 40 seconds, wind speed is 85-times play speed and shuttle is variable, from ¼-speed to 10-times play speed. Variable-speed forward/reverse "reel rocking" is also possible and audio from the aux track can automatically be routed to any source track output in Jog mode. So if Track 1 is selected, the cue track data routes to output #1 when in jog mode.

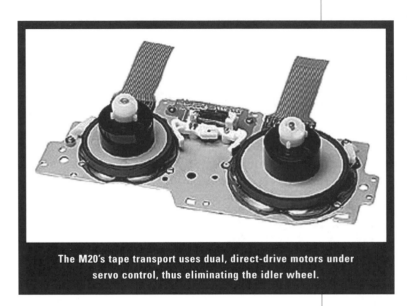

The M20's tape transport uses dual, direct-drive motors under servo control, thus eliminating the idler wheel.

The transport offers more than mere speed. Dual direct-drive motors under servo control move the tape efficiently, and this design eliminates the idler wheel, so tape handling is gentler yet provides for faster sync from stop and greater control in jog/shuttle mode. With no brake adjustments needed, no idler to clean/replace and an automatic head cleaning wand, maintenance needs should be greatly reduced. An off-line mode allows formatting on one deck while recording on others without repatching sync lines. After formatting, a "tape certify" function can check the tape and provide a count of tape errors.

The M20's analog Aux track acts as a "ninth track" to be used for various purposes ranging from a cue track to click track or slating, note taking or even recording tone pulses for triggering slide projectors in multi-image presentations. Additionally, the M20 provides a simple onboard mixer that can record the output of any combination of tracks to the Aux track whenever needed. Just select the tracks you want to copy, arm the Aux track and press Record. The Aux track has its own XLR input and output and is recorded on a linear track near the top edge of the tape in the same manner that linear audio tracks are recorded on a VCR. However, due to the ADAT's increased tape speed, which is faster than standard S-VHS transports, the quality of the Aux track is higher than that of most VCR linear audio tracks.

TO ERROR IS HUMAN

Like the ADAT XT, Fostex CX8 and Panasonic MDA-1, the M20 has an error rate display mode providing a count of the number of sync block errors per 14 drum revolutions (280ms). As there are 30 sync blocks per sector, 8 sectors per track and 2 tracks per revolution, the *maximum* number of errors is:

$$14 \times 30 \times 8 \times 2 = 6{,}720 \text{ errors!!!}$$

So what does this mean, really? Well, if you're getting 6,720 sync block errors, you've probably already figured out you have a problem, since you are getting 100 percent errors and 0 percent useful audio data. But consistently high error rates (in the 25-100 range and up) may simply indicate that the recorder's heads are dirty, especially when combined with a flashing or steady interpolation indicator (error icon) on the vacuum fluorescent display. From my perspective, the best use of this display is determining which brands of tape have the lowest error rate. Of course, there are numerous other factors that determine tape quality (shell quality, longevity, binder and lubricant quality, etc.), but this mode can give you some clues about where to start working.

AUDIO IS EVERYTHING

Soundwise, the M20 is impressive. The record electronics are based around 24-bit, 64x oversampling Delta-Sigma analog to digital converters; the playback side has 20-bit, 128x oversampling Delta-Sigma digital-to-analog converters. The sound quality is superb, sparkling and clear. In comparisons between the 20-bit M20 and 16-bit recorders (Alesis XT and various studio DAT recorders), there's an obvious difference that's immediately noticeable, even to the casual listener. And all of the DACs and ADCs used are single converter-per-channel chips.

The M20 has the same vari-speed range (±200 cents at 44.1kHz, -300/+100 cents at 48kHz) as the ADAT classic and XT models, although the M20 displays pitch change values both as cents and percent. By the way, there's a sneaky (no cost) way to further increase the M20's sound quality, and it's particularly effective when tracking with and mixing through a high performance analog console. By boosting the pitch shift range to its max during recording and playback, the recorder's effective sampling rate becomes 50.854kHz, thus increasing the deck's upper frequency response by another 1,000Hz or so, which roughly equates to a five percent increase in frequency response.

OPTIONS, OPTIONS, OPTIONS
Although the M20 offers a lot, a number of optional accessories are available, allowing users to customize an M20 system to fit various specific applications or installation/production needs. The M20 is shipped with removable rack ears, including power amp-style rear rack rails, which are required to safely support the M20's substantial 35-pound heft.

To simplify routine maintenance procedures, one useful option is a rack slider kit: Requiring a 22-inch deep rack with rear rails, the kit provides a pull-out, drawer-style mounting for the M20. The rack slider kit also includes new rack ears with handles. However, although these handles provide convenient hand-grips for sliding the ADAT when it's mounted within the rack slides, they should *never* be used to lift the ADAT when it's removed from the rack slides.

For facilities needing a digital interconnect in addition to, or in lieu of, the ADAT Lightpipe digital I/O ports, the M20's back panel has a slot for an optional AES/EBU interface card, which plugs in and installs in minutes by replacing four screws on the back panel. This relatively inexpensive option features eight XLR connectors, four stereo pair AES/EBU inputs and four stereo pair AES/EBU outputs.

Especially suited for users who need to transfer two (or multiple) channels of digital audio directly to or from a workstation or digital video recorder, or load/offload multichannel DVD or digital cinema surround mixes, the AES/EBU ports offer a simple way to access external converters, DSP units or digital consoles that don't have ADAT Lightpipe interfacing. Perhaps best of all is that the M20's audio output data is always routed to the analog outs, Lightpipe and AES/EBU ports. This provides all kinds of possibilities such as simultaneously monitoring through an analog console while transferring tracks to an AES/EBU-equipped workstation and making a safety clone with the Lightpipe connection.

An LRC mini-remote is included with the machines. For those requiring more, the optional Controller Autolocator Desktop Interface (CADI) can control up to eight M20s (64 tracks) with access to all controls, track arming and sync functions.

All the front panel controls of the M20, including the jog/shuttle wheel, are available on the CADI's front panel. A bright, vacuum-fluorescent display

shows machine status and alphanumeric information such as the names of location points. Individual M20s can be taken off-line from the remote (allowing tape formatting operations on two transports while recording or mixing using two other M20s in the chain). Individual "Locked" LEDs indicate all machines in a system are in sample-accurate sync.

Unlike the BRC control, CADI does not house all the system synchronization circuitry (SMPTE chase and MIDI sync is built into every M20). Communicating to any Type II deck via a single RJ-45 Ethernet-style cable (up to 300 meters), CADI merely acts as the interface telling the system what to do. The real power is in the M20 itself.

Also on the RJ-45 bus is display information for the redesigned 32-track optional RMD 32-channel remote meter display, which, like the new ADATs, provides a choice of metering modes (including a high-res 0.2dB/division setting) as well as error/interpolation indicators. The meter display's Peak mode and Peak Clear mode may be set from the front panel of the M20, or from the CADI. In addition, eight LEDs on the meter's front panel warn of any error conditions or tape problems.

WRAPPING IT UP
Priced at $6,999 (about double the cost of an Alesis XT) M20 puts the cost of a 24-track, 20-bit digital recorder below that of a new analog 24-track. Combined with some of the new 20-bit workstations, a variety of useful options (CADI, remote meter display, AES interfacing, rack slider kit, etc.) and an existing base of 100,000 machines, the ADAT Type II format should provide new choices for large and small studios alike.

Alesis Corp.
3630 Holdrege Avenue
Los Angeles, CA 90016
310-841-2272
fax: 310-836-9192
http://www.alesis.com

CHAPTER 14

Studer V-Eight

Studer's V-Eight provides versatile monitor mixing functions.

tuder Professional Audio AG of Zurich, Switzerland, a leading name in the broadcast and recording industry, has more than 40 years of experience in designing and manufacturing 2-track and multitrack analog and digital tape recorders. Despite this long tradition, Studer has never been shy of launching into new audio territories, such as its MicValve series of tube (!) microphone preamps, which have optional digital converters with ADAT Lightpipe outputs.

So with Studer's previous association with ADAT products, it came as a small surprise that Studer and Alesis announced an alliance for the development of ADAT Type II, a 20-bit recording system based on the S-VHS ADAT format. Released in late 1997, the first two Type II recorders are the Alesis M20 and the Studer V-Eight.

The V-Eight shares many of the same features as the Alesis M20, such as 20-bit linear recording (up to 67 minutes on a T-180 tape at 44.1kHz), as well as a mode that switches the new machines to 16-bit operation. The latter mode provides Type II decks with full compatibility for the recording and/or playback of tapes made on the 100,000 (or so) machines using the original 16-bit ADAT format. Any tape recorded in the 20-bit mode will not be playable on Type I ADATs (original Alesis ADAT, ADAT XT, Fostex and Panasonic decks). However, up to 16 ADAT decks (of any vintage) can be interlocked for as many as 128 tracks.

Housed in a die-cast, 4-rackspace chassis, the V-Eight has a large jog/shuttle knob, a keypad for entering SMPTE addresses or the 100 locator points. The tape transport is the Matsushita "IQ" used in Panasonic's high-end video editing systems, operating twice as fast as the Alesis XT. A 40-minute (T-120) tape rewinds in 30 seconds, wind speed is 80-times play speed, and shuttle is 10-times play speed. Variable-speed forward/reverse "reel rocking" is also possible. Dual direct-drive motors under servo control move the tape efficiently, eliminating the need for an idler wheel, so tape handling is gentler. With no brake adjustments needed, no idler to clean/replace and an automatic head cleaning wand, maintenance needs should be greatly reduced. An off-line mode allows formatting on one deck while recording on others without repatching sync lines. After formatting, a "tape certify" function can check the tape and provide a count of tape errors.

The V-Eight employs 24-bit, 64x oversampling Delta-Sigma A/D converters and 20-bit, 128x oversampling Delta-Sigma D/A converters from Studer's flagship D827 MCH reel-to-reel digital 48-track.

The V-Eight offers a dedicated time code track (time code can also be derived from the machine's absolute-time counter), an analog auxiliary track and onboard SMPTE/EBU time code chase-lock sync (all frame rates are supported), as well as MIDI Machine Control, video reference I/O (with 75-ohm termination switching) and word-clock in/out. Post-production pros will appreciate the pull-up/-down feature, which adjusts the sample rate by ±0.1 percent to compensate for film shot intentionally for video release at 30 fps (or 24 fps film transferred to video at 30 fps) and the standard NTSC frame rate of 29.97 fps. This makes a 0.1 percent change in the speed of the tape, while leaving the time code format/frame rate unchanged.

Analog interfacing is via balanced XLRs (including time code and aux tracks) or the 56-pin EDAC (Elco-compatible) connector used on all previous Alesis ADATs. ADAT Lightpipe digital in/out ports are standard; an optional 8-channel AES digital I/O interface is available. Other features include up to 170ms of delay on each track, auto-punch with rehearse mode, digital routing to/from any track on a machine or within a system and internal trim pots for precisely matching operating levels (±5dB) to your console. System status, locator information and metering are on two large fluorescent displays.

An LRC-style mini-remote is included with the V-Eight, but an optional Controller Autolocator Desktop Interface (CADI) can control up to eight ADATs (64 tracks) with access to all controls, track arming and sync functions. Communicating to any Type II

deck via a single RJ-45 Ethernet-style cable (up to 300 meters), CADI acts as the interface telling the system what to do. Also on the RJ-45 bus is display information for the redesigned 32-track optional meter bridge which provides a choice of metering modes (including a high-res 0.2dB/division setting) as well as error/interpolation indicators.

While the previous section explains the similarities between the Alesis M20 and the Studer V-Eight, there are many differences beyond the latter's silver faceplate.

The V-Eight employs 24-bit, 64x oversampling Delta-Sigma A/D converters and 20-bit, 128x oversampling Delta-Sigma D/A converters from Studer's flagship D827 MCH reel-to-reel digital 48-track. Also standard is a 9-pin port for control via the Sony P2 standard and a parallel port for direct transport control via high-end consoles, such as Solid State Logic's renowned E or G Series. (MIDI Machine Control is also standard for communication with other consoles.) One nice touch that most studio engineers will appreciate is the V-Eight's "Night Design" feature, which provides backlit illumination of its 80-plus

Spotlight

Studer V-Eight
- Product Introduction: March 21, 1997
- Deliveries Began: December 1997
- Format: ADAT Type II, using S-VHS videotapes
- Maximum Recording Time: 67 minutes (T-180 tape at 44.1kHz)
- Track Capacity: Eight, expandable to 128 (in multiples of eight)
- Digital System: Rotary head; switchable ADAT Type I (16-bit linear encoding) or ADAT Type II (20-bit linear encoding); 44.1/48kHz sampling frequencies
- Analog Connections: Audio: balanced +4dBu inputs/outputs on 16 XLRs and 56-pin EDAC (Elco-compatible) multipin; two XLRs (+4dBu) for aux (cue) track I/O; headphone output for monitor mix
- Digital Connections: ADAT Lightpipe (8-channels in and out on TosLink fiber-optic connectors); 8-channel AES/EBU interface optional on plug-in card
- Dimensions: 7x19x14.5 inches (HxWxD); 35 pounds
- Retail: $8,300, including LRC-style remote and two fiber-optic digital dubbing cables

transport and function keys for easier operation in dimly-lit studio control rooms.

For field listening or machine room applications, the deck also has a front panel 8x2 monitor mixer with headphone output. This feature will not appeal to everybody, but it's a godsend for those who need it. For example, I recently completed an album of an acoustic group, recorded live in a small coffee-house setting. My remote recording package consisted of a high-end, 8-channel preamp and an Alesis XT mounted in a road case. By assigning one track to each microphone, I had the luxury of *not* mixing on-location, yet I had to drag a mixer along just so I could individually monitor tracks using headphones. In this situation, the V-Eight's monitor mixer would have been a real time saver and would have greatly simplified the recording process.

The V-Eight's back panel also has an additional "return" input routed to the headphone mixer. This return input allows cascading the headphone outputs of multiple V-Eights, so a number of tracks can be monitored from headphones connected to one V-Eight recorder. In addition to remote recording applications, the headphone mix cascade would be ideal in machine room applications, where maintenance or tape operator personnel can monitor tapes, even if the control room may be hundreds of meters away.

Retailing at $8,300 (approximately ten percent more than the Alesis M20) the Studer V-Eight will surely find a market among those higher-end users who are attracted both by its expanded features and the prestige of the Studer name. These factors, combined with its compatibility with an existing base of more than 100,000 ADATs worldwide, will make the Studer V-Eight the machine to watch in the years to come.

Studer Professional Audio
1449 Donelson Pike
Nashville, TN 37210
615-391-3399
fax: 615-259-4452
http://www.studer.ch/studer

DTRS Format Recorders

Chapter 15 Tascam DA-88

Chapter 16 Secrets of the DA-88

Chapter 17 Sony PCM-800

Chapter 18 Tascam DA-38

Chapter 19 Tascam DA-98

Chapter 20 DTRS Accessories

Chapter 21 DTRS Maintenance and Troubleshooting

Tascam DA-88

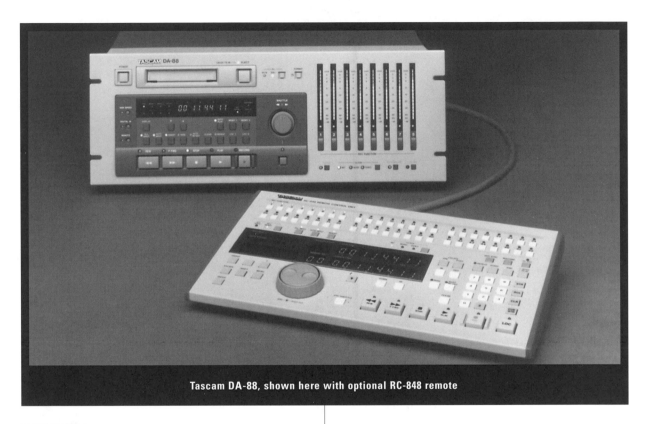

Tascam DA-88, shown here with optional RC-848 remote

or months before its arrival, rumors of a Tascam modular digital multitrack system circulated through the industry. Finally, on October 1, 1992, the Tascam DA-88 made its debut at the Audio Engineering Society Convention in San Francisco. Seven months later, when the initial DA-88 deliveries began, the low-cost digital multitrack market was no longer the exclusive domain of the Alesis ADAT. The audio community had another format, and those who had postponed the decision to go digital suddenly had new options to consider.

Tascam displayed its first line of affordable studio production products at the AES show in 1970. By 1972, this line included the 3340, the first simul-sync 4-track recorder using ¼-inch, reel-to-reel tape. Designed specifically for music production, as opposed to earlier 4-tracks, which were built for quadraphonic recording, the 3340 and its successors,

such as the 1979 Tascam Portastudio™ series of analog cassette multitracks, became the catalysts of the home studio revolution. It's no surprise that more than a few of today's top recording engineers and musicians got their first taste of recording technology on Tascam gear.

Tascam was no newcomer to the professional digital marketplace, either. In 1988, Tascam unveiled its $100,000 DA-800 digital 24-track, a ½-inch reel-to-reel design using the same DASH (Digital Audio Stationary Head) format as Sony's PCM-3324 multitrack. Tascam also made serious headway in the professional studio DAT market with its excellent DA-30 deck. This commitment to cost-effective, high-performance technology led to Tascam's development of the DA-88.

Still in production five years after its initial debut, the DA-88 initially found favor with the film/video post-production sound community, thanks in part to its fast transport and optional SMPTE time code sync card.

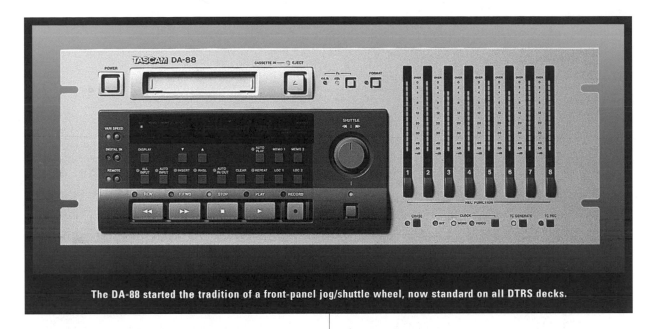
The DA-88 started the tradition of a front-panel jog/shuttle wheel, now standard on all DTRS decks.

The DA-88 garnered both Emmy and TEC Awards for technical excellence, and today a majority of the 50,000+ DTRS (Digital Tape Recording System) format decks in use worldwide are DA-88s.

SYSTEM BASICS

The Tascam DA-88 is an 8-track deck that can record 108 minutes of digital audio on a standard Hi-8mm videotape. Like other MDM designs, the DA-88 does not require additional audio tracks or expensive external synchronizers for multimachine lockup; a single cable between the DA-88s is all that's required for sample-accurate synchronization. Tascam's modular recording approach allows up to 16 of these machines to be interlocked, providing up to 128 tracks of recording capability.

The DA-88 uses a 4-head, rotary, helical-scan transport to store audio on Hi-8mm video tapes. It runs about ten percent faster than a camcorder, so a 120-minute tape provides an actual running time of ten percent less than that figure, or 108 minutes. The machine automatically ejects tapes that are longer than 120 minutes or are not Hi-8mm.

Hi-8mm tapes are readily available from electronics stores, and 3M recently showed a pro Hi-8mm formulation designed for digital audio use. Tascam has tested many tape brands and recommends the MP and ME designations of Hi-8mm tapes from Sony, TDK, Maxell and BASF, as well as the MP-types from 3M, Denon and Konica. As a price comparison, I checked a local discount shop, where TDK's ME-120, a decent-quality Hi-8 tape, was $9.99. With the DA-88's 108-minute running time, this works out to about 1.25 cents per track-minute. Remember that two-inch analog tape at 30 ips is about $7/minute (29 cents per track-minute).

Curiously, the erase-protect tab on the 8mm videotape (Hi or standard) must be slid into the open position to allow recording, the opposite of the way that floppy disks, DATs, analog cassettes, VHS tapes and everything else on the planet operates. This is a minor point, but it takes some getting used to.

Before recording, the tapes must be formatted, with the 44.1 or 48kHz sampling frequency selected ahead of time. On an 8-track system, formatting can

Spotlight

- Product Introduction: October 1, 1992
- Deliveries Began: April/May 1993
- Format: DTRS, using standard Hi-8mm video-tapes
- Recording Time: 108 minutes (P6/E6-120 tapes); 82 minutes (P5/E5-90 tapes)
- Track Capacity: Eight, expandable to 128
- Digital System: Rotary head; 16-bit linear; 44.1/48kHz sampling frequencies
- Analog Connections: Unbalanced -10dBV phono jack (RCA) inputs/outputs; +4dBm balanced I/O on 25-pin D-sub connectors
- Digital Connections: Proprietary bidirectional TDIF-1 on 25-pin Dsub port; AES/EBU-S/PDIF and SDIF-2 interfaces optional
- Dimensions: 7x19x15 inches (HxWxD); 31 pounds
- Retail: $4,799

take place during recording. However, a multimachine DA-88 system cannot run in sync while formatting; when using DA-88s for live 16-track (or more) recording, the tapes must be pre-formatted. The procedure itself requires several button presses, so there's little chance of accidental formatting, which would erase any audio information on the tape. One interesting bit of trivia is that tapes previously recorded with video information cannot be formatted for DA-88 use, so forget about tracking over your camcorder tapes of little Jimmy's birthday party!

The layout of the DA-88's 4-rackspace, 7-inch high front panel is uncluttered and logical. Operation is fairly straightforward, especially to anyone familiar with the locator operations on Tascam's other pro multitrack products. Besides the usual transport functions, the front panel includes controls for tape shuttle, sample rate select, two locator points, rehearse and auto-punch modes, clock source select (this should remain in the "Internal" setting for most applications), time code generate/record switches (these function only with the optional SY-88 SMPTE synchronization card) and arrow up/down keys. The latter are increment/decrement softkeys used in conjunction with a display button that allows the user to set pre-roll times, crossfade times, sync offset in a multimachine setup, ±6 percent pitch change and

playback delays on individual tracks. The numeric LED readout is large and bright, and in addition to displaying the softkey parameters, can be switched to show absolute time in hours/minutes/seconds/frames, as well as time code (if the sync card is installed) or the two memo/locator points.

The meters are 15-segment LED ladders, which are large and bright but slightly inset, making them difficult to read if the viewer is more than 50 degrees off-axis to the recorder. As an alternative to the onboard meters, a 15-pin rear-panel jack connects to the optional 24-track meter bridge, model MU8824 ($899, not including the PW-88M meter bridge connector cable at an additional $90).

MAKING CONNECTIONS

The rear panel's line-level analog inputs and outputs are unbalanced RCA phono jacks (-10dBV) and balanced +4dBm. However, to reduce manufacturing costs, the +4dBm I/O is via two 25-pin D-sub multipin connectors. These D-subs are commonly used on computers and peripherals; Tascam's high-end M-600 and M-700 professional mixing boards; mixers made by other companies, such as British manufacturer DDA; and also appear on the rear panel of the Fostex RD-8 and CX-8 modular digital 8-track recorders. D-sub connectors are inexpensive and readily available but can

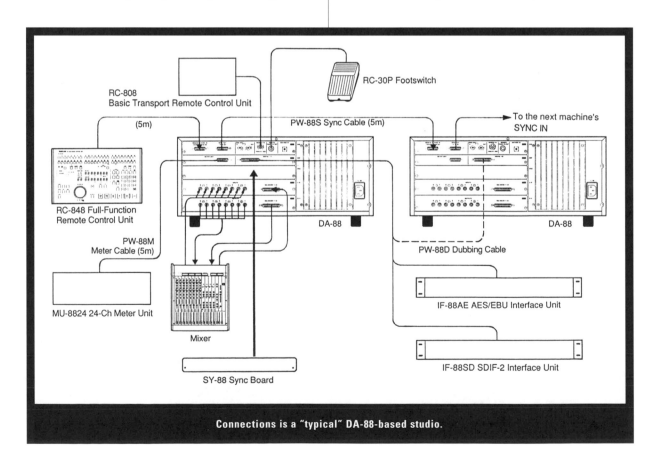

Connections is a "typical" DA-88-based studio.

be difficult to assemble, especially with larger-gauge cable. For those who hate to solder, optional Tascam PW8D/XM and PW8D/XF D-sub-to-XLR snakes (wired with pin #3 hot) are available, as are interface cables in a variety of lengths and configurations from Clark Wire & Cable (847-949-9595), Conquest Sound (708-534-0390), Hosa (714-522-5675), Pro Co (616-388-9675) and Whirlwind (716-663-8820).

Note that the hold-down nuts on all of the DA-88's D-sub connectors are fitted with ISO threads. Although common in Japan, the ISO threads will not mate with metric or USA-standard 4-40 threads. This leaves the do-it-yourselfer three options:

1. Find high-quality connectors with ISO threads (a difficult task).
2. Build connectors using top-notch American D-subs, such as those made by AMP, and then swap their 4-40 hold-down screws with some ISO-thread screws (an easier task).
3. Buy a tap and rethread the DA-88 hold-down nuts so they have 4-40 threads (the most permanent approach).

You may have heard of the S/PDIF and SDIF-2 digital interfacing standards, but get ready for TDIF-1 (Tascam Digital InterFace), a 25-pin D-sub port that connects to a second DA-88 for making clone copies of tapes, as well as providing the link to Tascam's optional AES/EBU and S/PDIF interface (the $1,099 IF-88AE) and the $1,299 SDIF-2 (IF-88SD) interface. TDIF-1 is a bidirectional, 8-channel interface, so only one cable is required for transferring digital audio materials between two TDIF-1-equipped units. TDIF-1 is currently a proprietary digital transfer format, so it's unlikely that you'll find many non-Tascam devices fitted with TDIF-1 connectors. With that in mind, the two optional interfaces are essential if you plan to transfer DAT, CD or workstation tracks into and out of the DA-88 in the digital domain.

The IF-88AE provides AES/EBU (professional-type) and S/PDIF (consumer-type) digital ports for connecting the DA-88 to workstations, DAT machines, CD players/recorders and signal processors with digital inputs/outputs. Included on the IF-88AE are four pairs of AES/EBU inputs and outputs on standard XLR jacks, each routed to a pair of DA-88 tracks. Also provided is an S/PDIF input and output on RCA phono-type jacks, a BNC word-clock output and a bidirectional 25-pin TDIF-1 port for connecting to the DA-88. The AES/EBU ports automatically route to any record-ready track pairs on the DA-88 when the Digital Input button on the DA-88 front panel is enabled. As there is only a single set of S/PDIF ports, a front-panel switch allows the user to select any track pair on the DA-88 for sending/receiving the digital information.

The SDIF-2 interface format used on the IF-88SD is compatible with high-end digital systems such as Sony's PCM-3324 (24-track) and PCM-3348 (48-track) DASH-format, reel-to-reel digital machines. The IF-88SD's front panel is simple, with a switch for selecting 44.1kHz or 48kHz sampling frequencies. The rear panel has the SDIF-2 input and output ports (on 25-pin D-sub connectors), BNC word-sync in/out jacks and the 25-pin TDIF-1 port for connecting to the DA-88. The BNC word-sync in/out jacks are only useful in a few practical applications without the AES/EBU or SDIF-2 interfaces.

Also, although not mentioned in the manual, a Tascam representative told me that the DA-88's ±6 percent vari-speed range can be expanded to +18/-12 percent by feeding an external clock source to the word sync input. In any case, whether adjusted from the RC-848 controller or from the DA-88 front panel, the ±6 percent pitch range can be fine-tuned in smooth 0.1 percent increments.

The optional SY-88 synchronization board ($799) is a plug-in SMPTE card for chase-lock to video or other time code sources and MIDI Machine Control. Time code is derived from subcode data, so no audio track is required for time code. A single SY-88 card provides SMPTE functions for the master recorder and up to 15 additional interlocked DA-88 units operating as slaves.

TAKE CONTROL OF THE DA-88

On the DA-88's front panel is a rotary forward/reverse shuttle control, which is similar in function to several DAT machines on the market. The small size of the shuttle knob takes some getting used to and, as with many other shuttle systems, audio is noticeably degraded in shuttle mode. Also, in multimachine chase operations, slaves do not shuttle exactly in sync with the master. The shuttle knob is best used for locating specific points, such as the exact beginning or end of a musical beat or dialog/narration line, when defining exact auto-punch/insert points.

The DA-88's punch-in/-out performance is seamless, even on difficult material. The DA-88 defaults to a crossfade time of 10ms, but users can change this in 10ms increments, up to a maximum of 90ms. Battery-backed memory stores crossfade times, pitch changes, memo points, track delays and punch-in/-out points, even when the DA-88 is powered down.

On the back panel, a ¼-inch jack permits remote punch-in/-out operations with an optional footswitch. Two 15-pin D-sub sync in/out ports allow multimachine lockup and connect to the optional RC-848 full-function autolocator; an 8-pin DIN jack connects to the RC-808 basic transport control, also optional. Priced at $225, the RC-808 is a compact 5.5x6-inch unit that duplicates all of the DA-88's front-panel transport controls except the shuttle wheel. While the RC-808 is designed as a single-machine controller (it only includes track arming buttons for channels one through eight), any additional DA-88s connected to the master DA-88 will follow the commands issued by the RC-808.

The RC-848 ($1,499) is a large, multimachine autolocator with record select buttons for up to 48 tracks (six DA-88s); all ready/all safe buttons can simultaneously arm or clear selected tracks into or out of record. Beyond the standard transport commands, the RC-848 also provides programmable pre-/post-roll, along with 9-pin RS-422 output for interfacing to video systems, ports for controlling Tascam analog decks, 99-point autolocation, a shuttle wheel, an LCD status screen and two time readouts. The latter are large, bright numerical LED displays indicating both tape time and the current/next locator point (or points captured on the fly) in hours/minutes/seconds/frames.

The RC-848's machine status LEDs indicate the number of the deck currently designated as the master, whether it be a DA-88 in the chain, a Tascam analog machine (such as the 238 and 488 multitrack cassette models) connected to the 37-pin parallel port, one of Tascam's TSR-8 or MSR-16/24 series of reel-to-reel machines controlled via the 15-pin serial port or a video deck wired to the 9-pin RS-422 port with standard parallel control protocol (this is used in high-end video recorders such as the Sony BVU-800). The VTR modes accessible via RC-848 control include assembly mode, video insert mode and independent control of audio insert on VTR tracks one and two.

The DA-88 transport is fast and generally smooth, although it emits some strange whirring sounds when going into and out of play and stop modes. In a quiet control room, machine operation noise was noticeable, but not objectionable. As with other MDM designs, the DA-88's machine noise level is comparable to the sound of a hard disk whirring. Transport operations happen very quickly, like a DAT recorder, where minutes of tape zip by in seconds. A 100-minute tape rewinds or fast-forwards in 80 seconds; during rewind, the transport slows down about three minutes before the end of the tape, presumably for better tape packing. The repeat (loop) and locator memories operate flawlessly in either single or multimachine chase mode and, in the latter, the DA-88s lock up quickly and efficiently.

DISASSEMBLY NOT REQUIRED

Beauty is only skin (or chassis) deep, so I disassembled a DA-88, and yes, Elmo, it operated perfectly after reassembly. The DA-88 uses modular construction, with all the major electronics mounted on cards that can be easily removed from the back panel. In addition to simplifying servicing, this allows future upgrades and may also open the door for third-party companies to create specialized DA-88 cards, such as custom sync modules or high-end D/A or A/D circuits.

The boards are easily removed with a Phillips screwdriver. The digital-to-analog converters are Analog Devices DA 1865N (18-bit, 16-times oversampled), while the A/D converters are good quality 16-bit Crystal 5339s. The outside of the card cage is enclosed in thick, heavy-gauge slabs of copper sheeting, which should provide excellent shielding from EMI, RFI and other such gremlins.

The power supply is a conventional linear design with a large power transformer, massive heat sinks that extend two inches beyond the rear panel and a muffin fan to keep heat under control. That large iron-core transformer is a major contributor to the unit's 33-pound heft: Make sure your roadies are in shape if your location recording plans require mounting three DA-88s in an ATA road case!

The transport is mounted at the top left front, easily accessible for maintenance or head-cleaning duties. Tascam recommends using a dry head cleaner designed for Hi-8mm video every 50 hours or so. (Complete information on the DA-88 head cleaning procedure is contained in Chapter 21.) The entire transport assembly removes with four screws; combined with the ease of removing the slide-out electronics cards, this should make servicing any part of the DA-88 no problem.

After a quick reassembly, it was time for a bench check. Measurements indicate performance (20-20k Hz) that is flat to ±0.2dB, much better than the ±0.5dB spec that Tascam claims. The Total Harmonic Distortion + Noise results were under 0.003 percent at 1kHz (nearly three times better than the 0.007 percent on the DA-88 spec sheet) and, even in the worst case (at 18kHz), the THD+N measurement is a quite respectable 0.025 percent. According to Tascam, the stated specs are typical for the life of its machines; DA-88 buyers should expect the decks to stay within specified performance ranges for years to come.

GETTING INTO SYNC

Up to 16 DA-88s can be interlocked for multimachine operation without any external synchronizing equipment. While the DA-88 uses 15-pin D-sub connectors for sync, an off-the-shelf computer cable will not work in this application and may damage the equipment. You can either get the optional Tascam PW88S sync cable ($85) or make one by connecting all pins except 12 and 13. After rolling my own, it occurred to me that I could have just bought a ready-made cable and cut or removed pins 12 and 13, an inexpensive, no-hassle alternative.

Note that tapes must be formatted at identical sampling frequencies to achieve proper multitransport synchronization. As explained in Chapter 1, intermachine sync between two DA-88s is achieved via electronic word sync: As data is read by two machines in close mechanical sync, the digital information from the tape heads is temporarily stored in a RAM

the card also provides MIDI sync for locking the DA-88 to computers, synthesizers, drum machines, samplers and other MIDI gear.

The SY-88 installs easily. Just power down the DA-88, unplug the power cord and remove the two Phillips screws holding the blank panel that covers the third (center) card slot. Carefully insert the SY-88 board into the empty sync slot, replace the two screws and power up the DA-88.

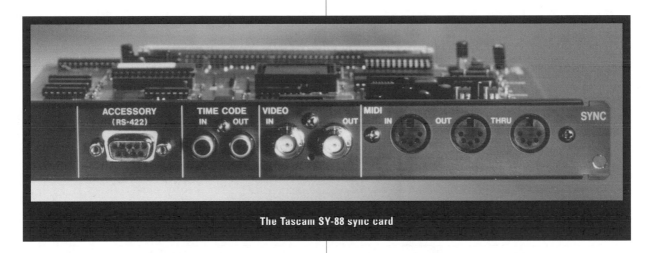

The Tascam SY-88 sync card

memory buffer. Word-clock timing information (carried over the PW88S sync cable) from the master machine controls the release of data from the second deck's buffer, thus enabling sample-accurate (±1/48,000 second) synchronization.

Machine lockup is easy. A tiny rotary switch on the rear of each machine selects a Machine ID (sort of like a SCSI ID number): ID #0 for master, #1 for the first slave, #2 for the second, etc. Once IDs are set, just load your tapes and push the Chase button on the slave decks, and the slaves faithfully follow the master transport. The increment/decrement controls can also be used to set offsets between the machines, up to ±1 hour in single-frame steps.

To confirm the DA-88's multitransport sync accuracy, I recorded a short burst of mono audio simultaneously on two interlocked machines, rewound the tapes, powered down and restarted the machines in chase mode. The audio burst, recorded at the 80-minute mark, was played back and dumped into a Digidesign workstation system for waveform analysis. The results, shown in Fig. 4, indicate that playback sync is sample-accurate. Note that the divisions on the horizontal axis are in milliseconds and that the elapsed time in the window is just over 0.003 seconds.

Synchronizing a DA-88 to a video recorder for music scoring or other post-production chores is a simple, cost-effective matter with Tascam's SY-88 plug-in sync card ($799). In addition to SMPTE chase-lock,

It's important to note that only one SY-88 sync card is required to synchronize as many as 16 DA-88s to one external sync source. For example, to sync 24 DA-88 tracks (three recorders) to a video deck, all you need is one SY-88 installed in the master (ID #0) machine and two PW-88S cables connecting the sync ports of the three machines, along with an appropriate cable routing the time code output of the video recorder to the RCA time code input/output on the SY-88. In the video chase-lock diagram shown in Fig. 5, the three DA-88s will chase to follow and match the incoming time code from the video deck, which is routed to the SY-88 card installed in the master DA-88.

In addition to SMPTE time code chase, the SY-88 card provides a 9-pin D-sub connection for external RS-422 video editor control. The card also carries video in/out sync on standard BNC jacks for locking to/from a standard video sync signal, such as composite video or a reference source (e.g., house sync or a black burst generator). Other features of the SY-88 include changing the master DA-88's display to show any incoming time code source, absolute time to SMPTE time code conversion and pull-up/-down. The latter is the ability to make ±0.1 percent changes in the sampling frequency (for example, dropping the 44.1kHz sample clock to 40.056kHz), which compensates for the difference between film running at 30 frames per second and NTSC video (USA standard), which operates at 29.97 fps.

The SY-88 also supports MIDI Machine Control, which allows the manipulation of many DA-88 functions from MMC-compatible MIDI sequencing software. In an MMC environment, the recorder becomes a transparent extension of the sequencer, and procedures such as punch-in/-out, looping and autolocation can be defined as musical events at specific measures, beats or bars in a song.

TRACK DELAY

One of the DA-88's most interesting features is the ability to delay the playback of individual tracks by up to a maximum of 7,200 samples (or advance by -200 samples). At a sampling frequency of 44.1kHz, this equates to a delay of 163ms, or 150ms at a sampling frequency of 48kHz. As the delay is displayed in samples, you'd better keep a calculator nearby, unless you have the RC-848 remote, which displays samples or ms.

To convert the sample display into seconds, try this simple formula:

$$\frac{\text{Delay in Samples}}{\text{Sampling Rate}} = \text{Delay time in seconds}$$

So if the DA-88's delay time display shows 5,000 samples, and you're recording at 44,100 samples per second, the track delay time is 0.113 seconds, or 113ms:

$$\frac{5{,}000 \text{ samples}}{44{,}100 \text{ samples/sec}} = 0.113 \text{ seconds} = 113\text{ms}$$

Conversely, if you need a delay of 12ms, you can calculate the required delay (in samples) by multiplying the delay time in seconds times the sampling frequency, which would yield the correct number of samples. In this case:

$$12\text{ms} \ \times \ \frac{1 \text{ second}}{1000\text{ms}} \ \times \ \frac{48{,}000 \text{ samples}}{1 \text{ second}} = 576 \text{ samples}$$

In addition to some fun signal-processing tricks, this onboard track delay is invaluable for all kinds of track delay fun. (See Chapter 43 for detailed information about track delay applications.)

FUN WITH TDIF-1

Another hip trick on the DA-88 involves the TDIF-1 digital port. Designed mainly for making clone tapes or attaching outboard digital interfaces, the TDIF-1 port (combined with the DA-88's sync offset feature) also allows multitrack digital assembly editing.

In addition to two DA-88s and a PW88S sync cable, you'll also need a TDIF-1 cable with double-ended, 25-pin D-sub male connectors. A typical computer cable won't work, as the bidirectional TDIF-1 port requires a special cable (see Chapter 26 for information on buying or building one).

One minor snag in the DA-88's digital dubbing process is that each channel must be delayed by 43 samples (less than 1ms) to adjust for an internal processing time delay in the DA-88. The manual says this should be done individually, track by track; however, by pressing the Up and Digital Input keys simultaneously, the 43-sample delay occurs automatically on all tracks. Of course, if you forget to enter the delay, the clone is still less than 1/1000 of a second out of sync; nothing to cry about.

As an example of the DA-88's editing capabilities, I once created an assembly-edited version of a full-length song from an 8-track digital cassette with the basic instrumental tracks of one verse and one chorus. I began by cloning the basics from machine one to a pre-formatted tape on machine two. Then I repeated the process, this time assigning a 37-second/11-frame offset to the slave deck, so the "new" verse and chorus would come in precisely after the first cloned tracks. A third pass, with a longer offset, yielded a finished track with three verses and choruses. I then placed the cloned, full-length song in the master deck, put a fresh tape in the slave and continued with overdubs on the 16-track project. Total time: under ten minutes, most of which was spent searching for the correct offset times.

One caveat: The digital cloning/assembly process requires setting the erase-protect tab on the master tape to the "nonprotected" position and then pressing Record on the master deck, which enables the record function on the slave deck. If any of the track arming buttons on the master are selected during this process, those tracks on the master will be erased; an unpleasant scenario that could occur if a tired engineer attempts to make a safety copy of tracks after an all-night session.

While the DA-88s can lock up to sample accu-

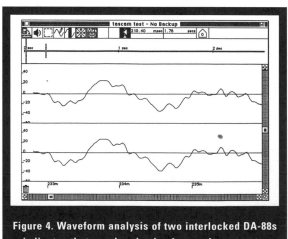

Figure 4. Waveform analysis of two interlocked DA-88s indicates that synchronization is sample-accurate.

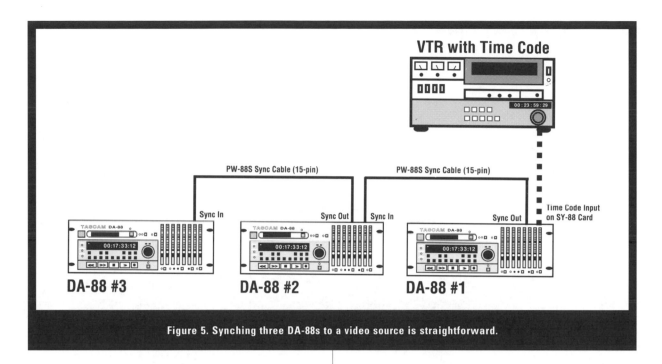

VTR with Time Code

PW-88S Sync Cable (15-pin)   PW-88S Sync Cable (15-pin)

Sync In   Sync Out   Sync In   Sync Out

Time Code Input
on SY-88 Card

DA-88 #3   **DA-88 #2**   **DA-88 #1**

Figure 5. Synching three DA-88s to a video source is straightforward.

racy, digital assembly is limited to frame accuracy, due to the fact that offset and punch-in/-out resolution on the recorder is defined in frames. However, if you're using the MIDI Machine Control to manipulate the optional SY-88 sync card, punch-in/-out accuracy could be determined by the sequencer's resolution, which is typically 20 times more accurate than SMPTE frames. Speaking of frames, be aware that the DA-88 operates at, or at least displays time in, the somewhat nonstandard rate of 33 fps.

The recorder is capable of multimachine, digital-domain editing, yet the DA-88 is currently unable to copy tracks on a single machine in the digital domain. For example, if you had only one DA-88 and wanted to combine several vocal takes into one seamless, perfect track, this would have to be done via analog. The solution to this shortcoming may eventually come through the bidirectional TDIF-1 interface: Either Tascam or some enterprising third party could build a matrix router or patch-bay array that would allow the user to redirect the TDIF-1 digital inputs and outputs to any desired track in the digital domain.

GENERAL OBSERVATIONS

The DA-88 manual is fairly sparse for a unit of this complexity. No system diagrams, flow charts, schematics or even a description of the format's basic technology are included. There are also no warnings about the danger of using standard computer cables for TDIF-1 or sync functions. There is, however, a detailed section bearing a warning of the danger of using this "appliance" near bathtubs and swimming pools.

Fortunately, the DA-88 sounds better than it reads.

Its specs are impressive, and my subjective sonic evaluation is that the machine sounds about the same as any high-quality DAT recorder. If you've heard Tascam's DA-30 studio DAT machine, then you have already had a preview of the DA-88's sound. If you're an audio purist who absolutely despises DAT mastering and will only mix to analog reel-to-reel machines at 30 ips, then you probably won't like the DA-88. But to me, the DA-88 sounds just fine. Of course, Tascam's AES/EBU-S/PDIF and SDIF-2 interfaces allow users to pick and choose from a number of outboard digital-to-analog and analog-to-digital converters to create their own sounds.

The Tascam DA-88 offers a lot for its $4,799 price: High-quality audio, a fast transport and special sync/offset functions combine to create a very attractive package for either the project room or commercial studio facility. Its 100+ minutes of record time should certainly appeal to location and concert recordists, who will also appreciate the versatility of the track delay feature. With the delivery of the DA-88, Tascam has taken a major step in advancing the state of modular recording.

Tascam Professional
7733 Telegraph Road
Montebello, CA 90640
213-726-0303
http://www.tascam.com

Note: Turn page for diagrams of the DA-88 front and rear panels.

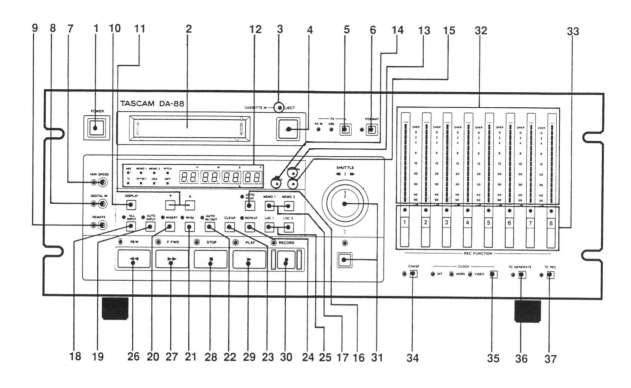

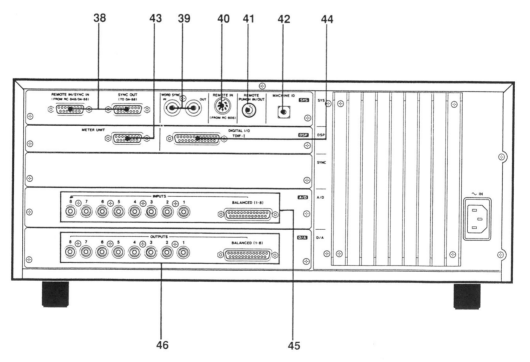

TASCAM DA-88 OPERATIONS

Front Panel
1. AC Power Switch
2. Tape Well
3. "Cassette In" LED
4. Eject Key
5. Sampling Rate Selector and LEDs
6. Format Key
7. Vari Speed Switch
8. Digital Input Switch
9. Remote In/Out Switch
10. Display Select Switch
11. Up/Down (Increment/Decrement) Keys
12. LED Time Display Window
13. Warning LED
14. Write Protect LED
15. Error LED
16. Auto Play Key
17. Memo 1/Memo 2 Keys
18. All Input Switch
19. Auto Input Select
20. Insert Monitor Switch
21. Rehearse Switch
22. Auto-punch-In/-Out Switch
23. Clear (Rehearse/Auto-punch Defeat) Key
24. Repeat (Memo 1 to Memo 2 Loop) Key
25. Location 1 and 2 Keys
26. Tape Rewind Key
27. Tape Fast-forward Key
28. Tape Stop Key
29. Tape Play Key
30. Record Key
31. Shuttle Knob/Shuttle In/Out Switch
32. Peak Level Meters
33. Track Arming (Record Ready) Switches
34. Chase Key
35. Clock Source Selector
36. Time Code Generate Switch
37. Time Code Record Key

Rear Panel
38. Remote In/Sync In and Sync Out Jacks
39. Word Sync In/Out Jacks
40. Remote In Jacks
41. Remote punch-in/-out Jacks
42. Machine ID Rotary Switch
43. Meter Output Connector
44. TDIF-1 Digital Input/Output Port
45. Input Connectors: RCA and D25-Sub
46. Output Connectors: RCA and D25-Sub

CHAPTER 16

Secrets of the DA-88

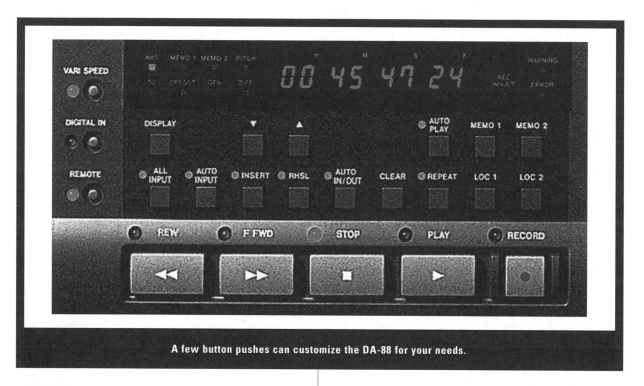

A few button pushes can customize the DA-88 for your needs.

ne of my favorite aspects of modular digital multitracks is their hidden functions. You can really amaze your friends by making your Tascam DA-88 or Sony PCM-800 (most of these also work with the DA-38) jump through hoops with these tricks, which, by the way, are not listed in the owner's manual.

NEW POWER-UP GREETING

Whenever a DA-88 is turned on, it's actually running a self-diagnostic test. During the power-up procedure, the meters will display the word "Tascam" (or "Sony" on the PCM-800). However, you can program your machine to display a different greeting, such as "George" (a particular favorite of mine), simply by doing the following:

1. Turn the recorder off.
2. Now, while holding down the Fast-forward, Stop and Play keys, turn the recorder back on.
3. Press Stop before the scrolling "Tascam" message appears. This causes the machine to enter test

mode and the meters should display the word "TEST."

4. Make sure the display is in ABS mode, then press and hold the following four keys, in this order: Up, Down, Display, and Remote.
5. The letter "A" should appear.
6. Using the Up/Down keys to select letters, enter your new message. For example, to enter the word "George" (this is highly recommended), scroll to G, then press Display; scroll to E, then press Display; scroll to O, then press Display; and so on.
7. Once you've entered all the characters in your new message, press the Up and Down keys simultaneously to exit the greeting mode.
8. To see your new message, turn the recorder off and power up again. This new message will be displayed every time you power up (unless you change it). Of course, if there's a typo or you just don't like the message, go back to Step 1 and start over.

CHECK THE MILEAGE!

Whether you're keeping a maintenance log or merely checking the odometer on a used DA-88 before buying it, you can find out the exact number of hours on the head drum by holding the Play and Stop buttons while powering up.

The number of hours that the deck has been operated in the shuttle mode can be determined by pressing the Stop and Fast-forward buttons while powering up.

Sometimes, you need to check the recorder's software version. To do this, hold the Stop, Play and Record buttons while powering up.

The deck's servo version is revealed by holding the Rewind, Fast-forward and Stop keys during power up.

If you need the software version of an SY-88 sync card, hold the Fast-forward, Play and Record buttons during power up.

The software version of an RC-848 remote controller connected to a DA-88 is displayed by powering up the DA-88, followed by pressing the Rewind, Fast-forward and Stop keys on the RC-848.

Obviously, knowing the software versions you have is vital when troubleshooting a system or calling in for technical support.

Amaze your friends by making your Tascam DA-88 or Sony PCM-800 (most of these also work with the DA-38) jump through hoops with these tricks.

METER TRICKS

To turn off the recorder's peak hold function, push the Rewind, Play and Record buttons while the deck is powered up.

To return to peak hold metering, push the Rewind, Stop and Record buttons while the deck is powered up. Then press the Up Arrow and Clear button. The deck will return to normal (peak hold) metering.

THE BEGINNING OF THE END

The following are all matters of personal preference, but the DA-88 allows you to customize your machine to suit the way *you* work. For example, if you'd like your recorder to automatically go into play after you've rewound a tape, press Rewind, Fast-forward and Play while powering the machine up. If you want to return to the "normal" operation (where the recorder goes into stop mode when a tape is rewound), simply hold down the Fast-forward and Play buttons on power-up.

Similarly, if you'd like your DA-88 to automatically rewind itself when the tape is finished, just hold the Rewind, Stop and Play buttons while powering up. To return to "normal" operation, where the tape stops at the end, hold down the Rewind and Stop keys while powering up.

In my studio, I want the decks to stop after rewinding or reaching the end of the tape, and most people prefer these modes. So why would anyone want to use the other modes?

Well, one very practical application for automatic playback operations involves theatrical or theme park applications, where an unattended DA-88 could play eight channels of sound effects for nearly two hours and then restart itself after a quick auto-rewind. Who says MDMs are strictly studio tools?

CHAPTER 17

Sony PCM-800

Sony's PCM-800 offers AES/EBU digital and XLR analog interfacing.

umors of its existence rumbled throughout the industry for months. Finally, the news of Sony entering the modular digital multitrack sweepstakes leaked out in September, 1994, at IBC, Europe's broadcasting convention held in late summer. The rest of the world waited until November 10, 1994, the first day of the 97th AES Convention in San Francisco, to see this digital marvel.

Known as the PCM-800, the $5,995 Sony machine is compatible with the Tascam DA-88, offering eight tracks of digital audio on Hi-8mm videotapes and the ability to interlock up to 16 transports for up to 128-track recording. And now that two decks are sharing the DA-88 recording scheme, Tascam and Sony christened the format with the name Digital Tape Recording System (DTRS).

An alliance between these two companies is not surprising. Tascam became a signatory of Sony's

DASH (Digital Audio Stationary Head) format for reel-to-reel digital machines when it announced the $100,000 DA-800 24-track in 1988. Tascam later based its DA-88 recorder on the Hi-8mm videotape that Sony pioneered. With two popular MDM formats already established (ADAT and DA-88), creating a new, incompatible format was not a viable option. Hence the DTRS format and the PCM-800.

Standard features of the PCM-800 include up to 108 minutes of recording on an NTSC 120 tape; 16-bit linear digital recording at 44.1 or 48kHz; ±6 percent vari-speed (in 0.1 percent steps); individual delay on any track (up to 7,200 samples); user-selectable crossfade times (10-90ms); jog/shuttle wheel; auto-punch-in/-out; and the ability to offset sync in a multimachine environment for multitrack assembly editing.

Looking at the front panels, the Tascam and Sony machines have a similar appearance, because

Tascam is supplying the decks to Sony on an OEM basis. From a cosmetic standpoint, Sony opted for a high-tech gray finish, replaced the DA-88 push-on power switch with a VCR-style rocker switch and swapped the position of the Play and Stop keys. However, one has to look to the PCM-800's back panel to see the real differences between the two machines. The PCM-800 replaces the unbalanced RCA jacks and (+4dB) D-sub multipin analog connections on the DA-88's analog-to-digital and digital-to-analog cards with electronically balanced, +4dBu inputs and outputs on standard 3-pin XLR connectors.

The Sony recorder uses the same Crystal A-D converters and Analog Devices DACs as the DA-88. However, the PCM-800's digital I/O configuration is different: Two 25-pin D-sub connectors carry eight channels of AES/EBU digital information (on stereo pairs), and breakout cables with XLR connectors can interface with other digital devices. A second BNC word-sync output on the back panel insures accurate data transfers, while a fiber-optic output is provided to keep track of errors in the AES bitstream. Unfortunately, it seems that the error port was intended for service applications only, and no outboard error indicator was ever offered.

In offering the AES/EBU ports, Sony has eliminated the TDIF-1 (Tascam Digital InterFace) connector from the PCM-800, so direct transfers from a PCM-800 to a DA-88 are impossible, unless you have Tascam's optional IF-88 AE AES/EBU interface. Cloning tapes from one PCM-800 to another is a simple matter of connecting the AES/EBU breakout cables. One advantage of the PCM-800's AES/EBU breakout is that individual track data can easily be copied from one machine to another. For example, you may cre-

The PCM-88 rear panel is clean and uncluttered.

ate a work tape with several solo performances. To copy the solo from Track seven on one deck to Track one on the other deck, just patch Track seven's AES output to the AES input channel you need, arm the track, hit the digital input switch and go into record.

Several PCM-800 options are available. The RM-D800 ($1,500) is a full-function autolocator/remote unit, with the ability to control up to eight PCM-800s. The Sony remote is essentially identical to Tascam's RC-848, save for a gray paint job and reversed location of the Play and Stop keys.

Another option is the DABK-801 sync board ($800), which is similar to Tascam's SY-88 sync card, and adds SMPTE time code chase, 9-pin RS-422 control, MIDI machine control, time code generation and MIDI sync capabilities. A minor difference between the two cards is that the DIP switches for selecting time code and sync modes have been moved to the back panel of the Sony card, making them accessible from the outside of the machine, while the SY-88's internal DIP switch requires removing the card to change frame rates or modes.

By the way, the Sony PCM-800 does *not* spell out the letters "Tascam" when it powers up. It says "Sony"—I've checked this out, just to be sure. You gotta be careful about some things.

Note: For more information about the Sony PCM-800, see the DA-88 section in Chapter 15.

Sony Corp.
3 Paragon Drive
Montvale, NJ 07645
201-358-4197
fax: 201-358-4907
http://www.sony.com/proaudio

Spotlight

Sony PCM-800
- Product Introduction: November 10, 1994
- Deliveries Began: April 1995
- Format: DTRS, using standard Hi-8mm videotapes
- Recording Time: 108 minutes (P6/E6-120 tapes); 82 minutes (P5/E5-90 tapes)
- Track Capacity: Eight, expandable to 128
- Digital System: Rotary head; 16-bit linear; 44.1/48kHz sampling frequencies
- Analog Connections: +4dBm balanced on XLRs (8-inputs; 8-outputs)
- Digital Connections: Two 25-pin D-sub ports, each carrying eight channels of AES/EBU digital interconnects
- Dimensions: 7x19x15 inches (HxWxD); 31 pounds
- Retail: $5,995, including two 25-pin to XLR breakout cables for the AES/EBU digital I/O

CHAPTER 18

Tascam DA-38

The DA-38 brings DTRS recording to a new level of affordability.

In 1996, Tascam unveiled the DA-38, an 8-track digital recorder compatible with the DA-88 format but priced at only $3,499. The savings were made possible by using shared parts between the two recorders to cut down manufacturing costs and by eliminating some of the DA-88's features. For example, the DA-38 does not offer a slot for the SY-88 sync card (which allows the DA-88 to be used as a stand-alone SMPTE chase recorder). Similarly, the DA-38 has no 9-pin Sony P2 serial control option and lacks the connection for feeding an optional meter bridge.

Despite these minor limitations, the DA-38 is a suitable addition to a DA-88-only environment and may be combined with one or more DA-88s in many applications. While the DA-38 cannot sync to SMPTE on its own, if it is slaved to a DA-88 that is equipped with the SY-88 sync card, the DA-38 will operate in precise, sample-accurate sync with the DA-88 master. For users in a MIDI-based facility, the optional MMC-38 adapter adds MIDI Machine Control and MIDI sync operations to the DA-38.

Further, the DA-38 adds some new tricks of its own, such as track-to-track copying within the machine, dither on/off switching, A440 digital sine wave/tuning tone generator and numeric error rate display. Features held over from the DA-88 include selectable 44.1/48kHz sampling, the ability to sync up to 16 transports for up to 128 tracks (with sample accuracy), machine offset for assembly editing operations, auto-punch-in/-out with rehearse mode, programmable pre-/post-roll, two locate points, user-definable cross-fades, individual track advanced delay (up to 150ms), shuttle wheel and a punch-in/-out footswitch jack.

The DA-38 is housed in a three-rackspace, 16.5-pound chassis, which is 1.75 inches shorter and about 15 pounds lighter than the DA-88. In the studio, this isn't such a big deal, but if you're toting three DA-38s around in a road case for remote recording, there's a huge difference between 49.5 and 93 pounds of hardware.

The DA-38's layout is similar to the DA-88, so if you're familiar with DA-88 operations, you'll be tracking in no time. One obvious difference is the DA-38's use of a Shift button to access secondary functions on the feature keys. In fact, other than a few operational differences (such as formatting the Hi-8mm tapes for digital audio recording), anyone who's used an analog or digital multitrack will have no trouble with DA-38 operations.

The front panel includes a bright LED display of hours/minutes/seconds/frames, along with various LEDs to indicate operational status: digital in, 44.1/48kHz sampling, track copy, word in, track delay, track offset and playback condition. The latter indicator is the same as the Error LED on the DA-88, but its name was changed to playback condition; a kinder, gentler phrasing. The shuttle wheel is the same as the DA-88, providing a playback range of ¼ to 8 times normal speed, either in reverse or forward.

The DA-38's meters and track arming buttons are nearly the same as the DA-88's; the only difference being that the DA-38 meters have 12 LED segments and the DA-88 has expanded 15-segment metering. On the DA-38 back panel are two D15-sub connectors for sync/remote in/out, BNC word-sync input, DIN socket for the optional RC-808 mini-remote ($225), unbalanced analog RCA inputs and outputs, balanced analog connections on two D25-sub connectors and a TDIF-1 port. Also mated via a D25-sub connector, TDIF-1 is a proprietary bidirectional interface that connects to a DA-38 or DA-88 for cloning tapes or to various AES/EBU and S/PDIF interfaces from Tascam and third party suppliers. TDIF-1 is also the essential link for direct interfacing with digital consoles, such as the Yamaha 02R, 03D, Mackie Digital, Soundtracs Virtua, Tascam TM-8000 or RSP's Project X. All TDIF-1 connections are made using the optional $110 PW-88D cable.

SOME DISASSEMBLY REQUIRED

For the "void the warranty" part of this test, I completely disassembled a DA-38. Remove seven screws and the top/sides panel comes off, revealing a clean, spacious layout. Maintenance access to the transport, for occasionally cleaning the heads and guides, is excellent. The DA-38 uses a switch-mode power supply, which is compact and produces virtually no heat. It's also a lot lighter than the 10-pound conventional iron-core transformer power supply tucked inside the DA-88. Best of all, there's a sizable empty space below the transport and power supply assemblies that is ideal for stowing spare parts or other necessary "supplies" that one occasionally has to take through customs on lengthy tours.

The DA-38's electronics consist mainly of two large boards located behind the meters. The Control PCB handles all the logic info, such as transport control, digital I/O routing and synchronization housekeeping. Here two large, custom ICs developed for the DA-38 reduce the parts count, while the all-surface-mount componentry on the control board reduces the overall size. Mounted two inches below the Control PCB (providing plenty of cooling airspace) is the Audio PCB. The A/D converters are

Asahi-Kasei 5340 (18-bit delta-sigma with 64x oversampling); the DACs are Burr-Brown PCM-1710U (20-bit delta-sigma with 8x oversampling). Both the ADCs and DACs provide superior performance to the converters used in the DA-88. In digital audio, five years seems like an eternity.

The transport is essentially similar to the DA-88's, with the exception of the head drum which now uses (no physical contact) rotary transformers rather than mechanical brushes to transmit the signal from the heads. But the biggest improvement in the DA-38 is its lack of a cooling fan, which on the DA-88 added to operating noise and increased air/dust flow through the head and transport assembly. Due to the reduced parts count and switching power supply, the DA-38 needs no fan and remains cool even after 15 hours of steady use.

FEATURES AND FUNCTIONS

Despite the apparent simplicity of the DA-38's user interface, there are times when a quick look into the manual is required, especially when accessing the "shift-key" functions. My favorite message is "StL.n off," which is supposed to mean the audio monitoring during shuttle operations is turned off. My advice? Keep the manual handy. Fortunately for users, the DA-38 manual is clear and fairly well-written. The documentation has several appreciated touches, including an appendix explaining how to interpret the DA-38's cryp-

Spotlight

Tascam DA-38

- Product Introduction: January 18, 1996
- Deliveries Began: June 1996
- Format: DTRS, using standard Hi-8mm video-tapes
- Recording Time: 108 minutes (P6/E6-120 tape); 82 minutes (P5/E5-90 tapes)
- Track Capacity: Eight, expandable to 128
- Digital System: Rotary head; 16-bit linear; 44.1/48kHz sampling frequencies
- Analog Connections: Unbalanced -10dBV phono jack (RCA) inputs/outputs; +4dBm balanced I/O on 25-pin D-sub connectors
- Digital Connections: Proprietary bidirectional TDIF-1 on 25-pin D-sub port; AES/EBU-S/PDIF and SDIF-2 interfaces optional
- Dimensions: 5.25x19x13.75 inches (HxWxD); 16.5 pounds
- Retail: $3,499

tic error messages. However, there are no pinouts given for the D25 connectors carrying the +4dB analog I/O in the DA-38 manual, so I've included these in Chapter 25.

Probably the DA-38's most powerful feature is intermachine track copying which, combined with the digital patching function, allows users of single recorder systems to create a seamless "comp" performance from several takes. Alternatively, a track could be copied in the digital domain in order to create a backup before a difficult punch is attempted. Such operations previously required single-machine users to go from digital into the analog domain (and vice versa).

In the analog domain, the DA-38's digital patching feature provides the means to reroute connections to any track, a useful feature for anyone tracking on a DA-38 from a 2- or 4-bus board. Pro users will probably skip this function entirely and use traditional patching to access inputs.

Like the DA-88, the DA-38 also provides ±6 percent of pitch shifting; however, this range can be expanded to +18/-12 percent by controlling the DA-38 from an external clock source.

The DA-38's tuning feature provides A440 (440Hz) from an internal oscillator. This can be used as a tuning reference and as a means of setting and calibrating levels within your system.

A much slicker and more useful feature is the block error rate function, which quantifies errors caused by tape dropouts or shedding, dirty heads, etc. Rather than merely depending on the playback condition LED, the block error rate displays whether block errors are within acceptable limits. This also provides instantaneous user feedback on which brands of tape provide optimal performance.

Without a doubt, the DA-38's most enigmatic feature is dither switching. Essentially, this allows the user to enable (or disable) a dithering circuit on any track during recording. The theory behind the dithering process is to add a randomized signal to mask low-level quantization noise that occurs when inputs higher than 16 bits (18-, 20- or 24-bit) are stored on 16-bit media. As to whether or not I'd use dither on the DA-38, the jury's still out. Tascam describes the net effect as "warmth." With dither, I heard an increase in clarity, particularly in low-level signals, but this was accompanied by a slight upper midrange bump that seemed to bring percussive background elements, such as cowbells, up in the track. The real solution here is to experiment and use it when you feel it's appropriate.

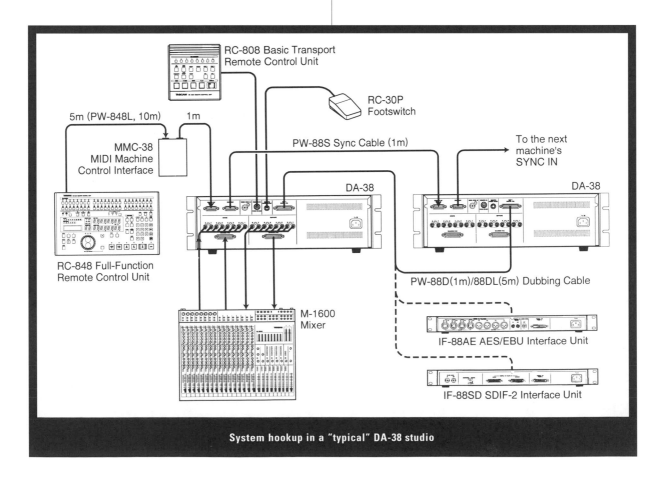

System hookup in a "typical" DA-38 studio

If you're using someone else's DA-38 and are unsure how many functions (track delay, dither, offsets, crossfades, etc.) are enabled, you can return the DA-38 to its default factory parameters by pressing the Shift key, and then pushing the Menu button until "init" appears on the display. Now press either the Arrow Up or Down key, which will bring up the "rEADy." Another press of either the Arrow Up or Down key and the DA-38 is reinitialized to its factory settings.

Anyone who's used a DA-88 already knows how the DA-38 transport performs: Both decks offer rapid, accurate tape handling, with fast multimachine lock-up times. The DA-38 transport seems quieter than the DA-88's, but this has more to do with the DA-38's no-fan operation than any differences in the transports themselves. Although both the DA-88 and DA-38 provide two locate points from the front panel, this number is too low, and five or six would be preferable.

Overall, the DA-38 is a winner. It packs most of the DA-88's features into a smaller package that operates quieter, sounds better and adds some new tricks. Best of all, the DA-38 retails at $3,499, which is hundreds less than the DA-88. Sounds like a good deal to me.

Tascam/TEAC Professional Division
7733 Telegraph Road
Montebello, CA 90640
213-726-0303
fax: 213-727-7635
http://www.tascam.com

Note: Turn page for diagrams of the DA-38's front and back panels.

Front Panel

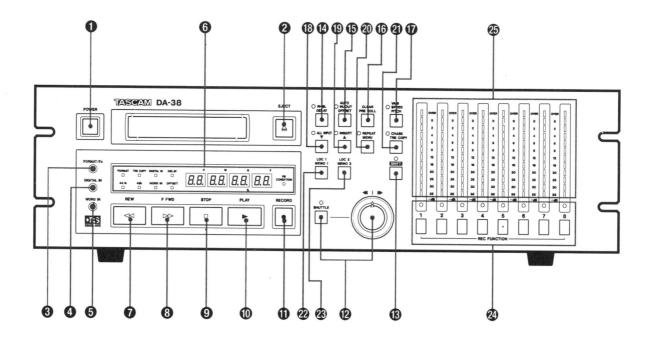

Rear Panel

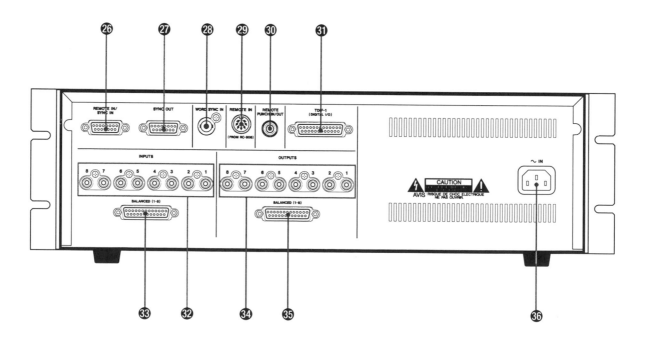

Front Panel

1. POWER switch
   Used to switch on power to the unit.
2. EJECT key
   Press to eject the tape.
3. FORMAT/Fs switch
   When pressed two times, puts the unit into tape format ready mode. During this mode, the switch is used to select a sampling rate.
4. DIGITAL IN switch
   Depending on whether this switch is pressed or not, recording is from the digital input or from the analog input.
5. WORD IN switch
   Used for referencing the unit to external word-clock. This switch does not operate when the unit is being used as a slave.
6. Display window
   Ensures smooth interaction between the user and the unit.
   FORMAT
   When the corresponding key is pressed only once, this indicator blinks. A second press causes the indicator to glow solid, indicating the unit is ready to format a tape.
   TRK COPY
   This indicator is lit to remind you that a track or tracks will be copied onto other tracks as you enter record mode.
   DIGITAL IN
   This indicator lights when the unit is switched to record from the digital input.
   DELAY
   If the output timing of any track is corrected at a menu, this indicator is lit.
   44.1k/48k
   Either is lit to show the selected sampling rate.
   WORD IN
   When pressing the corresponding key, this indicator lights to show the unit is referenced to external word-clock.
   OFFSET
   If the unit is used as a slave and an offset is entered, this indicator is lit.
   Numeric Display
   The ABS time and menus are shown here.
   PB CONDITION
   A persistent error condition in playback triggers this indicator.
7. REW button
   Press to rewind the tape.
8. F FWD button
   Press to fast-forward the tape.
   If you press F FWD or REW immediately after powering up or inserting a tape, the unit first configures itself for the reel hub diameter of the tape in use, during which the tape advances at low speeds. This takes several seconds. Thereafter, the transport momentarily goes into stop mode before the tape starts fast-winding.
9. STOP button
   Press to cancel the current transport mode. When pressed while in Chase mode, disables the mode and stops the tape.
10. PLAY button
    Press to begin playback. When pressed while RECORD is down, begins recording. When pressed during the autolocation process, causes the tape to start playing after completing autolocation.
11. RECORD button
    Begins recording when pressed together with PLAY or, if no REC FUNCTION switch is pressed, puts the unit into record ready mode. When pressed during playback, triggers recording.
12. SHUTTLE switch and knob
    Pressing the switch enables the knob for reel rocking to locate specific points on the tape.
13. SHIFT key
    Used to shift the following ten keys, #14 to #23, to their lower labeled functions. The associated LED will then blink.
14. RHSL or DELAY key
    RHSL is for a trial punch-in recording, and DELAY is used to correct the timing of each track.
15. AUTO IN/OUT or OFFSET key
    AUTO IN/OUT is used to commit a punch-in recording to tape, and OFFSET is used in a master/slave sync system to have the slave unit get synched up to the master with a distance maintained between them.
16. CLEAR or PRE-ROLL key
    CLEAR is used to disable Tape Format Ready, RHSL or AUTO IN/OUT mode. PRE-ROLL allows the user to enter an autolocation pre-roll time, a second press, to enter a punch-in pre-roll time.
17. VARI SPEED or PITCH key
    VARI SPEED allows you to enter a pitch change before starting playback. PITCH is simply used to change the current amount of pitch.
18. ALL INPUT or ▼ key
    When ALL INPUT is pressed, each output is fed directly by the same numbered input (primarily for alignment). The Ø key is used to enter numbers or switch on/off dome functions at menus.

19. INSERT or ▲ key
    INSERT causes the monitor to switch from tape to input at punch-in point and back to tape at punch-out point. The ▲ key is similar to the Ø key and used to enter numbers or switch on/off some functions at menus.
20. REPEAT or MENU key
    REPEAT is used to play user-selected segment over and over again, and MENU is used to have the display show menus.
21. CHASE or TRK COPY key
    Press CHASE for the unit to keep up with a master unit. A second press disables the Chase mode and stops the tape. TRK COPY is used to copy a track to another track.
22. LOC 1 or MEMO 1 key
    Press MEMO 1 when entering a punch-in point or an autolocation point. LOC 1 is used to autolocate the unit to a MEMO 1 point.
23. LOC 2 or MEMO 2 key
    MEMO 2 is used to enter a punch-out point or a second autolocation point, and LOC 2 causes the unit to autolocate to a MEMO 2 point.
24. REC FUNCTION switches
    Used to select tracks to record on. Also used to select in Track Copy mode the tracks onto which you want to copy or, In Track Delay mode, the tracks of which you want to adjust the output timing.
25. Level meters
    When recording analog input, adjust the level control on the source unit to keep the peak level as close to 0db as possible, without causing overscale reading on the meters. During recording the digital input as well, the OVER segment may light to indicate that distortion occurs; and during playback the same.

Rear Panel

26. REMOTE IN/SYNC IN connector
    For connection of the optional RC-848 remote control unit, or, when the DA-38 is used in a master/slave sync system, the optional PW-88S sync cable is connected here.
27. SYNC OUT connector
    For connection to another DA-38 by using the optional PW-88S sync cable to set up a master/slave sync system.
28. WORD SYNC IN connector
    Allows the unit to be slaved to the word-clock used by an external unit.
29. REMOTE IN connector
    Allows the unit to be controlled from the optional RC-808 remote control unit.
30. REMOTE PUNCH-IN/-OUT connector
    For connection of the optional RC-30P footswitch.
31. TDIF-1 (DIGITAL I/O) connector
    This I/O port is for interface to units conforming to the TEAC Digital Audio Interface Format (TDIF-1).
32. INPUTS, RCA jacks
    For connection of unbalanced analog signals.
33. INPUTS, BALANCED (1-8)
    This D-sub connector accepts the balanced analog signals.
34. OUTPUTS, RCA jacks
    For connection to the unbalanced inputs of external units.
35. OUTPUTS, BALANCED (1-8)
    For connection to the balanced inputs of external units.
36. ~ IN
    This is an AC power receptacle.

CHAPTER 19

Tascam DA-98

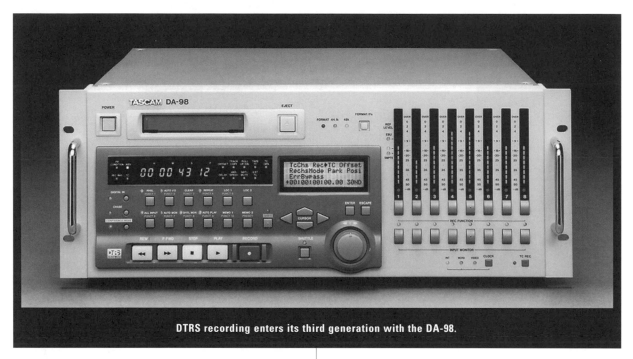

DTRS recording enters its third generation with the DA-98.

K, I'll admit it. When it comes to audio technology, I'm definitely the prying type. So on March 22, 1997, while walking through the 102nd Convention of the Audio Engineering Society in Munich, Germany, something interesting caught my eye. Over in a far corner of the Tascam booth was a prototype of the DA-98. I was impressed by its sleek lines and large, backlit LCD, but when I tried to take a snapshot of the unit, a polite, but no-nonsense, German woman mumbled something about *"photographie verboten,"* and explained that I wasn't allowed to see the recorder until its official launch at the 1997 National Association of Broadcasters show in Las Vegas two weeks later. So, while DA-98 made its first public showing in March, it's official debut was April 5, 1997.

The DA-98, Tascam's third-generation modular digital multitrack, is based on the proven 16-bit, Hi-8mm DTRS format and is fully compatible with the more than 50,000 other DTRS recorders (DA-88, DA-38 and Sony PCM-800) currently in use worldwide. However, while Tascam went downmarket from its

original DA-88 with its affordable DA-38, the $5,999 DA-98 is now the flagship of the company's MDM line.

As with other DTRS decks, up to 16 decks (any combination of DA-98s, DA-88s, DA-38s or Sony PCM-800s) can be interlocked for up to 128 tracks of recording. The DTRS format provides up to 108 minutes of record time on an NTSC-120 Hi-8mm videocassette and slightly more time with some of the new Hi-8mm tapes designed especially for DTRS recording, which offer a maximum recording time of 113 minutes. In addition to full tape interchange capability with other DTRS recorders, the DA-98 is also compatible with optional devices for the DA-88, such as the RC-848 autolocator/controller, MU-8824 meter bridge, and TDIF-1 accessories, whether they be Tascam's IF-88AE AES/EBU digital I/O adapter or third-party add-ons (Rane PAQRAT, Digital Audio Labs V8, etc.).

From a glance at the front panel, the DA-98 has a familiar look. There are some differences between the DA-98 and other DTRS decks, but anyone who's used a DA-88 or DA-38 should be cutting tracks on the DA-98 immediately without spending hours studying the manual. Although similar to the DA-88 and DA-38, the DA-98 offers much more, with numerous new enhancements and features.

Designed with audio post-production and high-end studio users in mind, the DA-98 features high-performance converters, built-in SMPTE/MIDI chase lock synchronizer, individual input monitor select switches (for source or off-tape monitoring), switchable reference operating levels, a comprehensive LCD display, dedicated function/numeric keys, and confidence monitoring.

GAINING CONFIDENCE

Confidence monitoring is one of the DA-98's most useful features. Merely press a front panel button and the DA-98 recorder enters "Confidence Mode." This switches the tape monitor during recording into a direct "read-after-write" mode, so what you hear during recording is exactly what's being read off the tape. The DA-98 is the first MDM to offer this feature. It's an appreciated touch, especially in mastering, live concert work, broadcast applications and other critical recording situations where there may be no opportunity for a second take, and you need to be sure that what you're listening to is actually going on tape.

For example, if you're recording on a system without confidence monitoring and you've recorded a 90-minute live set using a defective tape, you may not know about the problem until playback after the show. The term "confidence monitoring" refers to

Spotlight

Tascam DA-98
- Product Introduction: April 5, 1997
- Deliveries Began: Fall 1997
- Format: DTRS, using standard Hi-8mm videotapes
- Recording Time: 108 minutes (P6/E6-120 tapes); 82 minutes (P5/E5-90 tapes)
- Track Capacity: Eight, expandable to 128
- Digital System: Rotary head; 16-bit linear; 44.1/48kHz sampling frequencies
- Analog Connections: +4dBm balanced I/O on 25-pin D-sub connectors
- Digital Connections: Proprietary bidirectional TDIF-1 on 25-pin D-sub port; AES/EBU-S/PDIF and SDIF-2 interfaces optional
- Dimensions: 7x19x14 inches (HxWxD); 24 pounds
- Retail: $5,999

any read-after-write system, where you're confident that what's on the tape is exactly what you heard during recording.

Confidence monitoring is one of the DA-98's most useful features.

GETTING IN SYNC

Other DA-98 features of interest to post-production professionals include balanced XLR input and output for time-code; RS-422 Sony P2 (9-pin) port for control for interfacing with video editors, video sync input and thru ports with auto termination, word sync in/out/thru (also with auto termination) and a jog/shuttle wheel with an operating range of ¼ to 8 times play speed. Also standard is a 0.1 percent pull-up/-down sync adjust mode for telecine (film-chain) applications, such as 44.056 and 47.952kHz sampling for 29.97 fps resync.

The DA-98's onboard SMPTE time code reader/generator/chase synchronizer operates at a variety of frame rates, and all frame rates, sync modes and other synchronization parameters are accessible (and stored!) using the front panel controls and LCD screen. This will certainly be appreciated by users of DA-88/SY-88 sync card systems, which required pulling the sync card out of the recorder to change mode settings on its internal DIP switch.

Time code connections on the DA-98 are provided via balanced +4dB rear panel XLRs, a significant improvement over the unbalanced RCA time code connectors on the DA-88's optional SY-88 sync card. Not only does balanced time code operation allow improved signal integrity over long lines, but the interfacing with pro-level gear is easier. As an added plus, XLRs are locking connectors that won't pull out if the deck is moved or slid forward in a rack. The DA-98 also has optional RM-98 rackmount ear adapters (with handles) for use with the industry-standard Accuride 200 rail system.

Full MIDI synchronization capability is included (with in/out/thru ports on the rear panel), but equally important is the DA-98's MIDI Machine Control flexibility. This allows the recorder's transport and track-arming functions to be controlled from various external devices; not only MIDI sequencing programs but various consoles, such as the Euphonix CS-3000 and Mackie Digital which include built-in transport controllers integrated into each mixer's master section. In such applications, the beauty of

MMC control is that the user can remotely control all essential recorders without ever leaving the optimum listening position ("sweet spot") behind the console.

DIGITAL POSSIBILITIES

The DA-98's track copying feature, combined with the digital patching function, allows users of single recorder systems to create a seamless "best of" performance assembled from takes on several tracks, entirely in the digital domain. For example, if there are vocal takes on Tracks one, two and three, the verse from Track one could be comped with the chorus from Track three, the second verse from Track two, etc., into a digitally assembled "perfect" performance on Track eight.

When used with the DA-98's auto-punch and rehearse modes, the track copy/electronic patch bay functions become extraordinarily powerful, and users can insure that the final product is exactly as they intended.

A track could also be copied in the digital domain to an unused track, thus creating a backup copy before trying a difficult punch. In the analog domain, the digital patching feature can reroute connections to any track, a useful feature for anyone tracking on a DA-98 from a 2- or 4-bus board. Pro users will probably skip this function entirely and use traditional patching to access inputs.

Like other Tascam DTRS machines, the DA-98 also provides ±6 percent of pitch shifting; however, this range can be expanded to +18/-12 percent by controlling the DA-98 from an external clock source. Other standard amenities include individual delay (or advance) on any track, several metering modes (peak hold or release), a 37-pin parallel port for external control, dedicated numeric and function keys, up to 200ms of digital crossfade time (adjustable in 10ms increments) and a 4-line by 20-character backlit LCD screen showing other function menus while offering operational status at a glance.

INTERFACING

The DA-98 was designed for high-end pro recording applications, particularly in the audio-for-video/film post-production market. Tascam decided that the unbalanced -10dB RCA connectors found on the DA-88 and DA-38 would not be necessary on the DA-98, so analog interfacing on the DA-98 is available only via the D-25 sub connectors. However, this time Tascam has thankfully screened the pinout diagram on the DA-98's rear panel.

Users can select from three reference operating levels: Tascam (-16dB), SMPTE (-20dB) or EBU (-9dB); the DA-98's onboard digital tone generator/oscillator can be used as a tuning reference and as a means of setting and calibrating levels within your system.

In terms of digital interfacing, the DA-98's back panel includes the Tascam standard TDIF-1 ports for cloning tapes between any DA-98/DA-88/DA-38 combination. TDIF-1 is a bidirectional, 8-channel interface, so only one cable is required for transferring digital audio materials between two TDIF-1-equipped units. TDIF-1 is also the link to connecting one or more DA-98s to digital editing workstations or any affordable digital consoles on the market, such as the Yamaha 02R, Yamaha 03D, Mackie Digital, Ramsa DA7, Soundtracs Virtua, RSP's Project X and last, but certainly not least, the Tascam TM-D8000. All TDIF-1 connections are made using the optional $110 PW-88D cable.

AUDIO PERFORMANCE

The DA-98 is unquestionably the best sounding DTRS deck ever, thanks to its 64-times oversampling 20-bit Delta-Sigma analog-to-digital converters and its 8-times oversampling 20-bit digital-to-analog converters.

Meanwhile, the DA-98's dither feature allows users to enable (or disable) a dithering circuit on any track during recording. The theory behind the dithering process is to add a randomized signal to mask low-level quantization noise that occurs when inputs higher than 16 bits (18-, 20- or 24-bit) are stored on 16-bit media. So would I use the DA-98's dither function? Well, yes and no. Tascam describes its effect as "warmth." With dither enabled, I've heard an increase in clarity, particularly in low-level signals, but this was accompanied by a slight upper midrange bump that seemed to bring percussive background elements, such as cowbells, up in the track. As with any creative endeavor, I recommend trying dither in a variety of situations and discovering what works best with *your* application.

Offering the best converters ever built into a DTRS recorder and the world's only MDM with confidence monitoring, the Tascam DA-98 takes the format to its third generation. With numerous other features appealing to high-end users, the DA-98 should appeal to an appreciative audience ready to take the next step.

Tascam/TEAC Professional Division
7733 Telegraph Rd.
Montebello, CA 90640
213-726-0303
fax: 213-727-7635
http://www.tascam.com

CHAPTER 20

DTRS Accessories

The ultimate Tascam accessory: the TM-D8000 digital mixer

ll DTRS recorders offer a lot of flexibility right out of the box, adding appreciated touches such as jog wheel control, which is a standard feature on all decks. However, you can expand the capabilities of your system by adding from a diverse palette of accessories, offered either from Tascam or from a variety of third party vendors.

THE ULTIMATE TASCAM ACCESSORY

At the time this book was printed, Tascam was preparing to begin deliveries of its TM-D8000 digital mixing console mixer. The TM-D8000 has two 24-channel strips, providing a maximum of 40 TDIF (DA-88/DA-38/DA-98) inputs on mixdown, with 16 analog mic/line inputs, and AES and S/PDIF inputs. The board's auxiliary sends and returns are available as a combination of analog and digital. Two automation packages will be offered, with all console functions under MIDI control or an external computer/software package. Standard amenities include a huge backlit LCD panel showing parameters, 20 rotary encoders, jog/shuttle MMC transport controller with ten locate points; support of MTC, Sony 9-pin and DA-88 sync protocols are planned.

TASCAM REMOTE CONTROLS

The RC-848 ($1,499) is a large, multimachine autolocator with record select buttons for up to 48 tracks (six DA-88s); all ready/all safe buttons can simultaneously arm or clear any selected tracks into or out of record. Beyond the standard transport commands, the RC-848 also provides programmable pre-/post-roll, along with 9-pin RS-422 output for interfacing to video systems, ports for controlling Tascam analog decks, 99-point autolocation, a shuttle wheel, an LCD status screen and two time readouts. The latter are large, bright numerical LED displays indicating both tape time and the current/next locator point (or points captured on the fly) in hours/minutes/seconds/frames.

The RC-848's machine status LEDs indicate the number of the deck currently designated as the master, whether it be one of up to six DA-88s in the chain, a Tascam analog machine (such as the 238 and 488 multitrack cassette models) connected to the 37-pin parallel port, one of Tascam's TSR-8 or MSR-16/24 series of reel-to-reel machines controlled via the 15-pin serial port or a video deck wired to the 9-pin RS-422 port with standard parallel control protocol (this is used in high-end video recorders such as the Sony BVU-800). The VTR modes accessible via RC-848 control include assembly mode, video insert mode and independent control of audio insert on VTR Tracks one and two.

Priced at $225, the RC-808 is a compact 5.5x6-inch unit that duplicates the DA-88's front panel transport controls except the shuttle wheel. While the RC-808 is designed as a single-machine controller (it only includes track arming buttons for channels one through eight), any additional DA-88s connected to the master DA-88 will chase to follow the commands issued by the RC-808.

TASCAM DIGITAL INTERFACES

The Tascam IF-88AE provides AES/EBU (professional-type) and S/PDIF (consumer-type) digital ports for connecting the DA-88 to workstations, DAT machines, CD players/recorders and signal processors with digital inputs/outputs. Included on the IF-88AE are four pairs of AES/EBU inputs and outputs on standard XLR jacks, each routed to a pair of DA-88 tracks. Also provided is an S/PDIF input and output on RCA phono-type jacks, a BNC word-clock output and a bidirectional 25-pin TDIF-1 port for connecting to the DA-88. The AES/EBU ports automatically route to any record-ready track pairs on the DA-88 when the digital input button on the DA-88 front panel is enabled. As there is only a single set of S/PDIF ports, a front-panel switch allows the user to select any track pair on the DA-88 for sending/receiving the digital information.

The SDIF-2 interface format used on the IF-88SD is compatible with high-end digital systems such as Sony's PCM-3324 (24-track) and PCM-3348 (48-track) DASH-format, reel-to-reel digital machines. The IF-88SD's front panel is simple, with a switch for selecting 44.1kHz or 48kHz sampling frequencies; the rear panel has the SDIF-2 input and output ports (on 25-pin D-sub connectors), BNC word-sync in/out jacks and the 25-pin TDIF-1 port for connecting to the DA-88.

TASCAM MU-88 METER BRIDGE

As an alternative to the onboard meters, the DA-88, DA-98 and PCM-800 all feature a 15-pin D-sub rear panel port for connecting the optional MU-8824 24-channel meter bridge ($899, not including the PW-88M meter bridge connector cable at an additional $90). The MU-8824 displays level information on bright, 15-segment LED meters and includes switches for tailoring the display to personal preferences. These include a choice of fast or slow release times, peak hold on/off and, if peak hold is selected, either continuous hold or auto reset.

THIRD-PARTY ACCESSORIES

With more than 50,000 DTRS machines in use worldwide, numerous third parties have developed hardware accessories and peripherals to work with DTRS systems. Covering all of these would require more pages than this entire book, so here's a partial list with thumbnail descriptions of some of the available products, along with telephone numbers and Web site addresses (if available).

Ampex
- DA-8 (Quantegy brand)—Hi-8mm DTRS tape in various lengths

Apogee Electronics
310-915-1000; http://www.apogeedigital.com
- AD-8000—8-channel analog-to-digital converter with optional TDIF output
- FC8—format converter for transferring tracks to/from ADAT to Tascam TDIF format

BASF/JRPro Sales
805-295-5551
- DTRS Master—a DTRS tape available in 30-, 60- and 113-minute lengths

Digidesign
415-842-7900; http://www.digidesign.com
- TDIF Interface—interface for connecting TDIF-equipped decks to ProTools and Session-8 workstation products

Digital Audio Labs
612-559-9098; http://www.digitalaudio.com
- V8—8-channel I/O card for PCs, with optional TDIF I/O

Ensoniq

610-647-3930; http://www.ensoniq.com

- Paris—disk-based digital recorder/editor with optional TDIF interface

HHB Communications

310-319-1111

- DA113—high-quality 113-minute Hi-8 tape developed for DTRS recorders

JLCooper

310-306-4131; http://www.jlcooper.com

- Cuepoint remote controller for MDMs

Kurzweil

310-926-3200; http://www.youngchang.com/kurzweil

- DMTi (Digital MultiTrack interface)—TDIF to/from AES/EBU, S/PDIF, ADAT or Kurzweil K2500 sampler interface and sample rate converter

Mackie's digital 8-bus mixer offers optional TDIF I/O.

Mackie Designs

206-488-6843; http://www.mackie.com

- Digital 8-Bus—digital console with optional TDIF I/O interfaces

Mark of the Unicorn

617-576-2760; http://www.motu.com

- Digital Timepiece—Tascam sync to MIDI Time Code and SMPTE sync interface

Opcode Systems

415-856-3333; http://www.opcode.com

- XTC—MIDI/SMPTE sync box with TDIF and computer interfacing

Otari

415-341-5900; http://www.otari.com

- UFC-24—24-channel universal format converter TDIF to AES/EBU, S/PDIF, ADAT and vice-versa

PrismSound

973-299-7790; http://www.prismsound.com

- MR-2024T—adapter providing (with your external A/D converters) six tracks at 20-bits; four tracks at 24-bits; or two tracks of 24-bits at 96kHz on a DA-88

Rane

206-355-6000; http://www.rane.com

- RC24t—PAQRAT 20/24-bit recording adapter for Tascam decks

Ramsa

714-373-7277

- WR-DA7—digital mixer with optional TDIF I/O

RSP Technologies

810-853-3055; http://www.rocktron.com/rsp

- Project X—large format digital console with optional TDIF I/O

Sony Pro Audio

201-358-4197; http://www.sony.com

- PCM-800—DTRS format MDM
- DARS-MP—metal particle Hi-8mm DTRS tape
- DARS-ME—metal evaporated Hi-8mm DTRS tape

Soundmaster Group

416-741-7057; http://ourworld.compuserve.com/homepages/soundmaster

- ATOM—computerized multimachine synchronizer/controller for DA-88s
- ION/88—computerized multimachine synchronizer/controller for DA-88s

Soundscape

805-658-7375; http://www.soundscape-digital.com

- SSHDR-1—digital workstation with optional TDIF interface
- SS8IO-1—eight in/eight out box with TDIF, ADAT and Superclock/word clock I/Os.

Soundtracs

Distributed by Korg, 516-333-9100

- Virtua—digital mixer with optional TDIF I/O

Spectral

206-487-2931; http://www.spectralinc.com

- Translator Plus—TDIF to/from AES/EBU, S/PDIF, ADAT and Spectral interface

Yamaha

714-522-9011; http://www.Yamaha.com

- O2R—digital console with optional TDIF I/O
- O3D—digital console with optional TDIF I/O

CHAPTER 21

DTRS Maintenance and Troubleshooting

ll Tascam DA-88, DA-38, DA-98 and Sony PCM-800 machines use the 8-track Hi-8mm format known as DTRS. If your DTRS machine is acting erratically, replacing your transport with another deck may solve the elusive mystery of whether the problem is being caused by your recorder or by some peripheral device in the chain, such as a MIDI or SMPTE synchronizer. Since the DA-88's electronics are mounted on easily interchangeable pull-out cards, diagnosing problems within the deck becomes a matter of combining a logical series of board swaps with a simple process of elimination, assuming that you have access to a second (or third) deck.

TRY THE EASY STUFF FIRST!

So you've got a problem. Before you start dismantling your recorders, check the easy things first. Cables can come loose at inopportune times, and this is a frequent cause of MDM problems, particularly when those tiny screws on the D-sub intermachine sync cables aren't tightened all the way. Even the removable AC power cables can find a way to wiggle out of their sockets, and an intermittent connection here can cause every type of mysterious malady. Also, make sure the lockdown screws on the D-25 analog I/O multipin blocks are secure. Audio problems can sometimes be solved by simply tightening the connections, perhaps using a touch of cleaner/deoxidizer/conductivity enhancement treatment such as DeoxIT from Caig Laboratories (619-457-1799) on the contact pins.

On power-up, the DA-88/DA-38 is actually running a self-test/self-reset routine. So, if a problem occurs on the DA-88, the first thing to try is to power off the unit and then power it up again after waiting a minute or so.

HEAD CLEANING

According to Tascam, heads require cleaning whenever the front panel Error LED (marked with the kinder, gentler "PB Condition" designation in the DA-38 and DA-98) lights excessively. A *dry* cleaning

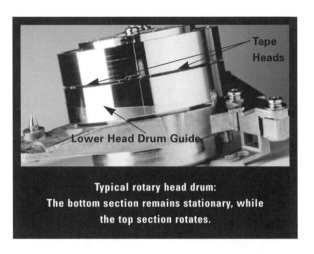

Typical rotary head drum:
The bottom section remains stationary, while the top section rotates.

tape, designed specifically for Hi-8mm video transports, should be used (Sony and TDK are recommended). Normally, the recorder automatically ejects tapes that are not recordable, such as cleaning tapes, regular 8mm formulations or tapes longer than 120 minutes, so the machine must be put into a special cleaning mode before the cleaning tape is used. Here's how this is done:

1. Eject any tape in the machine and turn the machine off.
2. Press the Arrow Up/Down keys simultaneously and turn the power switch on. The display will read "CLEAning" to indicate that the machine is in cleaning mode.
3. Insert the dry cleaning tape. Cleaning will start automatically. After 15 seconds, the process is completed: The cleaning tape is automatically ejected, the deck exits the cleaning mode. Now, power the machine down, wait 15 seconds and then power-up again before resuming studio operations.

DTRS decks incorporate an internal cleaning mechanism that cleans the rotary head *and* the tape as it enters the tape path. This significantly reduces the need for manual cleaning and all but eliminates the need to use the dry cleaning tape.

Use the cleaning tapes only as necessary. The use of a dry cleaning tape reduces the head life of a DA-88 by approximately five hours every cleaning cycle; use should be reserved for situations when play-back errors occur and a manual cleaning is not possible. If you elect to use the dry cleaning tape, *run one pass only,* not multiple cycles. If using a dry cleaning tape does not resolve the situation, a manual cleaning or alignment is required.

RECOMMENDED MAINTENANCE SCHEDULE

To display the number of hours on the head drum, hold the Play and Stop buttons while powering up. The number of hours that the deck has been operated in the shuttle mode can be determined by pressing the Stop and Fast-forward buttons while powering up.

The following is Tascam's suggested maintenance schedule. Note that the cleaning interval may be longer or shorter depending on your individual environmental conditions.

Every 350 to 400 hours: Perform manual cleaning of heads and guides.

At 1,000 Hours: During third manual cleaning, a complete alignment check is suggested. This requires proper test and measurement equipment and should be performed by qualified service personnel.

Remember, the duration between cleanings may vary depending on your environment. A dusty or smoky environment will shorten the cleaning cycle.

Although most name brand tapes are high quality, it is possible to receive some bad stock, typically tape that exhibits excessive shedding. If you encounter tape stock that sheds, immediately stop using it and clean your transport.

MANUAL HEAD CLEANING

Unlike the heads on analog decks, MDM tape heads are extremely fragile. Unless you are thoroughly trained in the methods of cleaning rotary-head assemblies, you'd better forget about popping the top on an MDM to do head cleanings. Besides, there are a couple of other issues to consider:

- Dismantling an MDM will void your warranty.
- The insides of such devices carry potentially lethal voltages.
- Worst of all, inexperienced hands mucking around in complicated electromechanical devices can seriously damage the equipment; it's all too easy to trash a very expensive set of rotary heads if you don't know what you're doing.

If you really want to clean your ADAT heads thoroughly, you should learn to do a complete manual tape assembly cleaning. What follows is my recommended procedure for head and tape path cleaning. (But if you are in any doubt about how to do this yourself, take the deck to an audio or video repair shop and ask them to show you the procedure

for manual head cleaning.)

There are numerous commercial preparations available for head cleaning, but I like using absolute (99+%) ethyl alcohol. This is commonly sold in drugstores as "denatured" alcohol, which is ethyl "grain" alcohol combined with a trace amount of a chemical that makes it poisonous to keep people from drinking it. Do not use rubbing alcohol, which is typically a mixture of isopropyl alcohol combined with water.

Note that ethyl alcohol is extremely flammable. Make sure it is sealed tightly after use. If it's left uncovered, it will draw water vapor out of the air and lose its purity.

The rotary heads should only be cleaned using Kimwipes (which look similar to ordinary tissues, but are sterile and lint-free); deerskin (chamois) swabs; or synthetic chamois swabs, such as Chamois Tips™ made by Chemtronics (800-645-5244). The latter are carried by broadcast and pro audio dealers and are available in convenient 15-swab packs. Do not use cotton swabs, as these shed lint and cotton particles, which will create havoc with rotary heads.

Begin by ejecting the tapes and disconnecting the power to the unit. Open the ADAT's top cover. Inside, the most prominent thing you'll see is the silver head drum, which looks similar to that shown in the photo on page 8. Note that the side of the head drum has a slot cut into it that goes around the entire drum. The tiny rectangular bits in the slot are the video heads.

Apply the absolute ethyl alcohol to the wipe or chamois and gently (but firmly) hold the wipe along the side of the head drum. Without moving the wipe, rotate the drum several times in one direction with your other hand, and then reverse the direction. Do not move the wipe up and down. Allow five minutes for the head drum to dry before using the recorder. The key to the head-cleaning procedure is finding the right amount of finger pressure: There is a fine line between properly cleaning and permanently damaging the delicate rotary head. If in doubt, take the deck to an audio or video repair shop and ask them to show you the procedure for manual head cleaning before attempting it yourself.

I suggest using a dental mirror to inspect the heads and tape path before and after cleaning, and if you don't have success with ethyl alcohol, try a commercial aerosol video head cleaner (if you use one of these, spray the aerosol cleaner onto the wipe, never directly onto the heads).

Make sure you clean the lower head drum guide. This is an indentation in the head drum that the tape rests upon as it travels around the head. It runs at an angle to the head slot, providing the precise angle for laying the audio track information in helical scans. If you're careful not to touch the rotary heads, an alcohol-moistened cotton swab can be used. Although the lower part of the drum does not rotate, I turn the top of the head drum several times as I clean the lower drum guide, so that the heads are away from the section I'm cleaning. It is critical that this part of the tape path is absolutely clean, as any dirt or crud that accumulates can push the tape up slightly, causing the tape to mistrack and resulting in an unplayable tape.

You can also use denatured alcohol and cotton swabs to clean the rest of the tape pathway: the fixed auxiliary and full erase heads, tape guides and capstan. Unlike the rotary heads, these parts can be cleaned with an up and down motion; just be gentle with the fragile nylon roller guides.

The rubber pinch roller wheel should be cleaned with a cleaner designed specifically for rubber parts, as alcohols degrade the life of rubber; TEAC/Tascam makes an excellent rubber roller cleaner, which I highly recommend.

ERRATIC OPERATION

Tascam and Sony MDMs store operational data, such as autolocation information, crossfade times and pitch-shift settings, in battery-backed memory, even when the units are switched off or unplugged. This useful feature operates thanks to a built-in lithium cell, which constantly supplies power to the onboard RAM. In my experience, such batteries last at least five years, so around the turn of the century, a senile DA-88 may merely be because of a dead battery.

TAPE WON'T FORMAT OR RECORD

If your DTRS deck won't format or record a tape, the problem may be simple to correct, and it may not cost you one peso! If you've never used an 8mm videotape system (audio or video), you should know that the erase protect tab on the back of such tapes (Hi-8 or standard) must be slid into the *open* position to allow recording, which is the opposite of how floppy disks, DATs, analog cassettes, VHS tapes and everything else on the planet operates. This is obviously a minor point, but it takes a bit of getting used to.

One interesting bit of trivia is that tapes previously recorded with video information cannot be formatted for DA-88/DA-38 use. So you'd better forget about tracking over your camcorder tapes of little Jimmy's birthday party when you're out of tapes and need to put down some killer licks in the middle of the night.

MY TAPE WON'T DUB!

When locking two DTRS transports to dub (clone), make certain that the master tape is *not* write-protected. If it is, you can't press the master deck's Record key; you also can't press the slave machine's Record key even if the slave tape is not write-protected. To fix the problem, simply slide the erase protect tabs on both tapes into the open position, and then continue the dubbing procedure.

GETTING INTO SYNC

Up to 16 DA-88, DA-38 and PCM-800s can be interlocked for multimachine operation without the need for any external synchronizing equipment. It's really a simple, plug-and-play operation. However, there are a few things to remember.

While the machines use 15-pin D-sub connectors for sync, an off-the-shelf computer cable will *not* work in this application and may damage the equipment. You should use the optional Tascam PW88S sync cable.

Machine lockup is easy, but if your DTRS decks won't sync, check the Machine ID switches and make sure they're set properly. A tiny rotary switch on the rear of each machine selects the Machine ID (sort of like a SCSI ID number): ID #0 for master, #1 for the first slave, #2 for the second, etc. Once IDs are set, just load your tapes, push the Chase button on the slave decks, and the slaves faithfully follow the master transport.

Another situation that can cause sync problems is poor quality sync cables or a chain of sync cables that is too long. Sync cables should be kept as short as possible; the maximum length of the sync chain should be shorter than 30 feet for reliable operation. If you have four DA-88s interconnected by 15-foot sync cables between each, you may encounter problems.

AUTODIAGNOSTICS AND ERROR DISPLAYS

The DA-88, DA-38 and PCM-800 have numerous error codes and autodiagnostic messages. Here are a few:

E. CLOC: No clock data is coming in or the clock switch is set incorrectly. This could also indicate a mismatch in the Machine ID numbers and the order in which the extra transports are connected.

E. t. cut: Tape is broken.

E. d io: Digital I/O error; check to see if cable is connected properly.

E. dE: Dew sensor has detected condensation on head drum. This sometimes occurs when a DA-88 or DA-38 is moved from a cold area to a warm one, such as from a car trunk in winter to a heated studio environment. Leave the deck powered up, and let the machine heat up gradually.

E. HI-8.t: Tape inserted is not Hi-8mm.

E. thin.t: Tape inserted is too thin; use 90- or 120-minute tapes.

The DA-88's dynamic servo checking system uses a binary 4-bit code to indicate many different conditions from a few parameters. Servo errors are indicated by a code such as "S-Err-01," where "S" refers to Servo, "Err" is error and "01" is the specific error number:

S-Err-01: Mechanical problem: tape path, guide, drum, motor, etc.

S-Err-02: Irregular drum rotation speed.

S-Err-03: Combo of Errors 1 and 2.

S-Err-04: Capstan motor problem.

S-Err-05: Combo of Errors 1 and 4.

S-Err-06: Combo of Errors 2 and 4.

S-Err-07: Combo of Errors 1, 2 and 4.

S-Err-08: Reel (take-up or supply) problem.

S-Err-09: Combo of Errors 1 and 8.

S-Err-10: Combo of Errors 2 and 8.

S-Err-11: Combo of Errors 1, 2 and 8.

S-Err-12: Combo of Errors 4 and 8.

S-Err-13: Combo of Errors 1, 4 and 8.

S-Err-14: Combo of Errors 2, 4 and 8.

S-Err-15: Combo of Errors 1, 2, 4, and 8.

S-Err-21: The reel tables did not wind the tape back into the tape shell in preparation for eject.

S-Err-31: The tape is loose or stuck. Tape manufacturing tolerances vary somewhat, and this error display (that also halts the transport) is the result if the tape is slightly too wide or too stiff and gets caught in the guides. Changing tape brands may help; there is also a possibility that the recorder's tape path is out of adjustment.

S-Err-41: Solenoid did not engage during fast-forward or rewind.

S-Err-59: Reels do not drive (or lock for more than 1.5 seconds) in eject mode.

S-Err-68: Reels do not drive (or lock for more than 1.5 seconds) in play mode.

As you've probably figured out, there isn't much the user can do if such errors are indicated. After a servo error is displayed, the user should power the DA-88 or DA-38 down, wait a minute and then turn the power switch back on. If a normal display reappears, the self-reset feature cured the problem. However, the DA-88 and DA-38 refuse to allow tapes to be ejected while a servo-check error is displayed. This is for the protection of the user's master tape. For example, if the servo check shut the deck down because of an S-Err-05 capstan motor problem, then attempting an eject without correcting the error could damage the tape. In this case, the cassette should be *manually* removed by a competent technician.

THE FINAL WORD

Having made hundreds of recordings on all types of MDM systems, I can conclusively state that tape is an important factor. Experiment a little, find a brand that works and stick to it. But no matter what brand you use, be aware that tapes will occasionally fail, jam or simply disintegrate. Backup tapes are a part of life in the digital lane, and if you care about your work, then take the time to make safety copies. If you're having strange symptoms, such as a continuous or flashing error light, try another tape before calling the service department or dismantling your recorder.

Hopefully, the information presented here will keep you and your (growing) collection of DTRS decks safe, healthy and happy. By applying these tips, a little common sense and an occasional call to the manufacturer's service department, your digital system will stay running well into the twenty-first century. Just remember to check those lithium batteries around 2001 or so.

Yamaha Format Recorders

Chapter 22 Yamaha DMR8/DRU8

CHAPTER 22

Yamaha DMR8/DRU8

DMP Records studio, Stamford, Connecticut

I have seen the future, and it is digital. Not 16-bit but real 20-bit stuff. And not today, but years ago, in the form of the Yamaha DMR8 Digital Mixer/Recorder. Although the DMR8 system was unveiled to the world on October 18, 1989, on the eve of the 87th Audio Engineering Society Convention in New York City, the DMR8 story began long before that. Actually, the DMR8's development shouldn't have come as too much of a surprise: Since the company's introduction of the DMP7 and DMP7D mixers (the first affordable digital mixing consoles) some years earlier, you had to figure Yamaha was up to something big, and the DMR8 was that something.

Today we still owe a debt of gratitude to the Yamaha DMR8, because many of its design elements were later incorporated into Yamaha's 02R 20-bit digital 8-bus console, offering 24 analog inputs and 16 digital tape returns for a total of 40 inputs, with four card slots accommodating ADAT Lightpipe, Tascam TDIF, S/PDIF and AES/EBU signals. Moving faders are standard, as is instantaneous reset of all console parameters, limiter/compressor/gate on every channel and output bus, and two internal effects processors. Paired with a couple MDMs, the all-digital studio is no longer a fantasy.

SYSTEM BASICS

Even by today's standards, the Yamaha DMR8 seems pretty impressive: an 8-track digital recorder and automated digital mixer combination in a fairly compact package. However, the DMR8 is just the tip of the iceberg. It forms the basis of an expandable, digital production system with 8, 16 or 24 tracks of recording and 24-track digital mixing capability (with the clarity of 24-bit mixer resolution) in a virtual console design, with snapshot recall of all console parameters, moving fader automation and onboard digital effects (reverb, delay, chorus, EQ, compression, etc.). The console can mix up to 24 inputs of tape or outboard sources.

Along with the eight digital audio tracks, two aux audio cue tracks and a time code track are provided. The DMR8 can chase-lock to incoming SMPTE time code; additionally, the unit will slave to the DRU8 8-track recorder/system expanders with sample accuracy.

The system tape format is Yamaha's proprietary M20P metal particle cassette, which records 22 minutes at 44.1kHz or 20 minutes at 48kHz. Longer 8-track record times can be achieved through a serial slave mode, which automatically starts a second 8-track transport to provide continuous recording when the tape on the first deck runs out. The tape's running time of over 20 minutes is 20 percent longer than a 10.5-inch reel of analog running at 30 ips. Two erase-protect notches on the cassette for Tracks 1-4 and Tracks 5-8 are a nice touch, allowing vocal or rhythm tracks to be protected while overdubbing continues.

Audio data is recorded via a stationary head block, so the transport is mechanically much simpler than rotary-head schemes such as DATs or VCRs. Since the proprietary tape format is presently available through only a handful of dealers nationwide, users can order tapes directly from Yamaha, with overnight delivery if required. So what happens if you run out of tapes at 3 a.m. on a Saturday? You wait until Monday, just as you would if you ran out of 1- or 2-inch analog tape at some inopportune time. Analog or digital, some things never change.

Tapes for the DMR8 must be formatted, ideally in real time before recording (just as one would initialize or format a floppy disk before inserting it into a computer or sampler). Formatting includes the option to record a table of contents at the start of the tape, where automation, routing, setup and autolocation data can be stored. The DMR8 can also format while recording, in which case you can take 30 seconds to format the TOC and then let the rest of the tape format itself as it records.

CONNECTIONS

The DMR8's rear panel is packed with connectors of all sorts: digital, analog, MIDI, time code, word-clock, video sync and "video superimpose" jacks. The latter are two BNC in/out connectors used to superimpose the DMR8 LCD status display's data over a video picture. One minor quirk is the placement of the control room and cue headphone outputs on the rear panel, which is somewhat inconvenient. Also, you won't find any analog audio inputs except for the aux cueing tracks and a 2-track input that can be switched for playback through the control room outputs.

With this in mind, Yamaha has taken the modular approach to the limit: Users can pick and choose from a variety of rack-mount accessories to expand the input/output capabilities of the system. Among these options is the $3,599 AD8X analog-to-digital converter, with eight analog line inputs (+4dB) and a

---

Spotlight

Yamaha DMR8/DRU8

- Product Introduction: October 18, 1989
- Deliveries Began: November 1990
- Format: Proprietary Yamaha, using Yamaha M20P tapes
- Recording Time: 22 minutes at 44.1kHz, 20 minutes at 48kHz
- Track Capacity: Eight, expandable to 16 or 24
- Digital System: Stationary head; 20-bit linear; 32/44.1/48kHz sampling frequencies
- Analog Connections: On balanced line-level XLRs: two channel inputs, left/right control room out, two cue send outputs, time code I/O. XLR talkback mic input; two sets of aux inputs/outputs on RCA jacks; two headphone outs
- Digital Connections: On Yamaha format D-25-sub: 8 channels I/O, digital patch-bay output and digital I/O to slave deck. AES/EBU input/output; two sets of S/PDIF I/O; AES/EBU and S/PDIF out to control room monitoring system; AES/EBU or S/PDIF cue send output. In Yamaha MEL2 (8-pin DIN) format: three effects sends and returns, slave input, submix input, monitor/input/output insert points and multimachine digital cascade
- Dimensions: 10x26x27 inches (HxWxD); 55 pounds
- Retail (before being discontinued): $33,999, including digital onboard digital mixer with DSP and moving fader automation. The DRU8 8-channel recorder/expander is $13,999.

The DMR8 combined an MDM and digital mixer in a single package.

The 8-pin DIN MEL2 digital connectors on the DMR8's rear panel (three effects sends and returns, slave mix in, digital cascade in/out, channel insert in/out and monitor insert in/out) allow simple connections to other Yamaha gear with digital ports, such as the DMP7, DMP7D and DMP11 mixers, SPX900 and SPX1000 multi-effects processors and DEQ5 and DEQ7 equalizers. All you have to do is plug and go.

Interfacing the DMR8 to external digital, which are not equipped with Yamaha-format I/O, can be both simple and convoluted at the same time. During one session, I wanted to transfer a stereo DAT recording to the DMR8 via the S/PDIF "DAT Input" port, which only routes to the control room monitor bus. It was no problem hearing the track in the control room, but getting it to tape required connecting an 8-pin DIN cable (Yamaha format) from the "out insert" point to the "sub in" return jack. *Note: Yamaha's FMC2 format converter would be invaluable in solving such digital routing problems.*

On the other hand, other digital routings can be extraordinarily flexible. For example, both the control room and cue monitor outs are available as analog XLR pairs, as well as digital AES/EBU and S/PDIF ports. Normally, a cue system wouldn't be used during mixdown, but the DMR8 offers other possibilities: A cue mix could be employed for submixes, or simply as an additional routing bus, with multiple analog and digital outputs. On a pop project I produced with the DMR8, I wanted to use a Summit tube equalizer (a nondigital device) on vocals, so I used the analog cue mix out as an effects send and returned the signal to the DMR8 via the AD8X A/D converter. The results were fine, although using a lot of analog outboard gear with the DMR8 can become expensive with the additional D/A converters required. However, with the DMR8's equivalent of three SPX1000s and plenty of flexible EQ on board, you probably won't need much outboard processing.

Yamaha-format digital output that connects to the 25-pin D-sub digital I/O port on the DMR8. If you need mic preamps, you can use any quality professional unit or Yamaha's HA8 8-channel mic preamp. Priced at $1,599, the HA8 has inputs for up to eight XLR balanced-line microphones and includes pad and gain controls and a switchable +48VDC phantom supply for powering condenser microphones. A 2-channel analog-to-digital converter, the AD2X ($1,699), transforms two balanced +4dB analog signals into Yamaha, AES/EBU or S/PDIF digital formats, while the $1,899 DA2X is a 20-bit D/A converter that can be used to connect analog gear to the insert and aux sends. Rounding out the line of conversion devices is the FMC8 Format Converter, a $1,999 unit that converts eight channels of Yamaha-format audio data to either the Sony DASH (SDIF-2) or Mitsubishi/Otari (Pro-Digi Melco) digital multitrack formats. The FMC8 can also be used as a standalone peripheral for transferring audio between the DASH and ProDigi recorders.

Yamaha later expanded its accessory line with two additional format converters: the FMC9 ($4,799), an 8-channel AES/EBU front end; and the FMC2, a 2-channel Yamaha-to-AES S/PDIF (and vice versa) converter that allows the DMR8 to be connected to digital processors and outboard gear with other formats, such as samplers and disk-based workstations. In the latter case, by combining the DMR8 with the 20-bit workstations from Digidesign and Sonic Solutions, the true 20-bit, entirely digital project becomes reality.

OPERATIONS

In spite of the DMR8's complexity, the top panel is startlingly simple, which is both a bane and a godsend. Let's say you want to make an equalization change. There are no dedicated EQ knobs, so you first punch the Select button to choose the channel you want to process, then hit the EQ button. The nine console faders become individual frequency, gain and bandwidth controls for the three bands of fully parametric EQ. Equalization changes are resettable and automatable in real time, and values are displayed on the LCD screen. The best part about this is that EQ changes can be made with the engineer sitting comfortably in the monitoring sweet spot without hunching over the console or groping to find the right knobs.

A similar procedure provides access to sends, monitor and cue mixes; control of the three onboard signal processors; and the effects available on every channel (EQ, highpass/lowpass filtering, delay, phase, emphasis, de-emphasis, compression, doubling, echo, flange). I found myself doing a lot of shuttling between the channel module, EQ, send, fader and monitor keys. Having ten automated moving faders in front of you for each of these operations really speeds up production.

The drawback of all this cool technology is the dreaded user interface: The DMR8's depth and power equates to a formidable learning curve. I needed about three days with the system before I was fully comfortable with recording, tracking and mixing operations. Yamaha provides a 22-page *Getting Started* booklet, an informative guide to DMR8 basics that accompanies the main (nearly 300-page) manual, which is well-written and complete. Unfortunately, the manual comes in a two-ring binder, which tends to tear pages. Access to the manual is much improved if you discard their binder and replace it with a garden-variety three-ring type.

Once you're into the system, though, production chores move along rapidly. Autolocation and sync capabilities are extensive, with 32 memory points and automated punch-in/-out and rehearse facilities. Of course, manual punching is possible, although the location of the transport controls (near the top of the unit) makes this somewhat awkward. I would prefer to have the controls closer to the edge or bottom of the unit, which would allow for resting the hand against the frame while the fingers do the walking. In any case, punches were seamless, with crossfade times adjustable from 1.33 to 2,730ms (by far the widest range of any MDM), with a default of 23ms.

Several track-bouncing modes are offered, allowing users to perform assembly edits, such as combining different takes of solo or vocal lines into one seamless track, or digital ping-ponging, where several tracks can be mixed internally to other tracks (with or without external sources). The DMR8 has write-after-read capability, so it is possible to record eight tracks and ping-pong them onto any two tracks (including the source tracks); just remember that this is a destructive edit. Fortunately, mixes and effects can be automated, providing ample opportunity to get it right before making irreversible track bounces.

The moving faders are a definite plus, but it should be understood that the faders only indicate relative positioning: Digital mixing and processing happens instantaneously within the DMR8 and is not limited by the mechanical speed of the faders.

The DMR8's audio quality is superb. After spending some time listening to 20-bit reproduction, going back to 16-bit digital recording was quite a shock. Certainly, the days of the phrase "CD quality"

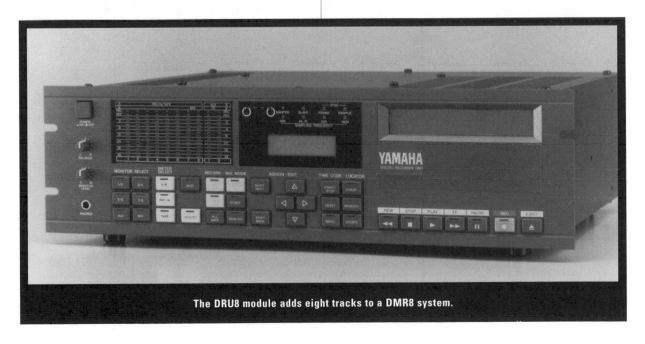

The DRU8 module adds eight tracks to a DMR8 system.

as a synonym for excellence are over.

As a modular system, the DMR8 allows users to start out with the basic recorder/mixer unit and then add DRU8 8-track recorder/expanders as necessary to form a complete 8-, 16- or 24-track production environment.

A few words should be said about the DRU8 recorder/expander. Priced at $13,999, this 3-rackspace unit incorporates all of the DMR8's recording and synchronization facilities. While the DRU8 has no built-in mixer, complete digital domain mixing becomes available when it is connected to the DMR8, and the units provide rock-steady, sample-accurate synchronization. The DRU8's front panel has full transport controls, and when teamed up with an appropriate analog-to-digital converter (such as the Yamaha AD8X), the recorder becomes an ideal location recording system.

For users who have a console they love, up to three DRU8 8-track expanders can be controlled from the RC24 ($2,999), a remote controller/locator that combines track arming, recording, transport and locator functions into one easy-to-use, compact device. Operations are monitored via two LED time code displays for tape time and locator points, and a 2-line by 24-character backlit LCD indicates system status and setting parameters. Priced at $1,199, the RC8 offers similar functions for controlling a single DRU8 for 8-track recording applications.

The price of the DMR8 ($33,999) may limit its appeal to the masses, but when you consider what comes with the package (digital recording, digital-domain mixing, dynamic moving-fader automation, onboard effects processing, SMPTE chase-lock, MIDI sync, etc.), it becomes an affordable step towards assembling a powerful, expandable production system.

Beyond Yamaha's original intended market of project studios and professional musician/composers, the DMR8 would certainly appeal to the video/film post market and pro audio studios, which might make the system the centerpiece of a "B" or "C" room. In the latter, the DMR8 would be an invaluable tool for overdubbing on a digital project. Why tie up the main room, big console and megabucks digital multitrack when the DMR8 can handle the same tasks, with better sound quality, at a lower price? Yamaha's DMR8 is a sensible approach that offers an impressive combination of power, flexibility and professional-level performance for the money.

One of the most significant aspects of the DMR8

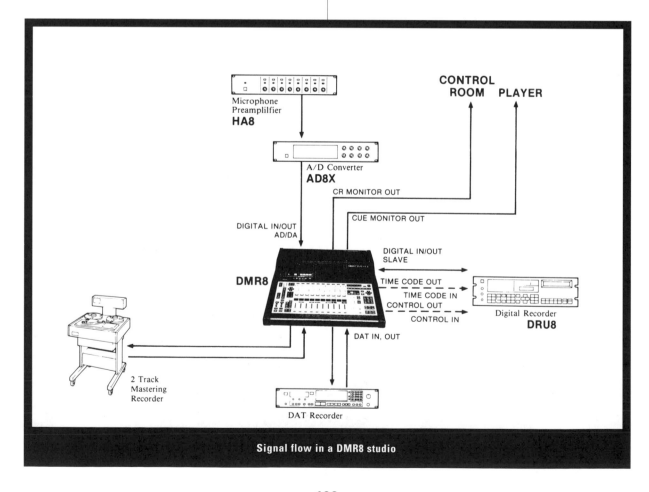

Signal flow in a DMR8 studio

is that the unit has proven the feasibility of the single-box studio. In the years to come, we may see more such wonders on the horizon, such as a 32-track digital studio-in-a-briefcase, with 24-bit audio, automated digital mixing, onboard sound sampling/synthesis and virtual signal processing, priced under $1,000 and $20 removable optical disks or biocubes for storing your creations. Too farfetched? Perhaps, but if I had told you a dozen years ago that a 24-track digital recording system would be within the budget of the average musician, you would have called the nice men in the white coats to take me away. It will be interesting to watch and see what tomorrow brings.

Yamaha Corporation of America
Pro Digital Products
6600 Orangethorpe Avenue
Buena Park, CA 90620
714-522-9011

Note: Turn page for diagram of DMR8 top panel.

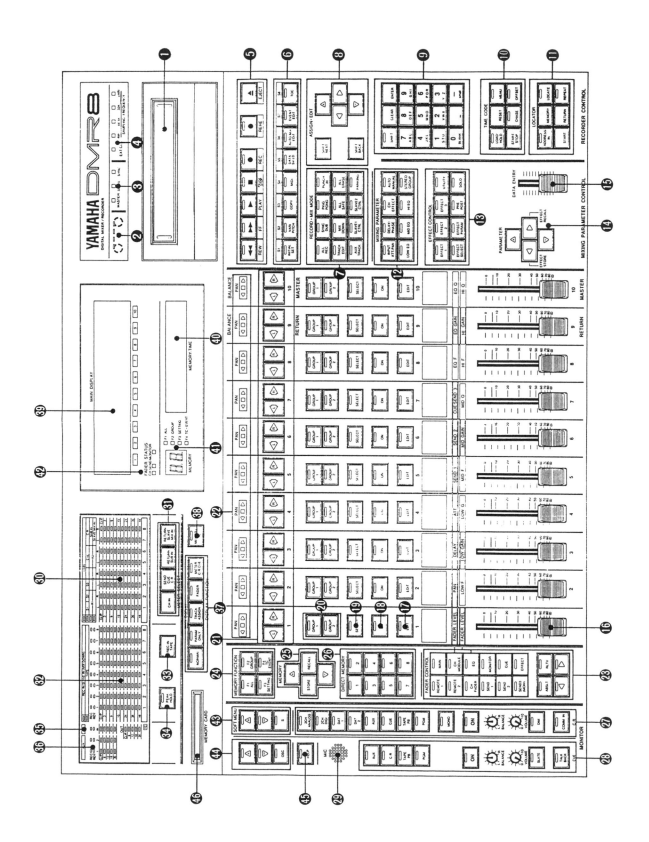

YAMAHA DMR8 OPERATIONS

Top Panel

1. Tape Well
2. Tape Motion Indicator
3. Master/Slave/Sync Status LEDs
4. Sampling Frequency Indicator
5. Transport and Eject Buttons
6. S1-S8 Menu Select Keys
7. Record-Mix Mode Select Keys
8. Assign-Edit Keys
9. Alphanumeric Keypad
10. Time Code Keys
11. Locator Keys
12. Mixing Parameter Keys
13. Effect Control Keys
14. Mix Parameter Cursor/Value Keys
15. Data Entry Slider
16. Motorized Fader
17. Channel Edit Key (for editing/bypassing automix data)
18. Channel On/Off Key (Mute)
19. Mix Parameter Select Key
20. Group Keys
21. Channel Pan Keys
22. Channel Pan Status LEDs
23. Fader Control Keys
24. Memory Function Keys
25. Memory Recall/Store Keys
26. Direct Memory Keys
27. Control Room Monitoring Section
28. Cue (artist mix) Monitor Section
29. Talkback Mic
30. Meter Bank 1
31. Meter Bank 1 Selector: Channel Inputs, Cue/Send/CR, Sub Returns or Returns from DRU8 expander.
32. Meter Bank 2
33. Meter Bank 2 Selector (Tape or External Inputs)
34. Peak Hold/Reset Switch
35. Time Code In/Out Meter
36. Meters for Analog Aux Tracks
37. Main Display Select: Mix Parameters/ Track Names, Parameters Only, Channel Assignments, Fader Positions or Multi-Segment CR/Cue Meter
38. Subdisplay Select: Time Code or Memory Data
39. Main Display: 4x40 LCD
40. Sub-display: 2x24 LCD
41. Memory Number Display: Two-Digit LED
42. Fader Status LEDs
43. Soft Menu Keys
44. Internal Oscillator
45. Help Key
46. Memory Card Slot

The MDM Power User

Chapter 23 The Power Demo

Chapter 24 The Buddy System

Chapter 25 Analog Interfacing

Chapter 26 Digital Interfacing

Chapter 27 Cloning/Tape Backups

Chapter 28 Tape Tips

Chapter 29 MIDI Sync

Chapter 30 MIDI Machine Control

Chapter 31 Understanding SMPTE

Chapter 32 The Whys and Hows of Crossfades

Chapter 33 Digital Assembly Editing

Chapter 34 MDM: The DAT Editing Tool

Chapter 35 The Built-in -10/+4dB Converter

Chapter 36 Mix to MDM!

Chapter 37 MDM: The Multichannel Mix Format

Chapter 38 Track Bouncing, Revisited

Chapter 39 The Submix Sync Trick

Chapter 40 Megatracking Without Bouncing

Chapter 41 The Workstation-MDM Connection

Chapter 42 The No-Console Tracking Trick

Chapter 43 Track Delay: Who Needs It?

Chapter 44 Fun With Pitch Shifting

Chapter 45 The 20-/24-bit MDM

Chapter 46 The Suicide Auto-Mute Squeeze!

Chapter 47 MDM: The Next Generation

CHAPTER 23

The Power Demo

This chapter is written for songwriters. Everyone else can skip to the next chapter, but I'd like to take a minute to give songwriters a tip that may just provide an inside advantage in the all-too-competitive world of getting your song placed with a major artist. I call this the "Power Demo," and it works equally well with country, R&B, rock, pop, gospel or virtually any style of music where performers are looking for outside material.

As a hypothetical example, let's say that Elvis is alive today and is looking for songs for an upcoming album. Like most songwriters, you'd record the hottest demo of your best tune and send a lyric sheet and cassette to his management, record company, producer, agent, hairdresser, chauffeur or anyone else who could possibly pass your song along to the King.

It's a month later. Elvis has picked about 25 songs from the 20,000 submissions, and yours is one of them. Unfortunately, the competition is going to be tough, because only 12 of the 25 finalists will make it onto the album. Before Elvis can decide which to use, he'll probably cut some quick demos of the tunes to hear how he sounds on the material. And before

he even lays a vocal on a demo of your song, he'll have to do the following:
1. Hire some musicians.
2. Hire an arranger to write out the parts.
3. Spend time teaching them your song.
4. Book the studio time.
5. Record the basic tracks.
6. Overdub the vocals.
7. Mix the demo.

With a little advance planning, this may just provide the extra incentive to get your next song placed on someone's chart-busting success.

Obviously, this represents a lot of time, effort and money just to see if your tune is right for the project. Fortunately, your MDM system can help encourage the artist to check out your tune first, allowing him or her to "try on" the song while skipping steps one through five. This method is based on the fact that there are tens of thousands of MDM systems throughout the world today, and nearly everybody in the music business either owns one or knows someone who does.

Here's how it works: After you mix the final version of your demo, run another pass without vocals, so you'll have an instrumental version. When you send in your cassette and lyric sheet, mention in your cover letter that you also have an 8-track MDM tape of the song with a stereo instrumental mix on Tracks one and two and a "scratch" vocal on Track eight. That way, Elvis can use your vocal track as a guide and have five additional tracks available for testing different lead and background vocal takes.

Insider's Tip

When you're mixing any music project, it's always a good idea to create an instrumental version of your song. You may not need it now, but someday, somewhere, someone might want to use your tune as a background theme in a video production, or later you might need instrumental tracks for creating an extended dance mix, or perhaps someone likes your song and wants to hear it with, say, a male vocalist rather than the female singer who's on your demo. By transferring the instrumental mix back to your MDM, all you have to do is record a couple new vocal tracks and you can create a quick demo for any occasion.

Depending on the equipment you have, this can be created in several ways. The simplest method is mixing directly to an MDM recorder, routing the instrumental mix to Tracks one and two and sending the lead vocal directly to Track eight. This assumes that you have an extra MDM laying around, which may be unlikely unless you have a friend with a similar system. However, if you have a 16-track (or larger) system and can get by with fewer tracks, you can record the lead vocal to Track 16 and mix the instrumentals directly to MDM Tracks 9-10. Later, you can make a clone and erase any other track material on the clone, so you have a clean copy with just the stereo instrumental tracks and a scratch vocal remaining.

A third, no-frills method is merely copying the DAT instrumental mix onto a new tape and re-recording a scratch vocal on Track eight. The downside of this approach is having to recut the vocal, but this isn't too much of a problem if you or a friend is the vocalist.

The Power Demo technique won't turn a bad song into a good one; creating a finger-snapping, foot-tapping demo is still up to you and your own creativity. But with a little advance planning, this may just provide the extra incentive to get your next song placed on someone's chart-busting success. And that's the name of the game.

CHAPTER 24

The Buddy System

et's say you have (or plan to buy) a modular digital multitrack recorder. If you have a friend with a similar-format deck, you can pool your resources and have access to more recording power. The beauty of MDM systems lies in their modular nature: Simply add more recorders to the system to increase the number of available tracks. Attempting that same trick with two analog decks usually requires adding an expensive outboard synchronizer and dedicating one track on each machine to SMPTE time code. In this case, synching two analog 8-tracks yields 14 rather than 16 tracks.

Obviously, if you want an easily expandable, cost-effective system, MDM is the way to go; and the more decks you have access to, the more fun you can have. The least expensive way to expand your capabilities is to find someone else with a similar system, hence, the Buddy System (TBS).

If you're in a band, TBS is ideal. Working individually, band members can use their MDMs as scratchpad recorders for experimenting with new song ideas. When the band needs to record an album or a serious demo project, the individual decks can be combined to form an ultra-high fidelity 16-, 24- or 32-track system.

However, TBS offers a lot more than simply megatracking. Access to two or more decks allows you to make perfect clone (safety) copies of important sessions, and lets you use two decks for assembly editing. And, every once in a while, TBS may provide a backup machine for that all-important session if your machine stops operating or is in the shop.

Another advantage of TBS involves troubleshooting. If your system is acting erratically, replacing your transport with another deck may solve the elusive mystery of whether the problem is being caused by your recorder or by some peripheral device in the chain, such as a MIDI or SMPTE synchronizer. And if you and your TBS pal both own Tascam DA-88s (with the electronics mounted on easily-interchangeable, pull-out cards), diagnosing problems within the deck becomes a matter of combining a logical series of board swaps with a simple process of elimination.

TBS does not need to be limited strictly to equipment sharing: Other knowledgeable users in your area may also be able to offer ideas and technical support based on their own experiences. Another source of information is Internet newsgroups, such as rec.audio.pro or the audio forums on Compuserve and AOL. In my experience, these forums are often quite informative, with lively, dedicated and highly opinionated users at every level.

If you want an easily expandable, cost-effective system, MDM is the way to go; and the more decks you have access to, the more fun you can have.

Getting started with TBS shouldn't be difficult. Alesis has formed the ADAT Worldwide Network™, an organization that provides free access and referrals to other users and ADAT-equipped facilities around the globe; call Alesis for details and/or registration forms. If you own a non-Alesis recorder, you might ask the dealer that you bought the machine from for the names of other users in your area. Other possibilities include posting a notice on a music-store bulletin board or running a classified ad in local musician-oriented newspapers. The investment is small, and the rewards could be great.

CHAPTER 25

Analog Interfacing

Analog snakes from Clark Wire & Cable

We live in a curious and rather complicated world: There are nearly 100 different sizes, formats and styles of audio connectors in use today. These range from simple variations on the XLR, ¼-inch (phone) and RCA (phono) connectors you've probably encountered on music and audio products to less familiar, more esoteric multipin connectors, such as the 56-pin EDAC/Elco (used on the Alesis ADAT) and the D-25 sub connector (borrowed from the computer industry and used on the Fostex RD-8 and CX-8 and the Tascam DA-88, 38 and 98).

Unfortunately, there is no universally accepted standard for analog connections or mixing console connections among MDM systems. However, the unbalanced ¼-inch and RCA jacks used on the Tascam, Fostex, Panasonic, Studer and Alesis machines are simple to use and a breeze to hook up: Just plug in and go!

If the rest of your gear is compatible with balanced lines, putting in a little work and wiring to

them is highly recommended: The hotter outputs require less console input gain, and the balanced lines reduce the possibility of noise/hum problems. Another advantage offered by balanced lines is that they provide superior signal transfer over long cable lengths (50 feet or more); this is especially important if you plan to locate your MDM system in a machine room that is some distance from the control room.

If your console offers +4dB, balanced-line operation, you'll need to purchase or build the proper "snake" lines before you can access the balanced connections. My advice is to buy the snake. Balanced line interface snakes are expensive, but the hassles of building the snakes are worse. I have built several, and you'd better believe it when I tell you that this definitely is not a for-the-beginner project: It's tedious, labor-intensive and *no fun at all!* Having said that, I also realize that electronics nerds like myself love a challenge, so I'm providing all the info you need to make these yourself. But don't say that you haven't been warned!

Several companies market MDM snakes with

XLR or ¼-inch (tip/ring/sleeve) terminations on one end and D-25 or Elco connectors at the other. Compatible interface cables are manufactured by Clark Wire & Cable (847-949-9595), Conquest Sound (708-534-0390), Hosa (714-522-5675), Pro Co (616-388-9675), and Whirlwind (716-663-8820).

Incidentally, these companies also build nice RCA-to-RCA, ¼-inch-to-RCA, and ¼-inch-to-¼-inch snakes for use with unbalanced systems. These get rid of the spaghetti-cable tangle in your studio and are generally inexpensive and wonderful.

Whether you have a small project room or a large world-class studio, make sure any snakes you build or buy are longer than what you think you need. Your setup may change in a couple years, and buying a couple extra feet of cable now may really pay off later. Whether you're building or buying cable, try to get the best possible quality cables and connectors, because you'll find that high-quality cables will serve you well for years to come. Isn't your audio worth it?

With that in mind, let's examine analog interfacing on a machine-by-machine basis.

AKAI A-DAM AND SONY PCM-800:
IT'S AN XLR WORLD, AFTER ALL

Originally developed by ITT/Cannon, XLR connectors (sometimes referred to simply as "Cannon" connectors) are the standard in professional audio: They provide secure locking to other XLRs combined with durability and three audio connections for handling balanced lines.

A balanced audio line consists of three conductors: Two carrying signal and a ground (shield) wire, where one of the signal wires carries the sound, while the other carries an inverted copy. When the signal reaches the destination, the inverted copy is flipped and added to the original. Any noise that has been induced into the signal also is inverted. When this inverted signal is combined with the "uninverted" noise, it cancels out. For this reason, balanced lines

are less susceptible to hum and can carry audio signals over longer distances.

The largest of all MDM transports, the 12-track A-DAM system, provides ample space on its back panel, with 12 female XLR connectors for recorder inputs and 12 male XLR connectors for recorder outputs. It does not accommodate multichannel connectors or unbalanced -10dB devices. The one exception is the auxiliary analog (time code) track, which has ¼-inch, unbalanced input and output jacks operating at a level of -10dB. Interfacing the A-DAM is straightforward: Merely connect the XLR tape inputs/outputs to the balanced inputs/outputs of your mixer, and you're on your way. The only thing to watch out for is that A-DAM XLRs are wired with Pin #1 ground, Pin #2 minus and Pin #3 plus.

The Sony PCM-800 is the only DTRS format machine with XLR inputs and outputs. The PCM-800 replaces the unbalanced RCA jacks and (+4dB) D-25 sub multipin analog connections found on the DA-88 with electronically balanced, +4dBu inputs and outputs on standard 3-pin XLR connectors.

ALESIS ADAT:
THE ELCO/EDAC CONNECTION

The original ADAT includes ¼-inch unbalanced (-10dBV operating level) jacks for the recorder inputs/outputs, while the +4dBu balanced lines are available only on a 56-pin connector made by EDAC Inc. (Scarborough, Ontario, Canada).

Interfacing on the Alesis XT was similar to the original ADAT but simply substituted RCA phono jacks for the ¼-inch unbalanced connectors; all balanced connections are made via the 56-pin EDAC.

The Panasonic MDA-1, Alesis M20, and Studer V-Eight are ready for anything, offering not only XLR inputs and outputs, but also unbalanced I/O on -10dB RCA jacks and a 56-pin EDAC connector for multipin connections directly to consoles or patching systems.

The EDAC connector (similar plugs are also

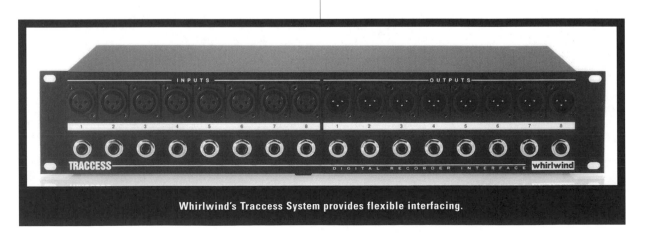

Whirlwind's Traccess System provides flexible interfacing.

manufactured by Elco) is available in female receptacle and male plug styles. You'll need a male EDAC or Elco to mate with the female receptacle on the back of the ADAT.

In addition to the male 56-pin EDAC connector, you'll also need the appropriate connector for the other end and a length of quality snake cable. The cable should be designed for audio use and should have individually shielded pairs of cable, with separate ground wires for each pair.

EDAC/Elco connectors are occasionally found on other pieces of professional audio gear, such as certain Soundcraft, Neve and Soundtracs mixers and the Alesis X-2 recording console. Unfortunately, there is no industry standard for the wiring of 56-pin connectors, but Alesis has printed the pinout both on the back panel of the original ADAT and in the manual. The pinout is also shown in Fig. 6. (Note that the pinout diagram refers to the *face* of the female connector or the *solder side* of the male plug.)

EDAC connectors tend to be hard to find and fairly expensive, but they're rugged, with large, gold-plated contact pins. These connectors are generally available *without* the pins installed, so the user has the option of selecting a particular style that is most suitable to the assembly method. Pin variations include solder (with a 0.098-inch wire hole), wire-wrap and crimp-on. The wire-wrap styles are not well-suited for use with audio snake cabling, so the only real assembly options are solder and crimp-on types.

Elco manufactures some high-quality crimping pliers which, cost about $100 (ouch!), but assembly time is much faster than soldering, and the connections are secure. If you are only going to make a couple snakes, then you're probably limited to the solder

route. These connectors cram a lot of pins into an extremely small area, so if you're using the solder pins, you'll also have to cover each solder connection with a small piece (about ¼ inch) of heat-shrinkable tubing to avoid the possibility of shorts between adjacent pins.

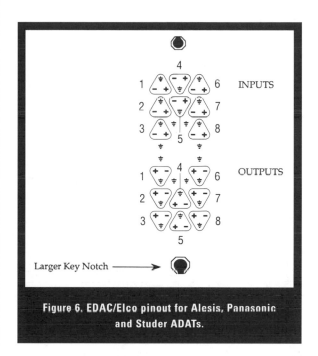

Figure 6. EDAC/Elco pinout for Alesis, Panasonic and Studer ADATs.

Elco also makes a line of contact (pin) insertion and extraction tools, although the pins are easily inserted into the connectors with a pair of needle-nose pliers. Removal is a bit more complicated: Slide a dental pick or other sharp, hard object into the front (nonsoldered side) of the connector, gently pry the locking edge of the pin aside and remove the pin.

When assembling an EDAC snake, don't insert all the pins into the connector before soldering or crimping, as this will make assembly difficult or impossible. If you complete all the soldering or crimping *before* inserting the pins, installation is much faster. And whatever you do, make sure you slide the cover (cable hood) over the snake cable before starting the job! While we're on the subject of connector covers, be aware that EDAC makes a line of covers that are convertible from rear to top/bottom cable entry. These convertible styles are convenient in installations where you may be unsure as to which cable routing is best.

Once you've stripped the wires, soldered or crimped the pins and made sure the connector cover is in place, you can insert the pins. But before you do, make a list of every wire, its color, where it's supposed to go and what signal it's supposed to carry. Then double-check everything before inserting the pins.

Insider's Tip

If you're planning to make EDAC/Elco snakes and the console end requires a fanout (breakout of multiple lines) with individual connectors for each tape send or return (such as ¼-inch or XLR connectors), build your snake using two 8-pair snake cables rather than one 16-pair cable. Your multipin connector will then have two separate cables exiting from the cable cover, but at the other end you'll appreciate having two cables (with one dedicated to recorder inputs/console sends and the other as tape outputs/returns) because, on most consoles, the input and output sections are located in different parts of the rear panel.

Note that the multipin connector has a larger key notch at the bottom and a narrow key notch at the top. Whenever I assemble such connectors, I use a marking pen to draw a stripe along the edge with the larger key notch, as the difference between the two is rather subtle, and it's easy to get confused while you're inserting the pins.

After you've completed inserting the pins, carefully slide the cover in place and tighten it down with the four screws on the face of the connector. Now, armed with your list of wire codes, you can do the other end, whether it be XLRs, tip-ring-sleeve ¼-inch plugs, EDAC/Elcos or whatever. If the console end requires an Elco and the console happens to be the Alesis X-2, the pinout will be the same as the ADAT. If you're wiring to a Neve, Soundcraft, Soundtracs or other non-Alesis, Elco-equipped console, you'll have to consult the manufacturer for the correct pinout.

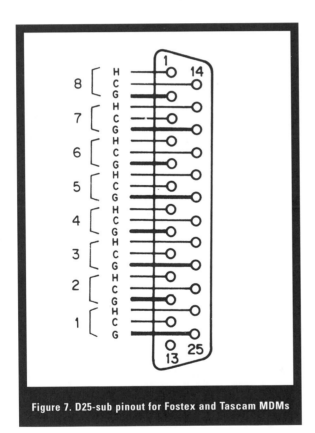

Figure 7. D25-sub pinout for Fostex and Tascam MDMs

FOSTEX RD-8 AND CX-8 AND TASCAM DA-88, DA-38 AND DA-98: THE D-25 APPROACH

These two manufacturers have incompatible tape formats but have much in common in terms of analog interfacing. Both provide unbalanced -10dB input/outputs on RCA (phono) jacks, which are inexpensive and readily available. As with the Alesis ADAT, the +4dB inputs and outputs are provided on multipin connectors, rather than a bank of bulky XLRs. Yet, unlike the single-connector EDAC on the Alesis machine, the Fostex and Tascam decks use two D-25 sub connectors, each carrying eight channels of +4dB input or output signals.

The Tascam DA-98 does not include any RCA or phono audio connectors; the recorder's only analog interfacing is via the D-25 connectors. It is also the first Tascam MDM to actually print the pinout of the connectors on the back panel. Thanks, Tascam!

Commonplace in the computer industry, the D-25 sub connector has been used with success over the years in some audio applications, appearing on products such as Tascam's high-end M-600 and M-700 consoles as well as mixers from other manufacturers, such as DDA. The D-25 sub has 25 pins, which provide for eight channels with three contacts (hot [+], cold [-] and ground connections) each. A pinout for the D-25 sub used on the Fostex and Tascam decks is shown in Fig. 7.

For those do-it-yourselfers who really want to make D-25 sub snakes, be forewarned: While the connectors are readily available, they can be difficult to assemble, especially with larger gauge cable, such as AWG 20 or 22. The crimping tools are not overly expensive, so only a true masochist should even think of soldering these connectors.

Before you begin, you need to be aware of a few facts. The D-25 sub hold-down nuts on the Fostex RD-8 and CX-8 and the Tascam DA-88, DA-38 and DA-98 use a different size thread. Made in the USA, the Fostex decks use the American standard 4-40 threads that are used on almost all PCs and computer peripherals. The D-subs on the Japanese-built Tascam MDMs are fitted with ISO threads. Common in Japan, the ISO threads will not mate with metric or USA standard threads. Therefore, even though they are electrically identical, any snake made for a Fostex deck will not mate with a Tascam recorder, and vice versa. This leaves the do-it-yourselfer four options:

1. Find high-quality connectors with ISO threads (a difficult task).
2. Build connectors using top-notch American D-subs, such as those made by AMP, and then swap their 4-40 hold-down screws with some ISO-thread screws (an easier prospect).
3. Buy a tap and rethread the DA-88 hold-down nuts so they have 4-40 threads (a more permanent approach).
4. Buy the optional Tascam PW8D/XM (male XLR termination) and PW8D/XF (female XLR termination) D-sub-to-XLR snakes. Incidentally, these are wired with pin #3 hot.

To get back to construction, you'll need a male D-25 sub connector, the appropriate connector for the other end and a couple lengths of quality 8-channel snake cable. The cable you use should be designed for audio use and should have eight individually shielded pairs of cable, with separate ground wires for each pair.

After you've stripped the wires, but *before* crimping the pins, make sure the connector cover (hood) is large enough to accommodate the comparatively large diameter of the snake cable, which typically is much larger than computer-type wires. Make a list of every wire, its color, where it's supposed to go and what signal it's supposed to carry. Then double-check everything before crimping the pins. Uncrimping a pin on a D-25 sub is virtually impossible, so if you insert one wrong wire, you'll probably have to start over from the beginning. Be careful, and have fun.

YAMAHA DMR8 AND DRU8: OPTIONS, OPTIONS, OPTIONS

The Yamaha DMR8 has only two analog inputs and two analog main outputs, which are balanced XLR +4dB line-level. Additional analog inputs/outputs generally come from one of the many optional outboard converters offered for the system, which use individual XLRs at line level. An 8-channel mic preamp is also available. No multipin connections are used for analog I/O on the Yamaha machine.

CHAPTER 26

Digital Interfacing

This is where it all comes together if you want to use your MDM to create backup (safety) copies of your work or clone tapes to send to friends. Also, if you need to transfer tracks to/from DAT recorders, CD players/recorders, workstations and signal processors with digital input/output ports, you'll need to understand some basics about digital interfacing.

While the industry has developed standards for multichannel transfer of audio data such as MADI and SDIF-2, all of the MDM systems in this book use non-standard, proprietary multichannel interfaces. And while transfers between these formats are hardly straightforward, copying and cloning tapes between two similar-format decks is a simple matter of connecting the right cable between the two machines.

AKAI A-DAM

The transport's rear panel includes a proprietary 37-pin digital I/O connector for making clones to another DR1200 recorder. The A-DAM interface is bidirectional, so only a single cable is required for digital transfers to/from a second A-DAM system. An optional accessory, the DIF1200 digital interface adapter, allows the transfer of two channels of digital audio into or out of the A-DAM system to peripheral devices equipped with AES/EBU digital ports.

THE ALESIS LIGHTPIPE

Unlike other MDM formats, the Alesis ADAT, Fostex, Panasonic and Studer systems use a high-speed serial bitstream that carries eight channels of digital audio through a fiber-optic cable. The digital data travels in one direction only, so each ADAT transport has separate digital input and output connectors. The connector is a standard Toslink optical, which is identical to those used for the S/PDIF optical digital I/O ports found on some consumer hi-fi equipment. However, the consumer optical and ADAT datastreams are incompatible, so don't plan on connecting the optical output of a CD player directly into an ADAT. The S/PDIF standard also includes a coaxial (nonoptical) interface with RCA phono connectors, which are commonly found on DAT recorders.

If you want to connect a device with an S/PDIF optical port to an ADAT, you should know about the Alesis AI-1 and a variety of conversion boxes, including the DMTi from Kurzweil (Cerritos, CA), the UFC-24 from Otari (Foster City, CA) and Translator Series from Spectral (Woodinville, WA), that have S/PDIF ports in both coaxial and optical forms, as well as the professional-standard AES/EBU digital connections. Apogee (Santa Monica, CA) also makes the FC-8, an affordable box that allows digital cloning between ADAT Lightpipe-equipped recorders and Tascam MDMs.

Copying and cloning tapes between two similar-format decks is a simple matter of connecting the right cable between the two machines.

Both optical interfaces (S/PDIF and ADAT) use similar connectors, so if you lose the one-meter optical cable included with your ADAT, you may be able to find a replacement at a stereo store. Alesis also offers a line of ADAT fiber-optic cables ranging from 21 inches to over 16 feet in length. These are especially useful for transferring sounds from the Alesis QuadraSynth keyboard (which has an ADAT-compatible optical digital output) directly into an ADAT system.

Transferring digital audio over fiber-optic lines is a simple, straightforward matter, and optical transfers offer the advantage of being immune to electromagnetic and radio-frequency interference that can occasionally play havoc with wire-based systems. However, fiber-optic lines are virtually impossible to repair without access to specialized tools, so protect the cables from sharp bends and turns. External damage from kinks and excessive weight, such as standing on the cable or routing it under heavy objects, may damage the delicate fibers, rendering the cable useless.

By the way, the digital ports emit a red light-beam, which is *not* a laser and is completely harmless. However, you should always make sure that the optical ports are covered, either by the small plastic plugs that came with the ADAT or with the digital cable in place, to ensure that the optical ports stay clean and free of dust and gunk.

Housed in a single-rackspace box, the Alesis AI-1 fiber-optic-to-AES/EBU and S/PDIF digital interface provides the pathway for bringing signals from other digital audio devices directly into the ADAT format entirely in the digital domain, without any signal loss whatsoever. The unit can also operate as a sample rate converter, outputting either 44.1kHz or 48kHz sampling rates, so if you want to transfer a sound effect from a CD player (44.1kHz) equipped with a digital output to an ADAT tape recorded at the default rate of 48kHz, the AI-1 will handle the necessary conversion. As an added bonus, the AI-1 will remove any SCMS copy protection flags (this is that horrid copy-code protection scheme implemented in most consumer-type DAT recorders) during the transfer process.

The ADAT fiber-optic interface becomes a powerful digital data exchange bus when the digital output of each ADAT is routed to the input of the next ADAT, and the digital output of the last ADAT in the chain is returned back to the input of the first machine to complete the circle. When connected in this manner information can be freely exchanged among multiple ADATs and, under BRC control, sophisticated multichannel editing becomes a reality. (For more on this, see Chapter 33.)

AES/EBU and S/PDIF ports transmit digital audio information serially in stereo pairs along a single cable. When connected to an ADAT via the AI-1, the audio information from a digital source can be routed to any enabled tracks, as long as the recipient ADAT's digital input switch is selected and the daisy-chained digital bus is connected between all ADATs in the system. Conversely, audio information from any two adjacent ADAT tracks can be sent to an outside digital device via the AI-1.

TASCAM TDIF-1

Used in the Tascam DA-88, DA-38 and DA-98, the proprietary TDIF-1 (Tascam Digital InterFace) is a 25-pin D-sub port that connects to a second DA-88 for making clone copies of tapes, as well as providing the link to Tascam's optional model IF-88AE interface (AES/EBU and S/PDIF) and IF-88SD (SDIF-2) interface. As TDIF-1 is a bidirectional interface, only one cable is required for transferring digital audio materials between two TDIF-1-equipped units. The two optional interfaces are essential if you plan to transfer DAT, CD or workstation tracks into or out of the DA-88 in the digital domain.

The TDIF-1 cable has 25-pin D-sub male connectors at both ends. A typical computer cable won't work, as the bidirectional TDIF-1 port requires the following pinout: Pin 1 to pin 13, 2 to 12, 3-11, 4-10, 5-9, 6-8, 7-7, 8-6, 9-5, 10-4, 11-3, 12-2, 13-1, 14-25, 15-24, 16-23, 17-22, 18-21, 19-20, 20-19, 21-18, 22-17, 23-16, 24-15, 25-14.

The Tascam PW88D dubbing cable is a high-quality accessory priced at $100, but in an emergency, you can easily make a TDIF-1 cable using two push-on, male D-25 sub connectors and 15 inches of 25-conductor ribbon cable. (If you plan to use this budget cable approach, it's essential that the cable length be as short as possible.) By attaching the D-25 plugs to the ribbon cable with one facing up and the other facing downwards (or putting a half-twist in the cable), you end up with the correct pinout. If you're timid about wires and electronics, any computer-savvy friend should be able to help you out. Using available parts from an electronics junk shop, I made one for less than two dollars; the assembly time was under two minutes.

Standard equipment on the optional IF-88AE interface includes four pairs of AES/EBU inputs and outputs on standard XLR jacks, with each routed to a pair of DA-88 tracks. Also provided is an S/PDIF input and output on RCA phono-type jacks, a BNC word-clock output and the bidirectional 25-pin TDIF-1 port for connecting to the DA-88. The AES/EBU ports automatically route to any record-ready track pairs on the DA-88 when the digital input button on the DA-88's front panel is enabled. As there is only a single set of S/PDIF ports, a front-panel switch allows the user to select any track pair on the DA-88 for sending/receiving the digital information.

The SDIF-2 format used on the IF-88SD interface is compatible with high-end digital systems such as Sony's PCM-3324 (24-track) and PCM-3348 (48-track) DASH-format, reel-to-reel digital machines. The IF-88SD's front panel is simple, with a switch for selecting 44.1kHz or 48kHz sampling frequencies; the rear panel has the SDIF-2 input and output ports (on 25-pin D-sub connectors), BNC word-sync in/out jacks and the 25-pin TDIF-1 port for connecting to the DA-88.

The FC-8 from Apogee (Santa Monica, CA) is a simple adapter that allows digital track copying between TDIF-1 and ADAT Lightpipe-equipped MDMs.

SONY PCM-800

Although the Sony PCM-800 uses the DTRS (Tascam) Hi-8mm tape recording format, the PCM-800's digital I/O configuration is different: Two 25-pin D-sub connectors carry eight channels of AES/EBU digital information (on stereo pairs) and the recorder includes breakout cables with XLR connectors for interfacing with other digital devices.

In offering the AES/EBU ports, Sony has eliminated the TDIF-1 connector from the PCM-800, so direct transfers from a PCM-800 to a DA-88 are impossible, unless you have Tascam's optional IF-88 AE AES/EBU interface. Cloning tapes from one PCM-800 to another is a simple matter of connecting the AES/EBU breakout cables that come with the PCM-800s. One advantage of the PCM-800's AES/EBU breakout is that individual track data can easily be copied from one machine to another. For example, you may create a work tape with several solo performances. To copy the solo from Track seven on one deck to Track one on the other deck, just patch Track seven's AES output to the AES input channel you need, arm the track, hit the digital input switch and go into record.

YAMAHA DMR8/DRU8

The Yamaha DMR8/DRU8 system is unique among MDM systems for many reasons, as its 20-bit resolution and the built-in mixing capabilities of the DMR8 combine to create a formidable production center. For these reasons, the digital interfacing is a critical part of its operation.

The main multichannel I/O is via a proprietary interface using a D-25 sub connector to carry eight channels of bidirectional digital audio data (24 bits per channel, serial lines with two audio channels per line) to/from a slave DRU8 recorder or optional 8-channel digital-to-analog or analog-to-digital converters. Cloning tapes requires little more than a single cable connection between two Yamaha recorders.

Two-channel digital ports are provided in a variety of forms: AES/EBU input; two sets of RCA-type S/PDIF inputs; AES/EBU and S/PDIF output to control room monitoring system; AES/EBU or S/PDIF cue send output; and 16 pairs in the Yamaha MEL2 (8-pin DIN) format—three effects sends and returns, slave input, submix input, monitor/input/output insert points and multimachine digital cascade.

A 2-channel analog-to-digital converter, the AD2X, transforms two balanced +4dB analog signals into Yamaha, AES/EBU or S/PDIF digital formats. Meanwhile, the FMC8 converts eight channels of Yamaha-format audio data to either the Sony DASH (SDIF-2) or Mitsubishi/Otari (ProDigi) digital multitrack formats. Additionally, the FMC8 can also be used as a standalone peripheral to transferring audio between the DASH and ProDigi recorders. Yamaha also offers format converters: the FMC9, an 8-channel AES/EBU front end, and the FMC2, a 2-channel Yamaha-to-AES/EBU or S/PDIF (and vice versa) converter for connecting the DMR8 to other digital systems and peripherals.

Perhaps the most exciting peripherals for use with the DMR8 system are not made by Yamaha at all. A recent resurgence in breaking the 16-bit audio barrier imposed by compact discs has led to the development of Sony's Super Bit Mapping and the Apogee UV22 Encoder. Such systems allow 16-bit mixing or playback systems to retain the sonic advantages of true 20-bit production, such as lower noise levels and improved audio clarity. So far, these devices show great promise and, best of all, the improvement can be heard in the living room of the final end-user. It will be interesting to see what other technical marvels lie ahead.

Insider's Tip

Some general advice: When making digital transfers between AES/EBU or S/PDIF devices, use a cable that's specifically designed for such applications. Don't use an XLR microphone cable for AES/EBU transfers or a phono patch cord for S/PDIF data. While a typical audio cable is designed for carrying frequencies over the audio range, digital audio datastreams require a much higher bandwidth. Common problems relating to poor cabling in digital audio systems range from mysterious and intermittent "tics" and "pops" to incoherent, garbled or distorted audio data. So get the right cable for the right job and keep the cable runs as short as possible.

CHAPTER 27

Cloning/Tape Backups

f all the information presented in this book, this chapter is probably the dullest, yet it's also the most important. No one wants to think about the day that disaster strikes, but it's better to be prepared than surprised when it occurs.

Think about the difference between these two sentences:

If my computer crashes, data will be lost.

When my computer crashes, data will be lost.

The first statement would be made by an idealist, while the second reflects the realist's viewpoint. Whenever you're working with complex, high-technology devices such as computers or MDM systems, the reality is that the system will eventually fail. It's inescapable. Murphy's Law says, "Anything that can go wrong will go wrong," but George's Law states, "In the entire history of recorded music, no master tape has ever been damaged when a digital safety copy was readily available." Safety copies have some intrinsic magical ability to protect master tapes: If you have one, you'll never need it; if you *don't* have one, your master tape will disappear in a puff of foul-smelling, burnt-insulation smoke. Guaranteed!

So what could possibly go wrong with these little MDM cassettes anyway? As anyone who's ever dug a crinkled tape out of a cassette deck or VCR can testify, there are dozens of horrible possibilities. Outside the transport, things aren't necessarily safe either: Set your precious master atop a warm power amp and, in a few minutes, the resulting slight warp in the cassette shell could render your tracks unplayable. Set a tape too close to a powerful magnetic field (from a studio monitor, guitar amp or P.A. cabinet), and you might be kissing those performances good-bye.

Need I say more? Here are three additional (and equally devastating) scenarios:

1. The keyboardist's little brother spills a Pepsi on the tape.
2. Bob the roadie rolls an amp rack over the tape.
3. Fido, the band mascot, eats the tape.

And there is always this time-tested, reliable disaster: "Great tambourine overdub! Now...which track had that smokin' guitar solo we recorded last night?"

By now, you probably get the idea about the need to make backup tapes. You'll sleep easier at night knowing you have backup copies of your tracks. But even if you're careful about dogs, Pepsi and overzealous tambourine overdubs, there are lots of *other* reasons to make backup tapes. Of course, all the techniques presented in this chapter require access to two or more similar-format MDM decks.

"Great tambourine overdub! Now...which track had that smokin' guitar solo we recorded last night?"

THE IMPOSSIBLE PUNCH

Let's say you've just cut some rhythm tracks and everyone thinks the take is hot except for the drummer, who's really bothered by one section where there's a slightly anticipated sixty-fourth note in the middle of the break going into the third verse. Punching in and out to fix one note won't be a picnic, no matter how good the engineer's chops are. Do you risk trashing the take just to please one player? "No problem," says the engineer, who makes a clone of the tracks and spends 15 minutes punching the drummer (that is, punching the cloned tracks of the drummer) to get it right. In this situation, cloning provides two obvious advantages:

1. The original tracks are protected while you experiment on the clone tape.
2. Since the original tracks are protected, there's less pressure on the drummer and engineer, so they can be more relaxed and concentrate on getting it right.

MORE TRACKS...FOR FREE!

I don't know about you, but I never seem to have enough tracks. Somehow, I'll wind up having only one track left for the soloist. But with this simple trick, you'll always have plenty of tracks to capture that wailing guitar flash or screaming sax. Here's how it works:

Let's say you have a 16-track MDM system with two 8-track decks. Fortunately, Track 16 is still free, so you start recording the solo. It's a pretty good take, but you're wondering if it could be better. With an old-fashioned analog recorder, you'd have to contemplate the agonizing decision of making that track a "keeper" or erasing it and trying a new one.

However, with an MDM system, you can make multiple clone tapes of the track 9-16 tape and record different solos on Track 16 of each clone. Best of all, this technique is cheaper than buying another transport, and once you record the perfect take, you can always erase or reuse any additional clone tapes that you don't need.

CUT YOUR TAPE COSTS IN HALF!

Back in the analog days, my grandpappy used to record one set of basic tracks per tune. And those of you who studied late twentieth-century history in school may remember that a $130 reel of 2-inch, 24-track analog tape running at 30 ips only provided about 16 minutes of recording time, so each 4-minute song consumed over $40 in tape. Therefore, these bands that grandpappy recorded would listen to the basic tracks very carefully and would record and re-record over the same stretch of tape until a suitable set of basic tracks was captured.

When recording with MDM systems, bands tend to record lots of basic tracks, especially when four minutes of tape costs as little as 35 cents. Compared to analog, this represents a cost savings in the range

of the hundreds. Not bad, eh? So, at least in the *beginning* stages of MDM production, tape is cheap.

Now let's look at an example of a band that records (and keeps) six versions of five songs for an EP release, with each song running four minutes long. That's a total of 120 minutes of tape time, not counting false starts, countdowns, joking between takes, etc. Let's assume that the tracks were recorded on a single 8-track MDM and used a total of four tapes. If the best takes are scattered over all 4 tapes, and the band starts overdubbing with 2 additional MDM transports (for 24 tracks), then 12 tapes will be required for the production. Of course, you'll probably spend more time shuttling, rewinding and searching than overdubbing.

There are several alternatives for saving time and cutting tape costs in this case. If the MDM system is capable of offsetting the playback between the transports, then the engineer could calculate the required offset times for each tune, time-slip the second and third transports, and the entire production could be completed using the 4 tapes of 8 basic tracks and 2 tapes for the extra 16 tracks. However, keeping track of the required calculations would probably drive the sharpest engineer crazy after a while and, of course, there's lots of extra tape-shuttling time involved in the process.

The preferred method involves copying the best set of basics from each song onto a new pre-formatted tape, using the digital output cable. (See Chapter 26 for details on digital interfacing.) This should *not* be done with the machines in sync or chase mode, as you want the resulting clone to be in the order you prefer. So while the best basics from Song A may start at the 18-minute mark on the original session tape, you'd want Song A to start at the beginning of the clone. I like to leave 30-60 seconds of space between songs (tape is cheap, remember?) on the clone, just in case I want to tack some musically worthless yet artistically poignant *mélange* at the end of the songs. More likely, I'll add some time at the end of each song, so that each tune starts at some easy-to-remember location like 00:00, 05:00, 8:00, 15:00, etc. I'll say it again: Tape is cheap.

Once you've got the songs set up the way you want, just start overdubbing with the second and third decks and you're on your way. Tape requirements: four original session tapes, one clone and two overdub tapes, for a total of seven.

Insider's Tip

If you live by the credo that "every bit of spontaneity is carefully rehearsed," you can space the clone-copied tunes fairly close together. Then when you overdub, add some (carefully rehearsed) ad-lib stage patter, tuning sounds, crowd noise, clinking glasses and applause. Mix it with way too much reverb (an airplane hangar setting is appropriate), and you've got a great "live" club demo. Apologize for the sound quality and say it was a stereo cassette deck in the back row. It'll fool them every time!

Tape Tips

Recording tape is a lot like our lungs: We rarely appreciate them when they're good and only notice them when they jam or won't play. Not a pleasant way to open a chapter!

So let's look at the bright side of things: Tape for video-based MDMs is cheap. *Really* cheap. And as you're going to spend lots of hours working on that tape, you'd better buy the best. A cheap tape is no bargain when the splice between the leader and the recording section separates and the tape wraps itself around the inside of your transport, gumming up the works and damaging the tape heads. The moral here is to find a good quality tape and then stay with that brand. Trust me, you'll sleep easier knowing your creations are safe.

> *Tape is a lot like our lungs: We rarely appreciate them when they're good and only notice them when they jam or won't play.*

FORMAT FORMAT FORMAT!!!

Back in the hardware section of the book, I said that you can record on MDMs while simultaneously formatting tape. While this is true, let me say that formatting the tapes *prior* to recording is a better idea, for a lot of reasons.

The first reason is convenience. When the muse strikes and you get that creative inspiration at three in the morning, it's nice to know that you can just throw in a tape and start working. But a more realistic scenario goes like this: You've finally filled up 16 tracks on two decks and you want to put some more tracks (17-24) on song number seven, which is 35 minutes into the tape. Now, unless you have some pre-formatted tapes lying around, you'll have to sit

Ampex was the first company to market tape for MDMs.

around for 40 minutes or so for that tape to format. This also comes up when you need to make a quick clone copy of one song on the tape so you can practice that difficult punch without messing up the original. It's a lot easier if you have a pre-formatted tape lying around.

The second reason for pre-formatting involves the tape itself. An old trick from those analog days of yore involves exercising the tape before using it. (By exercising, I mean rewinding and fast-forwarding the tape at least once before recording.) This way, any stickiness in the tape, which may be caused by too much humidity, adhesive "bleed-through" from the splice at the leader/tape junction or an excessive amount of force used in spooling the tape onto the reel at the plant, is eliminated. Of course, the pre-formatting process performs the exercising automatically as the tape is played (during formatting) and then rewound. If you really want to be careful, you can fast-forward and rewind the tape once before formatting, just to be sure. Isn't your music worth it?

TAPE STORAGE

Besides little brothers, dogs and master-munching tape transports, a tape's worst enemies are heat, dust and humidity. Pay careful attention to where you store your master tapes: Someday K-Tel may want to release all your early works for a 5-DVD set (also available on 15 CDs or 15 8-track cartridges) sold on late-night TV. This doesn't necessarily mean that you should build a thermally controlled tape vault in your backyard, but a good rule of thumb is that any place where you would be uncomfortable is also unsuitable for tape storage. So try and resist the lure of storing your tapes in an uninsulated attic space or in a damp basement. Ditto for leaving master tapes on your car's dashboard. A little common sense goes a long way.

If you make safeties of your master tapes, these should be stored at a different location from the masters. If the barn with the masters burns down and the safeties are stored next to the masters, the value of making the safety copies is significantly reduced.

Magnetic fields present another source of danger to recording tapes; a simple act such as laying a tape on top of a studio monitor, guitar speaker cabinet or high-frequency (horn) driver could spell disaster. Devices such as electric motors and power amps can also generate strong electromagnetic fields, which can potentially damage a tape.

MDM TAPE NOMENCLATURE:
KEEPING TRACK OF TRACKS

MDM recording techniques can create *lots* of tapes, such as original tracks, safety copies, clones to distant session players, collaborators, etc. In fact, I recently produced a 24-track session (with three MDM transports) and used over 12 tapes for a three-song EP! Things can get very confusing very fast, so here is my approved, time-tested method of keeping track of MDM tapes.

The process is based around the concept that an MDM system is like a very large, conventional tape recorder, so tapes from multiple linked MDMs would share a single "tape" number, differentiated by various suffixes and prefixes. For example, in a three-transport, 24-track session, all MDM tapes have the same tape number, just as all 24 tracks on an analog session would obviously have the same tape number. The original set of multitrack master tapes can be termed a "session tape." Consider the following IDs, where the tape number is 0072:

0072-8/24: The 0072 refers to the tape number, followed by a hyphen and the number 8/24, which means this session tape is the first eight tracks of a 24-track (three-transport) session.

0072-16/24: This is the same tape number but, obviously, this is the second set of eight tracks in a 24-track session.

0072-24/24: You got it! This is the third set of eight tracks from that session.

So far, so good, but how do we cover megatracking? Let's say we have a 16-track project, and only track 16 remains for the sax solo. By making two clones of the second set of tracks, we can record three variations of the sax solo, one for each new tape. So we have four tapes in our 16-track project:

0998-8/16
0998-16/16
C-0998-16/16A
C-0998-16/16B

The first two tapes are the 8- and 16-track session tapes. The last two tapes are clones of the 16-track session tape, hence the C ("clone") designation. The "A" and "B" suffixes are added to indicate that they contain the alternative A and B performances.

Finally, the producer decides that the B performance is the best, so two safety clones are made for the archives. These are designated as follows:

S-0998-8/16
SC-0998-16/16B

By looking at the numbers, we can tell that both of these are safety copies (a good reason to put the letter "S" first) and that the second tape is a safety of a clone that contains an alternate take.

So what happens when you record multiple versions of basic tracks and later clone the best takes onto a fresh new tape? Let's look at an example with three sets of basics, each on eight tracks:

01573-8
01574-8
01575-8

The tape numbers are sequential, reflecting the order in which they were recorded. Each carries a "-8" suffix, as these are 8-track sessions, and there is no "/16" or "/24" tag, because at this point we don't know how many transports will be required for the final production. So, since we now have a couple hours of basic tracks, we need to clone the selected takes onto a new tape, which may be given the following number:

01576-8

This edited clone is given a new number, and while it contains sections with cloned versions of the best basics, no C clone designation is needed before the number. A short note explaining the sources of the original material should be included with the track sheet and/or tape log. This information would be invaluable if our edited clone is damaged or lost.

Likewise, any tapes that result from bouncing tracks would also be given a new number. For example, let's say that you start with a 16-track system and record 14 tracks, leaving two tracks for the mix. The tape numbers might be as follows:

28456-8/16

28456-16/16

After routing the 14 tracks into a mixer and creating a stereo submix on Tracks 15 and 16, we have several options. If you think the mix is pretty good but you'd like to keep it and try another, you could simply make a clone of the 28456-16/16 tape and try mixing over Tracks 15 and 16 on the clone, which would be designated as:

C-28456-16/16A

If you want to try more mixes, just keep cloning and you wind up with:

C-28456-16/16B

and

C-28456-16/16C

…and so on. Finally, when you get the absolute killer submix, you could clone that tape and start erasing the tracks on the clone, which by this point would have the new number of:

28457-8

Again, the track sheet or tape log should indicate where the source material on Tracks 7-8 (these used to be tracks 15-16) originated. At this point, there is no need to put a "/16" or "/24" suffix at the end of the number, because we still don't know how many additional transports will be required in the final production.

WORK COPIES

If you weren't confused before, this section should do you in. You can increase the number of available tracks in any multi-MDM system through the use of "work copies," synchronous copies of session tapes which contain a rough "scratch" mix (a temporary or guide track) on one or two tracks and have the other six or seven tracks available for recording. Work copies are ideal for those instances when you want to send a tape to a long-distance collaborator, store lots of variations on performances, or merely continue working on a single-machine system when the project was started on a multi-transport setup.

Let's say you are in the middle of a project using a 24-track system. The first 16 tracks are full, and you want to add vibes, oboe and percussion, with a separate work tape sent out to three different session players. The tapes are numbered as follows:

0739-8/24

0739-16/24

0739-24/24

and

W-0739A

W-0739B

W-0739C

Once the desired performances are captured on the three "W" (work) tapes, the best takes on the work tapes could be digitally transferred to the 0739-24/24 tape. However, to further complicate matters and liven up the project, our percussionist friend returns the work tape with seven tracks of different instruments, the equivalent of a full samba section! We run all seven tracks through the mixer and create a stereo submix, which is recorded on Tracks 17 and 18 of the 0739-24/24 tape. The mono oboe is digitally transferred to Track 19, and the stereo vibes go to Tracks 20 and 21, which still leaves three tracks for the all-important mellophone, kazoo and zither parts.

Thanks to the work tapes, a total of 40 tracks are recorded, with 29 winding up in the final mix. Not bad for a 24-track system!

A "TYPICAL" 24-TRACK SESSION

Things tend to get weird before they get strange, so here's an example of a "typical" (yet gonzo) 24-track session using *lots* of tapes, like session tapes, work tapes, and of course, safeties of just about everything. By following the Rules of MDM Tape Nomenclature outlined above, you should be able to keep track of everything. Here we go…

This apocryphal session begins with some 8-track session tapes. Drums are recorded on six tracks: kick, snare, stereo overheads (mostly cymbals and hi-hat) and a stereo blend of six toms. Also on this tape is a scratch piano track coming from a sampled grand and an electronic metronome ("click") track. Over one grueling day, we record several hours of takes of four tunes. The tapes are numbered:

Insider's Tip

Go to an office supply store and buy some sheets of round, small-diameter, colored stickers. I use blue, but you can use any color you want, as long as you stick (pun intended) with that color. As soon as you format a tape, put one of the stickers on the top surface of the tape. This way, you'll always be able to tell the formatted tapes from the nonformatted ones. This may seem a trivial point, but when you get into a really complex production, this practice will pay off.

If you've partially formatted a tape, note the number of minutes formatted on the sticker. Also, those of you who work at various sampling rates should consider using two different colors for the formatting dots: I use blue for 48kHz and yellow for 44.1kHz.

00523-8

00524-8

00525-8

After a couple hours arguing over the best takes, we pick the coolest and clone the four tunes over to a new tape, which becomes:

00526-8/24

By now, the band members can't stand one another, so three work copies (each containing a stereo scratch track and six empty tracks) are handed out to the guitarist, bassist and keyboardist, who have single-transport MDM systems at home.

Note: If your system does not have the ability to reroute tracks in the digital domain, each player could be assigned one or two specific track numbers to work on. However, if track numbers can be reassigned during the dubbing process, the players could use any tracks on their work tapes.

The three work tapes would be numbered as follows:

W-00526A

W-00526B

W-00526C

The best guitar, bass and keys tracks would be transferred to tape number:

00526-16/24

This tape might then have bass on Track 9, two rhythm guitars on Tracks 10-11 and stereo keys on 12-13. Tracks 14 through 16 get filled with one lead and two background vocal tracks.

Something's missing, though. We need a little extra punch, so we make two work tapes for a saxophone player we know and our percussionist friend.

These are:

W-00526D

and

W-00526E

Meanwhile, we start working on the next eight tracks, which start off with a doubled lead guitar part on Tracks 17 and 18. This tape is:

00526-24/24

A few days later, the second set of work tapes comes back and we transfer the desired tracks to tape 00526-24/24. These are: stereo congas (two mics arranged in a stereo pair over three congas) on Tracks 19 and 20, mono shaker on Track 21, berimbau on Track 22 and a sax solo on Track 23. This leaves one remaining track, or three if you record over the scratch piano and quarter-note click track. Or we could save the latter and use it to trigger a sampled cowbell for the choruses. Just to be sure, we could record the sampled cowbell onto Track 24, in case we wanted to remix later and didn't have access to the drum machine at that time.

So far on this project, we've used 11 tapes, and we didn't even get to the overdubs on the other three

tunes! If we really want to be careful, we could make safety copies, named S-00526-8/24, S-00526-16/24 and S-00526-24/24. And if we made safeties of all the work tapes, we'd wind up with a total of 19 tapes on this project-in-progress. It's a good thing that tape is cheap!

MIDI Sync

ust over a decade ago, a not-so-quiet revolution took place. A group of musical instrument manufacturers agreed on a single, common protocol that allowed keyboards, drum machines, computers and signal processors to communicate with one another. Known as the Musical Instrument Digital Interface (MIDI) and fueled by the availability of low-cost, high-quality synthesizers and an ever-increasing ratio of computer performance to purchase price, the standard was soon adopted by hundreds of thousands of musicians worldwide. Suddenly, anyone with simple computer skills, a modest capital outlay and a desire to create could assemble a powerful music-production system.

The advantages of MIDI production were immediately obvious. Once a performance is stored in a sequencer, it can instantly be changed from harp to harpsichord, or from sax to sousaphone, with the touch of a couple buttons. Thinking of music production in terms of a finite number of tracks was quickly abandoned, as sequencers soon evolved into systems capable of dozens (or even hundreds) of tracks.

One thing that didn't change, however, is that we still needed to incorporate recordings of acoustic sources into MIDI production, whether vocals, narration, classical guitar or a '58 Les Paul Gold Top screaming through a Marshall stack turned up to 11.

In many situations, MIDI sequences synchronized to a multitrack tape recorder provide the best aspects of both worlds. This concept is known as virtual tracking, as the system has virtually as many tracks as are required (or can be accommodated by the available hardware). One major advantage to virtual tracking is that tracks played back through MIDI instruments are first-generation signals, as they have never been recorded. When virtual tracking takes place in conjunction with a digital multitrack recorder, the audio quality of the acoustic tracks can be as pristine as first-generation MIDI. The match-up of the two is ideal.

Synchronizing a MIDI sequence to a tape recorder can be achieved in many ways, ranging from the extremely simple to the excessively complex. The simplest is a converter box that takes the MIDI clock output from a sequencer and converts it to an audio signal known as FSK (Frequency Shift Keying). The FSK tone alternates between two frequencies, and the constant rate of the changing frequencies indicates the sequencer's tempo. While the sequence plays, the resulting FSK tone is recorded on an unused track of a tape recorder. Later, this sync tone from the tape is sent to the converter box, where the FSK is translated back into MIDI clocks to control the sequencer. This simplest of systems has several drawbacks. It requires "wasting" a tape track for the sync tone; also, the FSK signal carries no timing information, so synchronized playback requires playing the tape from the very beginning.

In many situations, MIDI sequences synchronized to a multitrack tape recorder provide the best aspects of both worlds.

A few years after the standard was created, an addition to the basic MIDI specification was adopted. Known as Song Position Pointer, this is a MIDI message embedded in a sequence's clock information that tells how many sixteenth notes have passed since the beginning of the sequence. This led to the development of "Smart FSK," which offers the ability to start an FSK-encoded tape at any point in the song and have the sequencer automatically chase to the tape, thus achieving perfect sync in a few seconds. It's cool, but it's incompatible with the SMPTE time code used in video production, and it still requires an audio track for the FSK signal. Smart FSK-based synchronizers include the Anatek Pocket Sync and the JLCooper PPS models. Additionally, many drum machines on the market provide some type of FSK synchronization, which is usually referred to as "tape sync."

Even if the sync type you use requires an audio track for recording a sync signal, whether it's SMPTE (see Chapter 31) or FSK, the advantages of locking an MDM to MIDI far outweigh the disadvantage of losing a track. This is especially true when you consider that a single lost track may add dozens of virtual tracks to your setup. Not a bad tradeoff, really.

A more recent enhancement to MIDI specification is MIDI Time Code, messages that allow MIDI synchronization to an absolute time reference in hours/minutes/seconds/frames that is unrelated to tempo. Unlike SMPTE time code, which can be recorded as an audio signal, MIDI Time Code is combined with the MIDI datastream and therefore cannot be recorded directly on tape. However, MTC can easily be created from a SMPTE time code signal. A few boxes even convert MTC to SMPTE, but for synching an MDM system to a sequencer, MTC is fairly simple to implement. With the right hardware, it doesn't necessitate wasting a digital audio track for the sync signal.

As SMPTE and MTC are not related to tempo, one drawback in using these methods involves the need to create a tempo map. If the tempo remains constant throughout the song, then making a tempo map involves little more than specifying the tempo and time signature (for example, 120 bpm and 4/4 time) at the first bar of the song. If the tempo and/or time signature of the sequence changes, then each new tempo/time signature is entered at the beat/bar locations where the change occurs.

It would be impossible to go into every combination of hardware, recorder, sequencer and synchronizer available on the market, so we'll just look at the basics of each MDM system.

SYSTEM SPECIFICS

On the Akai A-DAM, a dedicated analog aux track is provided for recording sync signals, which can be either FSK or SMPTE time code. From the SMPTE output, MIDI Time Code is easily derived with a simple SMPTE-to-MTC converter.

MIDI synchronization on the Alesis ADAT, ADAT XT, Fostex CX-8 or Panasonic MDA-1 requires either the BRC controller or the AI-2 synchronizer, both of which can output SMPTE and MTC data (the AI-2 also provides the ability to chase to any SMPTE source). Third-party accessories include the JLCooper dataSync, which converts the 9-pin ADAT sync information into MIDI Time Code; the dataSync Plus is an option that adds the capability of MIDI Clock and Song Position Pointer sync to those sequencers incapable of MTC operation. Another JLCooper box is

the dataMaster, which converts the 9-pin ADAT sync output to MTC or SMPTE, as well as adding a SMPTE chase feature.

The Fostex RD-8 has onboard SMPTE and MTC reader/generators for inputting/outputting these time codes; also standard is SMPTE chase-lock. The recorder uses the same 9-pin sync protocol as the Alesis ADAT, but no audio track is used for SMPTE.

SMPTE read/generate/chase and MIDI Time Code outputs for the Tascam DA-88 are provided by installing the optional SY-88 sync card. The Sony PCM-800 is similar to the DA-88, and requires the optional Sony DABK-801 sync board to handle SMPTE and MIDI sync functions. With the SY-88 or DABK-801 board installed, no audio track is required for time code operations. Tascam's DA-38 does not include any onboard SMPTE sync options but it will sync precisely to SMPTE if used as a slave in a system with a SMPTE-equipped DA-88 or PCM-800 as a master. Additionally, connecting the optional MMC-38 MIDI Machine Control Interface to a DA-38 (or DA-38 system) will convert the ABS (absolute) time output of the DA-38 and convert it to SMPTE or MIDI Time Code. Tascam's flagship DA-98 includes onboard SMPTE read/write/generate/chase functions, as well as MIDI sync and MMC features.

The Yamaha DMR8 can output either MIDI Time Code or MIDI clocks with Song Position Pointers, and SMPTE read/generate/chase-lock is a standard feature. Also standard is a dedicated analog track for time code and two auxiliary analog tracks that can be used for any other purposes, such as recording metronome "click" tracks, slide projector sync pulses, etc.

CHAPTER 30

MIDI Machine Control

dopted in January of 1992, MIDI Machine Control (MMC) is a general-purpose protocol designed to allow MIDI systems to communicate with and control traditional-style audio recorders. An MMC-equipped sequencer may, for example, be capable of sending play, stop, fast-forward, record and rewind commands to a single tape recorder; and more complex MMC systems may offer the potential to control synchronized multimachine setups. Additionally, a variety of new controllers for sending MMC commands have come to market recently, either as standalone units or built into mixing consoles.

Making the sequencer the central controller for an entire studio setup may initially seem like the ideal solution. However, in a simple MDM-synched-to-MIDI studio, MMC may be a case of putting the

> *MMC offers the ability to simultaneously control the record functions of the sequencer and recorder, which is an obvious plus when acoustic and MIDI sources are being tracked simultaneously.*

cart before the horse: Slaving a tape transport to a random-access system such as a sequencer is contrary to the way that the universe should operate. In such cases, it is much easier to have the sequencer slave to the tape transport.

Having said that, it is equally important to note that MMC does offer many advantages in the MDM stu-

dio. By itself, a recorder may only be capable of defining record punch-in/-out points in terms of SMPTE frames (1/30 of a second), yet with MMC, punch-in/-out times are limited only by the resolution of the sequencer. If the sequencer has a resolution of 384 ppqn (pulses per quarter note), then at a tempo of 120 bpm, punch-in/-out resolution equals 1/768 of a second, which is over 20 times more accurate than SMPTE frames!

MMC offers the ability to simultaneously control the record functions of the sequencer and recorder, which is an obvious plus when acoustic and MIDI sources are being tracked simultaneously. Too far-fetched? Not really, especially in a modern production setting, where the session players are using a hybrid of MIDI and actual instruments. If the drummer has a combination of electronic pads with real cymbals, then the cymbals could be miked and captured on an MDM system while the pad outputs track directly to a sequencer. The same goes for recording electric bass and a sampled piano simultaneously: The bass goes to MDM and the piano goes to a sequencer. A similar scenario could also involve recording a pickup (or miked amp) from a MIDI guitar while the MIDI performance goes straight to a sequencer.

Another benefit of working with MMC is the ability to define all studio operations from a musical viewpoint, in terms of bars and beats rather than minutes and seconds.

CHAPTER 31

Understanding SMPTE

I f you don't understand SMPTE, don't feel left out. SMPTE time code is one of the most confusing, misunderstood issues in the world of audio, even among the most seasoned production veterans. It's convoluted and complex, yet it's so simple that anyone can figure it out by remembering a few easy rules and examining some basic concepts. Ready? Here we go.

Back in 1972, the Society of Motion Picture and Television Engineers (SMPTE) adopted a simple digital coding system as a means of representing the exact time locations of video frames. Why? Locations on a strip of film are marked by sequential numbers that are printed at regular intervals along the edge of the film; by counting the number of frames between edge numbers, any location on the film can be positively identified because each frame has its own distinctive, unique number. However, video has no such means of "time-stamping" individual frames. The answer came in the form of SMPTE time code, which is used to express running time in hours/minutes/seconds/frames and occasionally subframes.

SMPTE time code is a limited-bandwidth signal that can readily be recorded on the audio track of any audio/video recorder. If it is recorded on the audio track of a video deck or on an audio recorder, it is referred to as Longitudinal Time Code, abbreviated as LTC. Some high-end professional VCRs record SMPTE in the vertical blanking interval between picture frames, so that no audio track is "wasted" for time code. Far less commonly encountered (unless you hang out at state-of-the-art video facilities), this method of recording time code is known as VITC

(Vertical Interval Time Code). One of the advantages that VITC offers is that the time code can be read at very slow speeds or when the tape is stopped; LTC, on the other hand, can be read at high speeds, such as during rewind/fast-forward operations. Most DAT recorders and MDMs typically "create" SMPTE time code by converting the ABS (absolute) time counter information to whatever frame rate is required.

Today, there are several forms of SMPTE time code: 24, 25, 29.97 and 30 frames per second, in standard and drop-frame (DF) varieties. Drop-frame time code regularly deletes frames from its display

Insider's Tip

Whenever you need to make a copy of a tape containing time code, route the time code signal through a "reshaper," a device that takes the incoming time code and generates a fresh new time code signal (at the same frame rate and format) that is recorded on the copy. The reason for this is that SMPTE time code uses a series of square waves to define its time signatures, and these square waves tend to be distorted from each generation of copying. While you're at it, try to avoid sending time code signals through patch bays: The additional connections degrade the signal but, more importantly, SMPTE time code has a nasty, raspy sound that tends to get everywhere you don't want it, including on your audio tracks.

to compensate for the difference between the USA color TV standard of 29.97 fps and what a real-time counter (such as a clock on the wall) would indicate. This difference is 108 frames per hour, so drop-frame time code skips two frames at the end of each minute except for the 10-, 20-, 30-, 40-, 50- and 60-minute marks.

The NTSC color TV standard of 29.97 fps is used in the USA and Japan. PAL, the European television standard, is based on 25 fps. 24 fps code is used primarily in motion-picture applications, since it precisely matches the projection speed used in 16mm and 35mm sound film.

The 30 fps rate was originally used for black-and-white television production, and creates a great deal of confusion because when video professionals talk about 30 fps time code, they are usually referring

SMPTE time code is one of the most confusing, misunderstood issues in the world of audio, even among the most seasoned production veterans.

to 29.97 fps. There are rare instances when actual 30 fps time code is required, such as posting a film that was transferred at 30 fps to video at 30 fps. Generally, if you're scoring a video, stick to 29.97 fps, nondrop-frame code, but for good measure, check with the producer or sound editor before you get too far into the project.

This brings up an interesting point: If you're working on your own projects and don't plan to interface or share tapes with any other facilities, use whatever time code standard you like. However, the moment that tapes leave your domain, such as when you send a time code DAT master to an edit suite or film mixing facility, you'll sleep better knowing that everything is copacetic.

CHAPTER 32

The Whys and Hows of Crossfades

nyone who has ever spliced an analog reel-to-reel tape will appreciate the concept of digital crossfades. When we're discussing crossfades here, we're not talking about the notion of one song slowly blending, or crossfading, into the next. In MDMs, workstations and other digital recording technologies, digital crossfades provide a means of making your punch-ins/-outs, edits and "splices" as seamless as possible.

Basically, the digital crossfade is analogous (pardon the pun) to using an angled splice (as opposed to a straight cut) for editing two pieces of analog tape: The longer the splice, the longer the crossfade.

THE WHYS

So what's the need for variable crossfades, anyway? Well, by matching the crossfade time to the material being recorded or punched in on, you can make the punch as inaudible as possible. Short crossfades are best suited to material where the audio on both sides of the punch is similar, particularly on sounds that have a lot of transients, such as percussion. Conversely, longer crossfades are best when the audio on both sides of the punch is dissimilar.

Longer crossfade times are also useful for cleaning up the tails of notes when you want an audio section to be preceded or followed by silence. For example, let's say you want to trim a sustained synth note at the end of a song. Ending it abruptly would create a chopped sound. However, if you punched from the end of the note into silence (no input on the record end) with a long crossfade time, the result would be a slight decay on the note, which would remove some of the harshness of the cut. A similar procedure could also be used on the beginning of a song, punching in from silence to the beginning of the first note. In this instance, you'd probably want to try a variety of shorter and longer crossfade times, depending on how much of the leading edge of the first note you want to retain.

In many such punch-in/-out applications, an MDM's rehearse feature comes in handy, as it allows you to audition several crossfades before committing the new recorded section to tape.

THE HOWS

Whether they're easily accessible or not, all MDM recorders provide a variety of digital crossfade times. The Akai A-DAM system defaults to a 23ms crossfade time but also offers 12, 46 or 93ms lengths, which are selectable from the DL1200 locator.

While the Alesis BRC offers quick access to four variable crossfade times, the original ADAT, ADAT XT, Fostex CX-8 and Panasonic MDA-1 units have no dedicated switch for this function. Nonetheless, non-BRC ADAT users can still select from four crossfade times (10.67, 21.33, 32 and 42.67ms) when recording at 48kHz. By pressing the Set Locate and Record but-

The digital crossfade is analogous to using an angled splice (as opposed to a straight cut) for editing two pieces of analog tape.

tons simultaneously, the display will read "FAd1" (which means the 10.67ms setting is selected). Press the buttons a second time and "FAd2" is displayed, meaning 21.33ms is selected, and so on for the 32ms and 42.67ms crossfade times. ADAT's default is to the 10.67ms setting.

Like the ADAT, the Fostex RD-8 also provides variable crossfade times of 10.67, 21.33, 32 and 42.67ms. These are accessed from page six of the Main Menu; just press the function keys and select the crossfade time you need.

The Alesis M20 and Studer V-Eight offer a choice of 32 crossfade selections, ranging from 5.4ms to 1,365ms (at 48kHz) or 5.8ms to 1,486ms (at 44.1kHz). The crossfade function is accessed by pressing the Utility key and going to page two. The selected crossfade time is displayed in milliseconds.

The Tascam DA-88 and Sony PCM-800 default to

a setting of 10ms, and eight other crossfade times are available in 10ms increments, up to a maximum time of 90ms. To change crossfade times on the DA-88, hold the Arrow Down key while pressing the Display button. The LED display will show "C.FAdE 10" to indicate that the 10ms time is selected, and the crossfade time will increase by 10ms each time the button is pressed. The Arrow Down key is used to lower the crossfade time. To check the current crossfade time in ABS (absolute) time display mode, hold the Arrow Up key and press the Display button.

Tascam's DA-38 offers up to 150ms of track delay, while the DA-98 provides crossfades from 10ms to a maximum of 200ms, adjustable in 10ms increments. Accessing the delay times can be done either via their front panels or remotely, by using the optional RC-848 controller.

In terms of crossfade times, the Yamaha DMR8 gets the prize, with crossfades adjustable from 1.33 to 2,730ms(!) and a default of 23ms. To change crossfade times on the DMR8, press the Punch-In key (it's in the bank of Record-Mix Mode buttons), press the Shift Next button until the crossfade menu appears on the main display and use the up/down arrows to select the desired crossfade time.

The ability to choose different crossfade times is useful for the professional, and a few minutes experimenting to find the times that work best in your projects will be time well spent. Try it—you may be pleasantly surprised by the results!

CHAPTER 33

Digital Assembly Editing

ASSEMBLY EDITING: ONE EXAMPLE

In this example, we have two takes of a song recorded on the original session tape, with the various sections of each indicated by letters of the alphabet. The song has an intro ("A" or "J" in the diagram) and three verses, each followed by a chorus. By selecting the best sections of the two takes and using the tape offset feature to selectively copy them into a new order, we create the composite master tape at the bottom of the diagram.

The edited version begins with the intro and first verse ("J" and "K") from Take Two, followed by the first chorus ("C") from Take One. In fact, we liked this chorus so much that we used it three times in the song, after the first, second, and third verses. Note that the only sections we used from Take Two were the intro and first verse (sections "J" and "K"). The last chorus ("I") had a retard ending, so "C" would not have been suitable.

ORIGINAL SESSION TAPE　　　　　　　　　　　　**HEAD**

| R | Q | P | O | N | M | L | K | J | | I | H | G | F | E | D | C | B | A |

TAKE TWO　　　　　　　　　　　　**TAKE ONE**

EDITED COMPOSITE MASTER　　　　　　　　　　　　**HEAD**

| | I | H | C | F | C | D | C | K | J |

ithout a doubt, the most powerful attribute of digital multitracking is assembly editing, the process of creating new versions of songs by using simple copy and paste techniques. However, thanks to digital technology, all edits are made on a clone copy of the original. This brings up two important points:

1. As long as the cloning is made in the digital domain, the sound quality should be pristine, as the clone is an *exact* copy of the original.

2. As the edits are made on a copy, the editing process is inherently nondestructive: No matter how many different edited versions are created, the original master tape remains unchanged.

So what's new here? Well, assembly-editing practices do not lend themselves to analog tape recorders, due to the unavoidable generational losses caused when analog tape is copied. If you have a great sounding analog multitrack tape, and you copy certain sections onto another analog tape, the copy is bound to be disappointing. Actually, the digital methods outlined here have been used by leading engineers and producers for years. These techniques are not really that new: Anyone with a couple hundred thousand dollars lying around to purchase two reel-to-reel digital multitracks has had access to this technology for more than a decade.

One advantage of MDM technology is that ownership of multiple digital tape transports is no longer solely in the realm of rich and famous recording superstars. In fact, as soon as you add a second transport to your system (usually to increase the number of recording tracks), you have the ability to do assembly editing. It's an extra bonus that originally you might not have thought about.

HARDWARE REQUIREMENTS

The required tools for assembly editing are a cable for transferring (dubbing) multitrack data in the digital domain, a sync cable for interconnecting the two decks, two similar-format tape transports and a means of offsetting the synchronization between the machines. Oh, and you'll also need at least one extra tape, preferably pre-formatted.

All DTRS format recorders (Tascam DA-88, DA-38, DA-98 and Sony PCM-800) have onboard sync offset functions, so all you'll need are two DTRS format machines and the optional dubbing and sync cables. Note that the Sony PCM-800 doesn't provide TDIF-1 interfacing, so dubbing between a Sony and a Tascam recorder can get fairly complicated, requiring the external Tascam IF-88AE digital interface to connect to the Sony recorder's AES/EBU breakout cable.

The most powerful attribute of digital multitracking is assembly editing, the process of creating new versions of songs by using simple copy and paste techniques.

Fiber-optic (Lightpipe) digital dubbing cables are included with all ADAT-format decks. All ADAT-format recorders are capable of offset recording, except the original "blackface" ADAT, which requires a BRC controller to perform digital assembly. The optional 9-pin sync cable (the same used for any multimachine sync) is also needed for assembly editing.

Multiple decks in the Akai A-DAM system synchronize flawlessly to one another, but creating time offsets between two decks requires an external SMPTE synchronizer, as well as the optional 37-pin dubbing and 50-pin sync cables. The Yamaha DMR8/DRU8 system includes offset capability; just add the optional dubbing and sync cables and you're ready to go. See Chapter 26 for detailed information on digitally interfacing these machines.

A HYPOTHETICAL CASE

Let's say you've used an 8-track system to cut basic tracks for a song entitled "Love, Love: Yeah, Yeah." Tracks are laid out as follows:

Track 1 Kick Drum
Track 2 Snare Drum
Track 3 Cymbals/Toms Left
Track 4 Cymbals/Toms Right
Track 5 Bass Guitar
Track 6 Rhythm Guitar #1
Track 7 Scratch Lead Vocal
Track 8 Click Track

After cutting three sets of basics for "Love, Love: Yeah, Yeah," nobody in the band can agree which is the best. Everybody likes different parts of each so before we start overdubbing on the next eight tracks, we use our 16-track system to do a little assembly editing. As the band cuts the basics to a click (metronome) track, tempo is not a problem (except in a couple bad spots where tempo *was* the problem) so we can pick and choose from the three takes.

We start out by dubbing the intro from take two onto our new clone tape. At this point, intermachine sync is not essential, so we merely advance deck one to the start of take two and dub the tracks to deck two. Unfortunately, during the first verse in take two, one of the following is clearly audible (pick one):

A. Pizza guy ringing the doorbell, or
B. Drummer drops drumstick, or
C. Bassist anticipates a sixteenth note in the four-bar fill, which no one but the bass player can hear.

Due to this disaster of epic proportions, the band finally decides to use the first verse, chorus, second verse and bridge from take three. At the end of the long intro, the time display for our clone on deck two shows a location of 01:14:06 (minutes/seconds/frames). Verse one of take three begins at 19:44:16, so the correct offset required for deck two to start recording precisely when verse one/take three plays is 18:30:10.

This offset is calculated by subtracting the time when the clone starts recording (the punch-in point) from the address of the new material. In this case:

01:14:06 - 19:44:16 = -18:30:10

The offset time is a negative value: The time address from take three is reduced by the offset amount, so that it plays immediately after the 01:14:06 mark on the clone. The length of the added section is 03:03:12, so this composite clone version is now 04:17:18 long.

In a flurry of creative hacking, we decide to put the intro from Take one after the second verse and chorus on the clone. We didn't use this intro in the beginning of the song because the rhythm guitar wasn't very tight with the drums and bass, but now we're using this (we'll mute the unwanted rhythm guitar track in the mix) as a drums/bass bridge into the solo, which will play over the basics in take one, verse one.

Now, the start time for the take one intro and verse is 00:32:05, so to calculate the required offset, we'll subtract this start time from the punch-in point (the end of the cloned section). So we have:

04:17:18 - 00:32:05 = 03:45:13

In this case, the offset time is a positive value: The time address is increased so that the intro/verse from take one precisely follows the composited cloned section. By now, you should have an idea how this works: We're going to allow verse one to continue copying over to the clone (we'll fade it out somewhere when we get to the mix). And now, having edited the basics just the way we want them, we can start overdubbing more tracks, using that second tape transport.

YOUR MILEAGE MAY VARY

Don't you hate those tag lines that are tacked onto the ends of TV commercials? You know, the ones where the announcer speaks as quickly as possible, informing the customer of some important, last-minute details such as, "Batteries not included" or "Your mileage may vary." Given that build-up, here are a couple pointers on assembly editing that are worth emphasizing:

1. Remember that these guidelines for calculating offsets are merely a means of *estimating* an approximate offset time from which you can tweak the exact offset times you need.

2. While fine-tuning the offset times, use the rehearse function, which allows the recorder to punch-in without committing the decision to tape. Once you find the right offset, turn the rehearse function off and let the machine's auto-punch feature handle the dirty work while you concentrate on the creative aspects.

3. Don't forget that selecting the right crossfade time is nearly as important as finding the right offset when it comes to creating a undetectable, seamless edit. (Turn to Chapter 32 for more information on digital crossfades.) Once you've gone through the drudgery of finding the perfect offset, auditioning crossfades is actually fun.

4. And, by the way, your mileage may vary.

CHAPTER 34

MDM: The DAT Editing Tool

ou probably bought an MDM system for music, broadcast or film/video post-production applications. Not once in the prepurchase stage did you consider using an MDM system for DAT editing, and the salespeople probably never mentioned it either. But the rumors are true: A dual-transport MDM system can indeed be used for editing DAT tapes.

DATs and MDMs have a lot in common: Both are cantankerous examples of new technology, with sealed cassettes and slow tape speeds that make them ill-suited for the razor-blade and splicing-tape editing methods. In fact, as MDM and DAT tapes are typically sucked inside some newfangled mechanism, it's even impossible to mark edit points with a grease pencil as the tape goes by.

So how *does* one go about editing a DAT tape? The usual approach has been to digitally transfer the DAT material onto a disk-based recording/editing (workstation) system. This has a lot of advantages, including automated looping, screen-based signal processing (EQ, reverb, etc.), playlist editing and the ability to look at the audio waveform when determining edit points.

However, a major drawback of a workstation system is that large audio files (such as a CD project) require large amounts of memory. Keep in mind that digital audio systems need about 10MB of disk space for every minute of stereo 44.1kHz/16-bit sound. So a one-hour CD project takes up a minimum of 600MB of disk space; that amount is even greater when you figure in the need to keep multiple versions on the disk during the editing process.

Another factor concerning workstations is cost. When packaged with a large hard disk, editing software, DSP hardware and a computer with enough power to adequately handle the job, even the least expensive workstation system may cost as much as adding another MDM transport to your studio.

Don't get me wrong. This is not to say that there's anything wrong with disk-based editing systems. However, if budgets are tight, your MDM system may be able to do some of the same tasks. If your editing needs are fairly simple, such as rearranging the order of DAT tracks or shortening or lengthening songs, then editing via MDM may be just the ticket. You may also consider using your MDM system for making safety copies of your precious DAT mixes, just in case the unthinkable happens.

HERE'S HOW

Assuming your DAT deck has a digital output, you'll need a similar-format interface (AES/EBU or S/PDIF) and a quality cable for transferring the audio into the MDM system in the digital domain. Your MDM system will also need two transports and a way to offset the playback between the two machines.

Another factor to consider is the maximum recording time of your MDM system. Obviously, if you're planning to assemble a full-length CD project, the longer the available recording time, the better. The Tascam DA-88's maximum recording time of 108 minutes (much longer than a CD can hold) is the winner in this category. Recording at 44.1kHz, the ADAT-format decks can record up to 45 minutes on a T-120 S-VHS cassette, 58 minutes on a T-160 cassette (using the T-160 mode, explained in the ADAT section of this book) or 67 minutes on a T-180 tape.

The comparatively short recording times of the Yamaha and Akai systems (approximately 20 minutes) would be unsuitable for CD editing, although these are certainly long enough to edit individual songs, radio spots and other short-form pieces. And, as the Yamaha DMR8 includes an internal digital mixer, crossfading one song over another is simple. In addition, since the signal remains within the digital domain, no signal degradation results from such operations. The onboard signal processing in the DMR8 also provides a lot of creative (and corrective) avenues for signal manipulation before, during and after the editing operations.

Once you've gotten your transports and the proper cables together, load the desired audio from your DAT into the MDM system and then follow the multichannel assembly-editing procedures outlined in Chapter 33. When you're done, simply offload your edited material back to DAT. And there you have it: easy, affordable DAT editing!

CHAPTER 35

The Built-in -10/+4dB Converter

his chapter is written for users of the Alesis ADAT or ADAT XT, Fostex RD-8 or CX-8, Panasonic MDA-1, and Tascam DA-88 or DA-38 systems; everyone else can skip to the next chapter.

One of the nice features built into these seven systems is that they include two sets of analog inputs and outputs, so they can interface with either semipro (-10dB) or professional (+4dB) equipment. In Chapter 25, we already went through the ins and outs of hooking these up to your system, but I left one thing out. I call this the Built-in -10/+4dB Converter.

In any studio, whether world-class or bedroom, there's a lot of gear that comes from a lot of sources. Some may be what industry insiders refer to as semi-pro gear, which means the device is equipped with unbalanced ¼-inch or RCA plugs. Most synthesizers, drum machines and affordable signal processors have inputs and/or outputs operating at -10dB levels, and home stereo gear, such as CD players and cassette decks, also falls into this category.

If you're confused about balanced and unbalanced lines, don't worry: Mozart couldn't understand the difference between the two either, and his music turned out OK.

The so-called "professional" devices operate at +4dB levels and typically have balanced 3-conductor lines with XLR or ¼-inch TRS (tip-ring-sleeve) connectors. Balanced lines operate by carrying three signal wires: a ground (shield) conductor, a wire

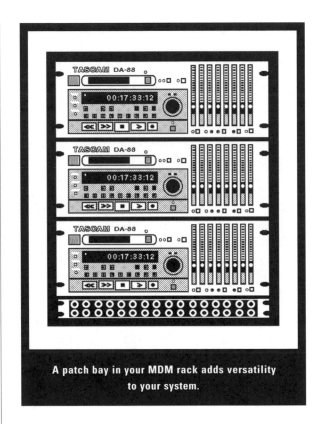

A patch bay in your MDM rack adds versatility to your system.

carrying the "normal" signal and another conductor carrying a phase-inverted copy of the signal. When the audio reaches its destination, the phase of the inverted copy is reversed, and this reversed signal is combined with the "normal" signal. This way, the original signal is made stronger, while any noise picked up along the line is canceled out. This is one of the reasons the signal from a balanced-line microphone can run through a 100-foot snake without ill effects, while running the unbalanced output of a bass guitar through a 25-foot cable is asking for trouble. The main advantage of a balanced line is this hum-rejection ability, along with the capability of sending audio over long cable runs without appreciable losses.

If you're confused about balanced and unbalanced lines, don't worry: Mozart couldn't understand the difference between the two either, and his music turned out OK. The key point to remember here is that there are two different systems in this world, and like it or not, you'll probably have to deal with both of them. The main problem you'll run across is level mismatch. Connect the relatively low output from a synth into an MDM's +4dB input and you'll barely get the LED meter to light up. At one time, there was a clear differentiation between pro and semi-pro products, but in today's studio, just about anything is bound to show up anywhere.

Today, more and more affordable mixers are incorporating balanced-line inputs for tape sends and returns, so taking advantage of an MDM system's balanced inputs and outputs is a possibility. However, if you want to record a sampler, synth, drum machine or other -10dB device, you have several options:

1. Connect the source to the console and boost its level up to the recorder's +4dB input.
2. Reach around to the back of your MDM rack and plug the source directly into the -10dB input on the recorder.
3. Install a patch bay at the bottom of your MDM rack and wire the patch bay points to the -10dB inputs on your recorder. This way, whenever you want to connect a -10dB device to your deck, it can be done easily from the front panel.

Obviously, number 3 offers the most possibilities. For example, you could install a patch bay with 32 ¼-inch jacks on the front and either RCA (if you have an Alesis XT or a Fostex, Panasonic or Tascam deck) or ¼-inch (for the original Alesis ADAT) jacks on the back. If you have a 16-track system, the 32 patch bay jacks could be divided between inputs and outputs for the most flexibility. However, the main attraction of the patch bay in the rack is access to the inputs, so if you eventually expand your system to 24 or 32 tracks, the patch bay could be reconfigured to handle inputs exclusively.

I suggest placing the patch bay in the bottom of the rack. That way, when the patch cords droop downwards, they won't obscure the MDM meters or controls.

Another advantage to the patch-bay-in-a-rack approach is convenience. Let's say a client or friend comes over one day with a rack of MIDI gear and wants to track. With the patch bay under the decks, it's a simple matter of plug and go. You don't have to reconfigure two-thirds of your board's wiring every time one of these sessions comes along. And, of course, anything coming directly into the MDM can be monitored through the tape inputs on your console.

It couldn't be easier.

CHAPTER 36

Mix to MDM!

What? You must be out of your mind! You don't mix to a multitrack! Mix to DAT, OK. Mix to cassette, maybe. But why would anyone in their right mind mix to multitrack?

There are lots of reasons, lots of *good* reasons, why we might want to mix to multitrack, or perhaps I should clarify that by saying *digital* multitrack.

Foremost on anyone's mind is money. After plunking down the bucks for your MDM system, you might not have enough money to buy a DAT deck, so by kissing off a couple tracks, you can access most of the advantages of DAT mastering at no cost. Another plus is that the final mix is stored along with the multitrack masters. And the money you *don't* spend on a DAT deck could provide a sizable down payment towards another MDM for your system.

> *There are lots of reasons,*
> *lots of good reasons, why we*
> *might want to mix to*
> *multitrack.*

Also, by recording to MDM, your mixes are already in the recorder format, so if you later want to edit the stereo tracks or sequence several songs, you're already set to start assembly-editing the tracks, as outlined in Chapter 33.

THE LONG-FORM AUTO-PUNCH
Let's say you're working on a long-form project such as a 20-minute instructional cassette program. Your system has 16 tracks, two of which will be devoted to the mix, leaving you with a remainder of 14: one for a narrator, four for sound effects and nine for music.

When you mix a three-minute song, you may run the tune down a dozen times before getting it right. But a dozen run-throughs of a 20-minute pro-

gram quickly adds up to a lot of time. So if you make a small mistake during the mix, do you live with it or make another arduous pass, hoping you get a perfect mix the next time?

If you're mixing to MDM, you don't have to face that decision, because the mix is automatically synched to the multitrack. Therefore, you can rewind to a spot before the mistake and punch into the mix. If you want, you can also use the MDM's auto-punch feature, perhaps even punching out after the missed cue or other mistake. This approach would be difficult or impossible using a separate mixdown deck. In this case, mixing to MDM turns out to be a real time saver.

CHAPTER 37

MDM: The Multichannel Mix Format

hroughout most of this book, I've talked about the promise of MDM technology and how cool it is as a replacement for pricey analog and digital multitracks. Now we're going to take a look at MDM technology as a multichannel mixdown medium.

LIGHTS, ACTION...MDM

Ironically, with all the interest in creating stereo soundtracks for film and video, there is no universally accepted format for storing 4- and 6-channel mixes created for film/video releases. Why not MDM? Offering sparkling audio in a portable, easily synchronizable package, an MDM deck is ideally suited to the task.

In fact, at the Fall 1991 AES Convention in New York City, a group of Mitsubishi engineers presented a technical paper on the development of a dual-mode digital recorder/player (four tracks at 96kHz or eight tracks at 48kHz) that would store up to 2.7 hours of audio on ½-inch video cassettes. Designed for specialized HDTV broadcast and exhibition applications, the system would have been the first compact, video-based digital audio transport (i.e., MDM) to be used as a medium for storing and playing multichannel mixes. The Mitsubishi system never got past the prototype stage, but today's MDMs should be able to fill the bill.

First, some words about motion-picture and television sound. Stereo motion-picture sound has been around since the days of Disney's 1939 classic *Fantasia*, which used multiple interlocked optical film transports synchronized with the projector to achieve its landmark 6-channel stereo presentation. In the 1950s, 4-channel 35mm and 6-channel 70mm films became popular, although the special prints, coated with thin stripes of magnetic material along the sprocket holes, were fragile, expensive to make and required film distributors to maintain a dual inventory of mono and stereo prints. The system was less than perfect, but it persisted for many years.

Under this system, a 35mm stereo theatrical film begins with a 4-channel mix, known as LCRS, which includes Left, Center and Right channels (located behind the movie screen) and a mono Surround channel, which is routed to speakers along the back and side theater walls.

In the 1970s, Dolby unveiled its Dolby Stereo system, which took the LCRS channels and used a matrixing system to encode the four channels into a stereo pair. This stereo pair is printed as two optical tracks that are placed close together so that they are picked up as a single mono signal in theaters not equipped for stereo. In a Dolby Stereo-equipped theater, a two-channel optical pickup sends the signal to a Dolby Cinema Processor, which decodes the two matrixed channels back into the original LCRS channels.

There is no universally accepted format for storing 4- and 6-channel mixes created for film/video releases. Why not MDM?

The Dolby Stereo prints are playback-compatible with mono theaters, so film distributors do not need to stock separate inventories of stereo and mono prints. Also, once the original stereo sound negatives are made, the costs of producing a stereo print are identical to making a mono print. For these reasons, film studios became very interested in stereo films, and with the success of early Dolby Stereo releases such as *Star Wars* and *Close Encounters of the Third Kind*, an increasing number of theaters began upgrading for stereo playback.

So what does this mean to the typical project studio? Well, for one thing, any Dolby-Stereo film released on a stereo video cassette also retains all the matrixed information for decoding 4-channel playbacks, and consumer interest in 4-channel home theater playback systems is on the rise. Because of this, opportunities for creating stereo soundtracks for lower-budget video productions may be available to the independent audio engineer/producer. Once you've mixed a project to the LCRS components (plus a time code track), it's possible to get access to a Dolby surround encoder (either through a rental company or by booking a couple hours at a larger studio that has one) and transferring the LCRS tracks to a Dolby-encoded pair for playback to the video master.

Fortunately, MDMs are fairly portable, so if you go to a larger studio for the transfer, bring your machine along with you, just in case the studio doesn't have the same type of deck you own. Another alternative is Rocktron's Circle Sound™ system, which offers a line of affordable surround-compatible encoders/decoders for the small studio market.

MDM-DVD

Whether you call it Digital Video Disc or Digital Versatile Disc, the DVD format includes audio storage (either standalone or with pictures) in the 5.1 surround format. Simply put, 5.1 includes five tracks (for the standard LCR left/center/right channels with stereo surround) *and* a separate subwoofer channel (the ".1" part of the designation). There aren't a lot of 6-track recorders around, but an 8-channel MDM has ample tracks and even leaves two channels left for SMPTE time code and popcorn.

While we're on the subject of 5.1, MDM is ideal for storing 5.1 mixes for use in the new digital theater release formats such as Dolby Digital and SDS (Sony Digital Sound). With MDMs, a new mix format is born!

OTHER MULTICHANNEL MIX APPLICATIONS

MDM systems provide an ideal storage format for multichannel playback systems in other situations as well. These include multichannel sound effects for theatrical applications, specialized exhibits such as planetariums, museums and conventions, and dozens more. To add an extra dollop of pizzazz, unused audio tracks could be used for recording automated sync-tone pulses for controlling slide projectors; while we're at it, a MIDI-equipped MDM or a recorded time code track routed through a SMPTE-to-MIDI converter could trigger MIDI Show Control data for lighting and other special effects. The possibilities are endless.

CHAPTER 38

Track Bouncing, Revisited

rack bouncing is one of the oldest tricks in the book. For those unfamiliar with the technology, I'll explain how it works before I get to the really cool ways to do it in the MDM milieu.

Let's say you're working on an 8-track recorder, which could be analog or digital at this point, and you need more tracks (doesn't everyone?). You've recorded the first six:

1. Kick Drum
2. Snare
3. Toms and Cymbals Left
4. Toms and Cymbals Right
5. Bass Guitar
6. Rhythm Guitar

Now you submix the six tracks down to a stereo pair on Tracks seven and eight. Once you get the perfect submix, you record over the original six tracks, replacing them with new sounds. At the end of the session, you now have:

1. Synth (mono)
2. Lead Guitar
3. Lead Vocal
4. Background Vocal
5. Background Vocal
6. Percussion
7. Stereo Submix Left
8. Stereo Submix Right

So we've recorded a total of 12 tracks on our little 8-track.

The main problem with bouncing analog tracks is that they noticeably degrade in sound quality whenever you bounce them into another generation. With a digital system, however, the effect of track bouncing on the audio quality is negligible: It's there, but it's extremely subtle compared to analog bouncing.

Of course, the major drawback to traditional track bouncing is that once those original tracks are erased, they are gone forever. So if mixing the final version of our song above, you decide that the bass guitar is too low or that the snare is too loud, you're out of luck. This isn't to say that bouncing is impossible, but you have to be *really* careful about that submix.

If you still need more tracks, you can always

record eight tracks in the original session, mix them to DAT, and then copy the DAT tape onto two tracks of a new tape. This method gives you six more tracks, and if you later decide you don't like the submix, you can redo it and start over from that point.

The major drawback to traditional track bouncing is that once those original tracks are erased, they are gone forever.

BOUNCING, MDM-STYLE

Track bouncing on an MDM system offers new avenues for fun and excitement. As I mentioned earlier, when you're working on a digital multitrack, the degradation effects of track bouncing are substantially reduced. MDM also offers other advantages.

Let's look at an example similar to the 8-track case presented above: You record six tracks and submix to Tracks seven and eight. Now, just to be sure, you call up a friend who has a similar-format machine (as explained in Chapter 24) and make an exact digital clone of the tracks. Later, working on the clone (so the original tracks remain intact) you record over Tracks one through five but, during the process, you realize that the snare in the submix isn't loud enough. Rather than start over, you bounce the two background vocal tracks into a mono track on Track six. Then you borrow your friend's machine and sync the two decks.

At this point, you have two options:

1. Mix the tune while you have the two decks available. You have the choice of mixing from the submix on tape two (adding more of the snare from tape one) or ignoring the submix entirely and using the other tracks to mix.
2. Use the second deck to transfer the snare from

tape one onto the background vocal (tape two, Track four); since you have a blended background vocal on Track six, Track five is now available for overdubbing the percussion part.

Whichever you might choose, you get the idea: MDM bouncing has a lot to offer. In fact, if you have a 16-track system, things get even more flexible. For example, you could record 12 tracks and mix them down to two stereo submixes, possibly with one for stereo drums and the other for the rest of the rhythm section. By cloning tape two, you could begin the process of replacing sounds on the four available tracks. Drop a new tape into deck one and you have another eight tracks to work with. The number of tracks recorded on this session would be 24 (12 + 4 + 8), and if you needed access to the original 12 tracks, any of these could be digitally transferred to open tracks on the clones.

Finally, when combined with synchronized MIDI tracks, the multi-MDM bouncing process gets really fun, really fast. Need more tracks? No problem with MDM.

CHAPTER 39

The Submix Sync Trick

ere's an idea that isn't really all that clever. In fact, if Sherlock Holmes were alive to comment on the Submix Sync Trick (assuming he ever lived in the first place), his observation would be, "I was expecting something ingenious; this is ingenuous."

Still, this technique will speed up your productions, extend the lives of your machines and make your life a lot easier. Best of all, it's free!

The Submix Sync Trick requires two or more machines, so only users with access to multiple transports will be able to take advantage of this. In fact, the more transports in your system, the more you'll need to use the Submix Sync Trick. You'll also need sync cables to interlock your decks. Ready? Here's how it works.

This technique will speed up your productions, extend the lives of your machines and make your life a lot easier. Best of all, it's free!

Let's assume you have a three-transport, 24-track system. After you've cut the basic tracks (say, on ten tracks) you create a scratch submix (mono should work nicely) on the last track of your second transport. As you begin overdubbing on Tracks 11-15, use the scratch track on Track 16 as a reference, and you won't need to run both transports during the overdubs. Once you've filled all 15 tracks, you can go back to dual-transport operation and replace the scratch mix on Track 16 with something else. When you start working on the final eight tracks, you can make another quick scratch mix, put it on Track 24 and continue the single-machine overdubs.

By now, you should get the idea. In addition to reducing wear and tear on your decks, the Submix Sync Trick also cuts down on the transport lockup time. You'll really notice this when you're working in a system that's synchronized to an external time code source.

Overdubs also become much more pleasant when the engineer has only a few tracks rather than 16, 24, 32 or more to worry about when setting up the performers' monitor mixes.

You'll benefit from this trick whether you have a 2- or 16-module system. As an added plus, the amount of mechanical noise emanating from the transports really drops when the number of on-line decks is cut from three (or more) to just one.

So give the Submix Sync Trick a try, and tell 'em you heard it from an old friend in the detective business. The game's afoot!

CHAPTER 40

Megatracking Without Bouncing

ere's where it all comes together: By combining most of the techniques we've learned so far, you can make your MDM system into a production powerhouse. Now, this chapter could be just a cheap setup for talking about virtual tracking, but it's not. Oh, I lied about the "Without Bouncing" part in the title, because some these techniques also involve the submix sync trick (see Chapter 39) style of bouncing to create a scratch track. However, these "bounced" tracks never appear in your finished work, so maybe I was just bending the truth rather than lying.

To start with, there are lots of ways to get more tracks: You could buy more transports, sync to MIDI or bounce tracks. But there are even more alternatives.

SINGLE-TRANSPORT MEGATRACKING

Unfortunately, this first method requires finding a second (similar-format) transport for long enough to make a few quick scratch mixes and maybe a couple clones of your tracks. This could be accomplished via the buddy system (see Chapter 24), renting a machine or booking time at a studio that has a system like yours.

Having started out with eight tracks, you find you need more. Buy a bunch of blank tapes, format them and make a couple of work copies; synchronous copies of your original tapes that contain a temporary "scratch" mix on one or two tracks, leaving the other six or seven tracks available for recording.

Once you have several work copies, return the borrowed machine or end your session at the bigger studio. When you get back to your little single-transport system, do overdubs on the work copies. After you've filled the tracks or completed your overdubs, whichever comes first, you're ready to mix, which will again require borrowing or renting additional transports or booking time at a larger studio.

If the latter is your option, you can sleep easy knowing that you've done as much as you could at home. This way, you got to take as much time as necessary to get your tracks done the way you want, without the constant sound of a cash register ringing up overtime in the background. Then, working at a nicer studio, you can complete the mix (usually the shortest phase in a project) and have access to a decent console, gobs of cool outboard gear and an experienced engineer. It's the best of both worlds.

MULTIMACHINE MEGATRACKING

It's funny, but some things are always true, no matter how big your studio. There's some peculiar law that states that if you need X number of tracks, then the number available will always be exactly X minus one. Yet, with a multitransport MDM system, we can usually get around such limitations without the obvious solution of renting or borrowing machines.

By combining most of the techniques we've learned so far, you can make your MDM system into a production powerhouse.

There's a method I refer to as "megataking." No, it's not a typo for megatracking; this useful technique allows you to do as many *takes* of a track as you want, limited only by your tape budget.

Let's assume you have a 24-track system, and you've filled all the tracks. On playback, you wonder if the sax solo on Track 22 could be better. It's the classic producer's dilemma: "Should we erase a perfectly good take on the chance that we could do a better one?" You're out of tracks, so this is no easy decision. Fortunately, you're working on an MDM system, so you do a little megataking (not to be confused with *meditating*, which is recommended after a tough session).

Grab a new, pre-formatted tape and make a clone copy of Tape three, containing Tracks 17-24. Now replace tape three with the clone, and you can record over the old solo on the clone without jeopardizing the original performance. Once you get a performance you like, you can either keep it or stick with the original solo. If you're really undecided, you can continue this process with as many clones as you wish.

Another variation of the megataking technique involves making a clone of tape three and then filling all of the tracks *except* Track 22 with different sax solos. Later, the producer could pick from these and copy the selected track onto Track 22 of the original tape. As an alternative, the engineer could do an assembly edit, copying the best sections from different solos into one seamless composite performance on clone Track 22, and then copying the composite back onto Track 22 of the original tape.

I have found these megataking techniques to be especially useful for lead vocals, where I have the opportunity to choose, say, the first verse and chorus from take one, the bridge from take two/track two, and the second and third verses and choruses from take three/track three. With a little cutting and pasting, just about any vocalist can sound like Pavarotti. Well, *sort of* like Pavarotti.

CHAPTER 41

The Workstation-MDM Connection

MDMs are the ideal adjunct to any workstation system.

In 1985, the first commercial disk-based digital audio recording/editing system appeared on the market. Known as SoundDroid, it was developed by a team of visionaries working at Lucasfilm. It was years (Han Solo would have said "12 parsecs") ahead of its time. It was revolutionary. It was a complete commercial failure.

But don't be too quick to fault the creators or the product. The concept of storing audio inside a computer and manipulating it onscreen was a little too outré for the audio community of 1985. Eventually, audio producers and engineers did get hip to the idea of the digital audio workstation and, today, such products are offered by dozens of manufacturers worldwide.

Predictions from the 1985 era stated that ten years hence, tape transports would be dead, analog recording would be forgotten and we'd all be storing audio on biocubes. Well, that day has long since come

and gone: Tape is still with us, high-end analog systems still reverberate in the very souls of audiophiles, and biocubes...well, the jury is still out on that one. Check back around the year 2005, and I'll tell you all about it.

Meanwhile, the tape-versus-disk argument has been settled: Each has its relative strengths and weaknesses, and there's plenty of room for both technologies in this here town, pardner.

Certainly, the best thing about tape is that it is an inexpensive, removable medium with enormous storage potential. The Tascam DA-88 packs over 4GB of storage (more than 4,300MB) on a tape that costs under ten dollars. I don't know if you've priced 4GB hard drives lately, but they ain't cheap! So, using a multichannel disk-based system to record weekly garage-band rehearsals and keep all the recordings would quickly become a very expensive proposition.

However workstations do certain things very well, and such systems provide an excellent complement to any MDM system.

For one, while MDMs offer multichannel assembly editing, the process (outlined in Chapter 33) can be tedious when it involves looping-type chores. Let's say you have four tracks of drums (kick, snare and a stereo mix of toms and cymbals) and you want a four-bar pattern to repeat through the entire song. (Don't worry, you can always overdub some live percussion later so the drums don't sound so sterile.)

The tape-versus-disk argument has been settled: Each has its relative strengths and weaknesses, and there's plenty of room for both technologies.

At 120 beats per minute in 4/4 time, the four-bar section would need to repeat every eight seconds, which means 30 repeats for a four-minute song. With a linear (tape-based) system, building this track would take over an hour. On a disk-based system, it could be completed in minutes, including transferring the material from the MDM to the workstation, editing and setting the loop points, experimenting with a couple of crossfade times and transferring the loop back onto the MDM.

Workstations also excel in the accuracy of screen-based editing systems, many of which have the ability to zoom into the waveform to the point where individual samples are visible. As such, workstations are an excellent complement to an MDM system, especially when the two can be synchronized via SMPTE or other methods. If a singer flubs a single note in a chorus, that section can be transferred in sync to the workstation, where a snip from another chorus can be inserted into the edit point for a flawless transition.

Other corrective surgery made possible via the workstation-MDM connection includes the removal of occasional clicks, pops or other problems, either through the "cut and paste" method or through DSP functions features such as the ability to redraw a flawed section of a waveform or pitch-shift correction on less-than-perfect vocal notes.

CHAPTER 42

The No-Console Tracking Trick

his technique is more an application than a trick, but "The No-Console Tracking Application" just didn't seem like a zingy enough title.

THE ANALOG SIDE

One of the neatest things about digital recording is the incredible clarity of the sounds it captures and reproduces. However, digital also has an amazing ability to capture every bit of hissing, buzzing and other forms of audio distortion created by everything else in the recording chain. Some of these may come from your console, so when you plug a mic into the board, you should make sure that the audio runs through the shortest possible pathway (meaning the least amount of circuitry) on its way to the recorder.

There is a common myth that consoles require one bus (subgroup) for each tape track, but this is simply not true.

There are several ways to achieve this. The simplest, although not necessarily the cheapest, is to buy two or more channels (they're usually sold in pairs) of high-quality, external mic preamplification. Plug the microphone into the preamp, connect the preamp to the input(s) on the MDM, and away you go. Of course, instruments and other sources with line-level outputs can usually connect directly to the MDM without a mic preamp.

If the console preamps are good quality, you should certainly use them, but whenever you are printing mono mic sources (or two single mics used as a stereo pair), you should connect the MDM inputs for those tracks to the direct output or insert point send from the mixer channel. The signal will go through the least amount of circuitry on its way to the MDM, resulting in a cleaner, clearer track.

One problem with modern mixing consoles is that they are typically designed for the convenience of the operator. There is a common myth that consoles require one bus (subgroup) for each tape track, but this is simply not true. Still, I have witnessed numerous sessions (including some for major-label artists) where the engineer, through ignorance or neglect, has routed all the signals through the buses. Yuck!

Let's look at a "typical" recording setup (believe me, there really is no such thing), with a 16-channel mixer with eight buses and an 8-track MDM recorder. We're just laying down eight tracks of basics on this session; we'll bring in a second deck later for the vocals and solo overdubs.

The channel assignments (inputs) on the mixer are as follows:
1. Kick (direct out to tape Track one)
2. Snare (direct out to tape Track two)
3. Hi-hat (bused into mixer subgroup 1/2)
4. Overhead L (bused into mixer subgroup 1/2)
5. Overhead R (bused into mixer subgroup 1/2)
6. Tom 1 (bused into mixer subgroup 1/2)
7. Tom 2 (bused into mixer subgroup 1/2)
8. Tom 3 (bused into mixer subgroup 1/2)
9. Gong (bused into mixer subgroup 1/2)
10. Bass (direct out to tape Track five)
11. Rhythm guitar (direct out to tape Track six)
12. Organ (bused into mixer subgroup 3/4)
13. Piano L (bused into mixer subgroup 3/4)
14. Piano R (bused into mixer subgroup 3/4)
15. Synth L (bused into mixer subgroup 3/4)
16. Synth R (bused into mixer subgroup 3/4)

So the track assigns on the MDM are:
1. Kick
2. Snare
3. Drum Submix Left (from sub one)
4. Drum Submix Right (from sub two)
5. Bass
6. Rhythm Guitar
7. Keys Submix Left (from sub three)
8. Keys Submix Right (from sub four)

The moral of the story is that even though we're using an 8-bus mixer, we only had to use four buses. If we were lazy, we could have used those eight subs for everything, but with a little extra patching, the kick, snare, bass and rhythm guitar are cleaner than they would have been running through the subgroups.

THE DIGITAL SIDE

Now that you're all excited about mic preamps, we can talk about digital converters or, more specifically, analog-to-digital converters. As their name suggests, these devices convert analog input signals coming into the tape deck to digital signals. The ADCs in MDMs are really good stuff: On a scale of 0–100, I'd give them an 85. Back in high school, that equated to somewhere between a B and a B+; these will do the job every time and do it well. However, if you're interested in picking up an extra ten points or so (extra credit, if you will) and reaching the 95 mark, you'll need a high-performance external ADC.

Now, such performance doesn't come cheap, but if you're willing to shell out $1,000 or more, you can get an ultra-high-quality outboard ADC and bypass the internal converters on any two adjacent channels. An ADC's output is either AES/EBU or S/PDIF, and both of these digital interface standards specify that the signal be carried as a stereo pair, so the output of the ADC will be routed to any pair of adjacent inputs: 1/2, 3/4, 5/6, 7/8, etc.

And while we're spending money, you should also know that only the Yamaha DMR8 includes digital inputs, so if you have an Akai, Alesis, Fostex or Tascam unit, you'll have to buy an optional AES/EBU or S/PDIF adapter in order to use an external converter. However, there is a growing number of analog-to-digital converters and mic preamplifier/converter combo units on the market, offering optional ADAT Lightpipe and/or TDIF-1 digital outputs and optional AES/EBU and S/PDIF digital outputs, such as the AD1000E from Apogee Electronics (Santa Monica, CA).

While adding an external ADC is not an inexpensive proposition, the extra margin of performance may appeal to those who seek the ultimate. As an extra inducement, remember that once you've used the converter to cut your MDM tracks, you can also use it in the mix to bypass the converters in your DAT machine. It's worth considering.

CHAPTER 43

Track Delay: Who Needs It?

ne of the most interesting yet misunderstood features on MDM systems is track delay. This function is available on the Akai, Fostex, Panasonic, Studer, Tascam, Yamaha and all but one of the Alesis ADAT systems right out of the box (the original Alesis ADAT needs the BRC controller to access its track delay feature). Most of the recorder manuals mention something about the wonderful advantage of sliding tracks in or out of the "pocket" or groove, which looks great on the brochure but in truth offers almost nothing.

So why can't we use track delay to fix a drummer who's out of the pocket? If the drummer's out of the pocket, then that player's timing is probably inconsistent, and no amount of track delay will help out. Even if the drummer's timing was steady but somehow out of the pocket, you'd have to delay not only the snare track, but also any other mics that could pick up the "bleed-through" of the snare sound, like the rhythm guitar, kick, overheads, hi-hat, toms, etc. By the time you delayed all those tracks to compensate for the snare, any direct (non-miked) tracks, such as electronic keyboards and bass guitar, would then be out of the pocket. Get a decent drummer (preferably one who also knows how to tune a drum kit), and your sessions will be heaven.

FUN WITH TRACK DELAY

The most obvious use for delay is as an effect. If you have an extra track (or tracks) left over when you're ready to mix, copy a track that you'd like to delay, such as a lead vocal, guitar or solo sax. When you mix, assign a track delay to the "new" track, bring it into a console input and treat it as you would any other track. Then adjust the delay to taste. If you think that this application seems obvious, think back to the last few mixes you've done: Was there an empty track slot you could have used for a delay effect? Probably!

Track delay can come in handy in post-production applications: If that door slam or gunshot comes in a little too soon, then track delay may fix the problem. Unfortunately, track delay has a limited range (under a fifth of a second), and the delay won't help if the

effect comes in too late. The latter could be addressed by delaying all the other tracks, but if you're doing a video project, this may put everything else out of sync. In such cases, it may be better to try "time-shifting" the track by using assembly editing with a second MDM or flying in/out via a workstation.

If the drummer's out of the pocket, then that player's timing is probably inconsistent, and no amount of track delay will help out.

Track delay can also be used as a corrective measure when you've replaced a drum part with a MIDI sample. For example, I frequently record drum parts using an electronic kick drum combined with a standard acoustic kit. Sometimes I'll decide to change the kick sound by using the playback of the kick track (not to be confused with a click track) to trigger a new sound, using an outboard trigger-to-MIDI converter such as my Roland Octapad or Alesis D5. Unfortunately, any triggered MIDI replacement suffers a slight but perceptible delay; with an MDM system, you can delay all the tracks *except* the kick to compensate for the difference. Depending on the MIDI system you're using, such delays are typically in the 3-15ms range.

As there is no bleed-through into other mics from the electronic kick drum, I can later change the kick *pattern*, sometimes putting in a new part that replaces the typical half-note (beats one and three) pattern with a steady quarter-note kick or something cooler, maybe triplets or alternating dotted eighths. Whatever you do, it's always easier to slip a track when there's no bleed-through to spoil the effect.

DELAY AS PHASE CORRECTION

Compared to electricity and light, which move at 186,000 miles per second, sound creeps along at just over 1,100 feet per second. When we see lightning strike, we can count the numbers 1001, 1002, 1003, 1004, 1005, and, if we hear thunder after that five-second count, we know that the strike was about one mile (5,280 feet) away. Now, armed with the fact that sound moves about 1,100 feet per second, we know that it would move approximately one foot in one millisecond, or 1/1000 of a second. Who cares? You should, and here's why.

When recording two tracks of bass guitar (combining a direct box with a miked amplifier) a time delay occurs, because the direct-box signal arrives sooner than the signal that goes through the amp, out of the speaker and into the mic. It's only a couple milliseconds but combining these usually results in a muddy sound. Adding a slight delay to the direct-box track will improve the sound immensely, making it full and powerful.

The same technique can be applied to guitar tracks. I've done sessions where I've combined two guitar mics; one a foot away from the amp, the other 20 feet away. By applying a 20ms delay to the close mic track, the result is a massive sound where the reverb of the ambient mic occurs simultaneously with the sharp attack of the close mic. Guitarists love this one.

Drums also benefit from track-delay adjustment. When recording drum tracks, try delaying the close mics on snare, hi-hat and toms to align with the overhead and/or room mics. So, if the room mics are 20 feet back and the overheads are 3 feet above the kit, add a 20ms delay to the close mics and a 17ms (20 feet minus 3 feet) delay to the two overheads, and you'll really notice the difference. If you are using only overheads, with no long-distance room mics, then delay the sound of the close-miked tracks by 3ms or so.

When doing live jazz, choral or orchestral recording, the close mics can be delayed to coincide with the sound arriving at the back-of-hall or audience mics. As a first estimate, use the formula of 1ms of delay per foot of separation distance. The best part about track delay is that experimentation can be done during the mix, when you normally have the most time to experiment with different combinations. Be creative!

CHAPTER 44

Fun With Pitch Shifting

ost professional recorders are capable of pitch shifting, or changing their playback speed, to compensate for variations in tuning or timing. Unfortunately, MDM decks can't play at half-speed, so if you're planning to remake "The Chipmunk Song," you'll have to go analog. However, the pitch-shift range of MDMs (Akai, ±6 percent; Alesis ADAT/XT/Panasonic MDA-1/Fostex CX-8, +6/-16 percent; Fostex RD-8, ±6 percent; Tascam/Sony, ±6 percent; and Yamaha, ±10 percent) is wide enough to handle a variety of other (non-chipmunk) situations.

Although the ADAT normally has a pitch-shift limitation of +100 cents, you can instantly set the pitch shift to +200 cents by simultaneously pressing the Set Locate and Pitch keys. This is the only way to pitch up to +200 cents. If you want to access +199 cents you're out of luck, as whenever the Pitch button is pressed while in +200 cents mode, the ADAT automatically reverts back to its +100 maximum. Unfortunately, this feature cannot be selected in the middle of a recording, but this is one of the best hidden ADAT functions.

One major difference between MDMs is the way that they numerically define a change in pitch. Some display pitch changes in terms of percentage, others define pitch changes in terms of musical cents while others allow users to define pitch changes in cents or percentage values.

The pitch conversion charts in this chapter list some approximations of percent-to-cents and cents-to-percent values. It's not a linear scale: The change in frequency from one note to the next is determined by multiplying the frequency of the first note by the 12th root of two, which is approximately 1.059. If you're confused by the math, just use the chart.

Everybody understands the concept of percentage, but for those who didn't take Music Theory 101, here's the 30-second lowdown on cents. As defined in terms of the traditional Western (meaning as opposed to Eastern, not country and western) music scale, an octave is divided into 12 notes, or semitones. Each semitone is divided into 100 cents, so there are 1,200 cents in an octave. Therefore, if we want to go

up one semitone, say from C to C#, that is a change of +100 cents. Mathematically, this works out to be approximately six percent.

Obviously, defining pitch changes in cents is extremely useful from a musical standpoint. For example, a beginning guitar player may hate a song that has the chords B, E and F#. However, the same tune could be recorded with a C, F and G chord pattern using a 100-cent pitch change. When the recorded tracks are played back at normal pitch, the chords are transposed to B, E and F#.

Pitch shifting can really save the day when the 30-second radio spot you're creating comes in at 32 seconds.

Pitch shifting is also useful when you record a song that is not precisely at concert pitch and want to overdub a difficult-to-retune instrument, such as an acoustic piano, Fender Rhodes, Wurlitzer electric piano, pipe organ or accordion. Just bump the pitch control up or down until you find the correct tuning. This trick is also a lifesaver when your song is at exact concert pitch and you want to add an instrument such as an ocarina, whistle or gong that has a pitch that is slightly off or conflicts with the song. Or say you've got a singer who just can't hit a certain high note. Try bumping the pitch control down a bit when recording, and they'll think you're a recording genius.

I occasionally use pitch shifting to alter the tempo of basic tracks, making them faster or slower. The pitch of the other instruments may make those tracks unusable, but the drums should be OK. For example, when tracking basics with bass, drums and an electric keyboard, I may elect to do a pitch change on the track and just keep the drums, replacing the bass and keys parts later. However, make sure that all later overdubs are made with the decks set at the proper pitch shift and jot it down on your tape log, track sheet or tape box.

The simple pitch-shift control can also improve the fidelity of your tracks. If you're concerned about getting the ultimate fidelity out of your MDMs, then pitch shift them all the way up during recording and mixing. This has the net effect of increasing the machine's sampling rate, and, as we all know from reading Chapter 2 (you *did* read Chapter 2 didn't you?), this will increase the frequency response of the deck by a couple thousand Hertz or so, which makes an audible improvement in performance. However, the drawback is that the tape's running time will be decreased by whatever amount you increased the pitch. If you use this technique, mark the tapes clearly, so you'll know what to do if you work on them at some later time.

On a non-musical note, pitch shifting can really save the day when the 30-second radio spot you're creating comes in at 32 seconds. When you mix, speed up the tape slightly and you'll be right on time. There will be a slight change in the musical key, tempo and timbre of the narrator's voice, but 99 times out of 100, no one will notice. And if the spot is for a local drag strip, stereo store or used-car lot, who's gonna care?

Another cool application is speeding up or slowing down the tape speed for recording sound effects. Bump it all the way up before recording and you can stretch out sounds such as explosions, gunshots and the like while emphasizing the lower frequencies of the sound. Pitch shift down before recording and you get the opposite effect: faster, shorter, shriller and more staccato. This gives a wonderful bite to things like glass breaking or fingernails going down a chalkboard. Screeeech!

Pitch Change Conversion Tables

%	Cents	Cents	%
+15	+242	+1200	+100
+14	+227	+1100	+89
+13	+212	+1000	+78
+12	+196	+900	+68
+11	+181	+800	+59
+10	+165	+700	+50
+09	+149	+600	+41
+08	+133	+500	+33
+07	+117	+400	+26
+06	+101	+350	+22
+05	+84	+300	+19
+04	+68	+250	+16
+03	+51	+200	+12
+02	+34	+150	+09
+01	+17	+100	+06
00	00	+050	+2.9
-01	-17	000	000
-02	-35	-050	-2.8
-03	-53	-100	-5.6
-04	-71	-150	-8.3
-05	-89	-200	-11
-06	-107	-300	-16
-07	-126	-400	-21
-08	-144	-500	-25
-09	-163	-600	-29
-10	-182	-700	-33
-11	-202	-800	-37
-12	-221	-900	-41
-13	-241	-1000	-44
-14	-261	-1100	-47
-15	-281	-1200	-50

CHAPTER 45

The 20-/24-bit MDM

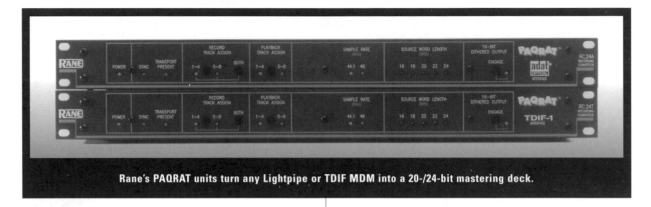

Rane's PAQRAT units turn any Lightpipe or TDIF MDM into a 20-/24-bit mastering deck.

wenty-bit recording will change your life. In 1990, I had the opportunity to try the first 20-bit MDM, Yamaha's DMR8. Since that time, I've never listened to 16-bit in the same way. The 20-bit playbacks in the control room were glorious: thick, rich and full of detail. When those same mixes were released on CD, the magic was gone. I knew it then. I wanted more. I had become a 20-bit-recording junkie.

These days, 20-bit MDMs have arrived in the guise of the Alesis M20 and Studer V-Eight (see Chapters 13 and 14 for full details), but not all of us are ready to shell out $7,000-8,000 for an 8-track MDM. Fortunately, there are ways to access 20-bit technology without the big price tag, and it comes by mixing to 20-bit 2-track. Intrigued? Here's how.

ENTER THE PAQRAT
Invented by famed Steely Dan engineer Roger Nichols, the PAQRAT series from Rane (Mukilteo, WA or www.rane.com) is a collection of outboard converters that transforms any 16-bit ADAT or DTRS format MDM into a 20- or 24-bit, 2-track mastering deck. Two models are available: The RC24A ($999) has optical ports for interfacing with ADAT-compatible machines; the RC24T ($899) has TDIF ports for connecting to the Tascam DA-88, DA-38 and DA-98. (PAQRAT will not function with the Sony PCM-800 as it does not have TDIF interfacing.)

The single-rackspace PAQRAT takes an AES/EBU or S/PDIF digital input from your digital mixer or 20-/24-bit A/D converter and stores the signal onto four tracks of an MDM. During recording, MDM Tracks one and three store the top 16 bits of the signal (the most significant bits), while Tracks two and four store the least significant bits (LSBs). Con-

After working in 16-bit for so long, one almost forgets what recording realism is all about.

versely, tracks could be recorded on MDM Tracks five through eight or, if you're really concerned about your masters, you can switch the PAQRAT to simultaneously record on Tracks 1-4 and 5-8 for redundancy in the event of dropouts. On playback, the digital output connects to the PAQRAT converter and is output in AES/EBU digital format on an XLR connector. Alternatively, the AES/EBU output can be switched to provide a 16-bit dithered signal for convenience in making standard DAT copies, transferring audio into 16-bit workstations for editing, etc.

Recording audio requires little more than assigning the tracks (1-4, 5-8 or both) on the PAQRAT and hitting record on your MDM. Playback is just as simple, and anyone who can operate a cassette deck can handle PAQRAT operations. One minor difference is that the even-numbered meters on your MDM will display a continuous -20dB reference signal to indicate that the LSBs are present, so make any required level adjustments based on the MDM's odd-numbered meters.

Although not mentioned in the manual, the PAQRAT can be used as a standalone 20- or 24-bit input/dithered 16-bit output converter by looping the MDM digital output directly to the MDM digital input and pressing the dithered output switch. Such a function could come in handy when offloading tracks from a 20-/24-bit workstation and making standard DAT copies.

Of course, the PAQRAT needs an external 20-bit A/D converter to operate: I use my PAQRAT with the $995 Symetrix (of Lynnwood, WA) Model 620, a pro unit with true 20-bit, delta-sigma conversion technology. But beyond its A/D functions, the 620 offers a choice of several outputs (linear 20-bit, dithered or noise-shaped 16-bit and 8-bit); along with 44.1-to-22.05kHz downsampling conversion, S/PDIF-to-AES/EBU (and vice versa) format conversion, digital black generator and 23-step LED headroom metering (active from digital or analog inputs).

PAQRAT delivers true 20-bit performance, with all the clarity, depth and punch that you'd expect from high-resolution recording. The additional dynamic range provided by high-bit-rate recording is impressive, but what you'll really notice is the utter disappearance of the noise floor, along with a tenfold increase in low-level detail such as instrument decays and reverb tails. After working in 16-bit for so long, one almost forgets what recording realism is all about, and PAQRAT delivers so much for so little money. Isn't that the way things are supposed to be?

APOGEE AD-1000

Retailing at $3,790, including outboard power supply, the AD-1000 20-bit analog-to-digital converter from Apogee Electronics (in Santa Monica, CA, at http://www.apogeedigital.com) offers a variety of tricks, including two high-quality mic preamps and Apogee's proprietary UV22™ coding (for retaining much of the punch of 20-bit when data is stored on 16-bit media, such as DATs and CDs.)

The AD-1000's 20-bit recording mode includes Rane PAQRAT technology, storing 20-bit audio on four adjacent channels of an ADAT. Users of TDIF-equipped MDMs (Tascam units) can also store PAQRAT signals from the AD-1000, but only via Apogee's ($495) FC-8 format converter.

PRISM MR-2024T

Designed for use with any TDIF-equipped (Tascam) MDM, the Prism MR-2024T from PrismSound (in Cambridge, UK at www.prismsound.com) is an interface adapter that provides full AES3 (and assignable S/PDIF) digital inputs and outputs for the DA-88, with some important additional features aimed at high-quality applications. The recording mode of the MR-2024T can be eight tracks at 16-bits, six tracks at 20-bits, four tracks at 24-bits or two tracks of 24-bits at 96kHz. All you add is a high-quality outboard analog to digital converter and the MR-2024T automatically tags the tape so that the correct mode is always selected on playback.

Beyond that, the MR-2024T's other features are numerous: A second DA-88 can be connected to the MR-2024T as a security backup, which is especially important for live and location work; sync options include using DA-88 sync, where the transport runs free or locked to video or word clock while the MR-2024T provides sync outputs. The MR-2024T can also synchronize the DA-88 to an AES3 or S/PDIF input if required.

The standard DA-88, DA-38 and DA-98 features are unaffected by the MR-2024T metering, 16-bit analog monitoring, full remote control and time code operation (without tying up a track for SMPTE code). Up to 16 transports can be slaved for more tracks: If you have enough money and/or resources, up to 96 20-bit tracks or 64 24-bit tracks are possible.

Now, who said that MDMs were strictly kid's stuff?

CHAPTER 46

The Suicide Auto-Mute Squeeze!

his slick trick allows you to add automated muting capability to any multitrack system equipped with auto-punch-in-/out and rehearse functions. This includes all MDMs right out of the box except the original Alesis ADAT, which requires a BRC controller to pull off this stunt.

Let's say you're mixing a 24-track session and there's a lot of background noise, buzzing amps and the typical 1-2-3-4 countdown before the tune starts. If you wanted, you could have erased all this pre-song clatter before mixing, but sometimes there are things, such as the countdown, that you should keep in case you ever want to add more instruments. If your mixer had automated faders or mute-grouping, this would be no sweat, but your mixer doesn't have these. To make things worse, you're mixing alone and don't have an extra two, four or eight hands to help out. You're sunk, right?

Add automated muting capability to any multitrack system equipped with auto-punch-in/-out and rehearse functions.

Not a chance, because you know all about the Suicide Auto-Mute Squeeze. (I'm sorry, but I just couldn't resist giving this technique such a juicy name!) Here's how it works:

The first thing you do is press the Rehearse key on your recorder or remote. This way, when you put your finished tracks into record mode, they won't be erased. Now press the record-ready (track arming) buttons on any tracks you'd like to mute. Set up an auto-punch-in-/out sequence so that the punch-in point is five or ten seconds before the first downbeat of the song, and ensure that the punch-out point

occurs as close to the first downbeat as possible. Set the track monitor switch so that the recorder inputs are monitored during recording, and make sure that no inputs are routed to the decks.

When the punch-in occurs, you will hear five or ten seconds of silence, and when the punch-out ends the "recording" (with the rehearse key selected, nothing will be recorded, so don't worry), the monitor select will switch back to monitoring the track playback.

Another possibility is locking your MDMs to a MIDI sequencer that is able to arm tracks via MIDI Machine Control commands, which would allow clearing the beginning of a song and, by selectively turning on and off auto-punch sequences throughout the song, would provide complete mute automation at no cost!

If this doesn't make sense, try it a few times on some unimportant tracks until you get the hang of it. Of course, if your finger slips and turns off the rehearse function, you'll send part of your creation on a one-way ride to degaussing oblivion. But hey, that's what living on the edge is all about. *Note: If you're timid, you could clone your tracks before doing this and mix from the clones, but then all the excitement would disappear!*

CHAPTER 47

MDM: The Next Generation

In Fall, 1993, while writing a chapter with this name for the first edition of *Modular Digital Multitracks: The Power User's Guide* (published in January of 1994), I made four predictions about the future of MDM technology and, it so happens, all of these became reality. Of course, if none of them came true, would I be really bringing these up now? Here's what those predictions were:

"Over time, expect more MDM recorders to enter the market, as other manufacturers enter the race and established companies unveil new models."

- *Since January of 1994, eight new MDMs (all featured in this book) have come to market, with newcomers Sony, Panasonic and Studer entering the MDM race, while Fostex, Alesis and Tascam all debuted new MDMs.*

"The field of third-party products for MDMs will also expand, as the user base grows and demands accessories for specialized applications, such as format converters, synchronizers and exotic A/D and D/A converters."

- *The field of third-party products for MDMs not only expanded, it went completely wild with dozens of companies offering hundreds of accessories and add-ons; so many that covering all of them would fill an entire book.*

"A little further (maybe a lot further) down the road is the low-cost, all-digital console, but present technology precludes this possibility for the time being."

- *The low-cost digital console did arrive (starting with the 1994 Yamaha ProMix 01, 02R [1995] and 03D, followed by the RSP Project X, the Korg 168RC, Soundtracs Virtua, and Mackie Digital Console) and as I write this, there are several more slated to debut in the next year.*

"Also being discussed at this time is a new breed of personal, 4-track digital recorder/mixers, as well as interfaces that link the MDMs to PC-based multimedia programs."

- *The 4-track MiniDisc recorder/mixers from Yamaha, Sony and Tascam arrived in 1996; as for the PC-to-MDM interfaces, there are well over a dozen on the market today, with more to come.*

When I first previewed the Akai A-DAM system at the New York AES show on October 16, 1987, I knew I was seeing the beginning of something special. But truthfully, I had no idea that ten years later, this 12-track digital recorder that stored audio on 8mm consumer videotapes would lead to the MDM movement that has changed the way that records

Will laser-modulated, interactive biospheres replace tape-based modular digital multitracks?

(and film/video post-production) are created. Perhaps more importantly, MDM technology has brought a democratization to the recording process, making the high-quality recording gear available and affordable to anyone who wants it.

But is it over yet? Will laser-modulated, interactive biospheres replace tape-based modular digital multitracks? The answers to both questions is no; at least not for some time. I'm not such a fool as to say that it will never happen, but when you can buy a ten-pack of 100GB floppies at K-Mart for $9.99, then we'll have a *real* revolution in recording.

However, the future does hold one certainty: With the rate that technology is changing, we're in for an interesting ride in the days, weeks and months ahead. Bet on it.

And keep your seat belt fastened.

A Music Bookstore At Your Fingertips...
FREE!

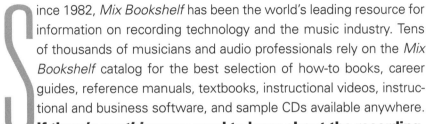

Since 1982, *Mix Bookshelf* has been the world's leading resource for information on recording technology and the music industry. Tens of thousands of musicians and audio professionals rely on the *Mix Bookshelf* catalog for the best selection of how-to books, career guides, reference manuals, textbooks, instructional videos, instructional and business software, and sample CDs available anywhere. **If there's *anything* you need to learn about the recording, technology, business, or composition of music, *Mix Bookshelf* has the information.**

We offer:

• The most comprehensive listing of resources for music industry professionals and hobbyists

• Convenient and cost-efficient "one-stop shopping" for retailers and school bookstores

• Discounts and review copies for educators and established music business and recording programs

For a free *Mix Bookshelf* catalog call (800) 233-9604

or write to
Mix Bookshelf; 6400 Hollis St; Emeryville, CA 94608
International (510) 923-0370 Fax (510) 923-0369
or check us out on the Web! You can browse our catalog and order Bookshelf items at **http://www.mixbookshelf.com**

MIX
BOOKSHELF
INFORMATION RESOURCES FOR MUSIC PROFESSIONALS